Bushwalking in Papua New Guinea

Yvon Pérusse

Bushwalking in Papua New Guinea

2nd edition

Published by
    Lonely Planet Publications
    Head Office: PO Box 617, Hawthorn, Vic 3122, Australia
    Branches: PO Box 2001A, Berkeley, CA 94702, USA
                 12 Barley Mow Passage, Chiswick, London W4 4PH, UK

Printed by
    Colorcraft Ltd, Hong Kong

Photographs by
    Janet Baldwin (JB), Richard Everist (RE), Judy Gordon (JG),
    Anne Jelinek (AJ), Jon Murray (JM), Yvon Pérusse (YP)

    Front cover: The Aiwara Valley near Tapini, Central Province (YP)
    Back cover: Mendi woman from the Southern Highlands (YP)

First Published
    March 1983

This Edition
    July 1993

National Library of Australia Cataloguing in Publication Data

Pérusse, Yvon.
    Bushwalking in Papua New Guinea

    2nd ed.
    Includes index.
    ISBN 0 86442 052 8.

    1. Hiking – Papua New Guinea – Guidebooks. 2. Mountaineering –
    Papua New Guinea – Guidebooks. 3. Papua New Guinea –
    Guidebooks. I. Title. (Series: Lonely Planet walking guide).

919.5304

text & maps © Lonely Planet 1993
photos © photographers as indicated 1993

Yvon Pérusse

Yvon Pérusse grew up in Lévis, Quebec. He has travelled extensively, including a six-year journey throughout the South Pacific. He has made three visits to PNG, totalling nearly 2½ years, and has made what might have been the first full crossing of the mainland on foot.

Not surprisingly, he likes the outdoors, camping and canoeing. He's a bird-watcher and has a plant collection of several thousand species, mainly from Quebec.

From the Author

This book is dedicated to all Papua New Guineans.

From the Publisher

The 1st edition of *Bushwalking in Papua New Guinea* was written by Riall W Nolan and published in 1983. This 2nd edition was completely rewritten by Yvon Pérusse with some additional updating by Jon Murray, author of *Papua New Guinea – a travel survival kit*.

The editing was done by Jon Murray and Katie Cody. The maps were drawn by Vicki Beale, Ralph Roob, Sandra Smythe, Valerie Tellini and Dave Windle. Map corrections were completed by Louise Keppie, Matt King, and Jacqui Schiff. Ann Jeffree was responsible for design and illustrations, with additional illustrations by Glenn Beanland. Margaret Jung designed the cover. Tom Smallman, as usual, gave his good advice willingly.

To those travellers who wrote to tell us of their experiences bushwalking in PNG – thanks! Your contributions have been acknowledged in *Papua New Guinea – a travel survival kit*.

Disclaimer

Although the author and the publisher have done their utmost to ensure the accuracy of all information in this guide, they cannot accept any responsibility for any loss, injury or inconvenience sustained by people using this book. For example, they cannot guarantee that tracks and routes described here have not become impassable in the interval between research and publication.

All walking times *exclude* rest stops, and are minimum walking times.

The fact that a trip or an area is described in this guidebook does not necessarily mean that it is a safe one for you and your walking party. This applies to both walking conditions and security. Warnings given in this guidebook about security problems should be used as a guide only, and you should always seek local information on the current situation in a particular area.

You are finally responsible for judging your own capabilities in the light of the conditions you encounter. Good walking!

Warning & Request

Things change – prices go up, schedules change, good places go bad and bad places go bankrupt – nothing stays the same. So if you find things better or worse, recently opened or long since closed, please write and tell us and help make the next edition better.

Your letters help us update future editions and, where possible, important changes will also be included in a Stop Press section in reprints.

We greatly appreciate all information that is sent to us by travellers. Back at Lonely Planet we employ a hard-working readers' letters team to sort through the many letters we receive. The best ones will be rewarded with a free copy of the next edition or another Lonely Planet guide if you prefer. We give away lots of books, but, unfortunately, not every letter/postcard receives one.

Contents

MAP LEGEND

—·—··	International Boundaries	⌢⌢⌢⌢	Escarpment or Cliff
—··—··	National Park Boundaries	●	Settlements
———	Major Roads	■	Places to Stay
-------	Secondary Roads	⚲	Church
+++++++++	Railways	⛺	Camping Area
·········	Major Walking Track	⌂	Hut, Refuge
·············	Minor Walking Track	▲	Mountain, Peak
~	Rivers, Creeks	)(	Pass, Saddle
⬭	Lakes	⊢⊢	Bridge
~	Waterfall	✳	Lookout
→ →	Water Flow	✈	Airport
☁	Marsh, Swamp	✛	Airfield
▦	Sand Bank or Gravel Bed	⚓	Jetty
500	Contour, Contour Interval		

Note: not all symbols displayed above appear in this book

Introduction

Papua New Guinea (PNG) is truly the 'last unknown'; it was virtually the last place on earth to be explored by Europeans and has captured the imagination of explorers, anthropologists and visitors for more than a century.

The country's unique cultural and linguistic diversity accounts for much of this attraction. Thousands of tribes speak more than 700 different languages; perhaps a third of all the languages spoken in the world.

There are few roads in PNG. Walking is often the only way to get from place to place, and is a fascinating way to discover the country. Each step rewards the walker with close contact with people whose lifestyle has changed little in generations and reveals a little more of PNG's unique tropical rainforests.

From the towering, wide-crowned trees of the luxuriant lowland rainforests, home to beautiful cockatoos and hornbills, to the moss-laden trees of the montane rainforests,

where wild orchids and possums abound, to the alpine grasslands where prehistoric-looking tree ferns and cycads grow among daisies and tussock grasses, PNG's vegetation and unique fauna are always entrancing.

The 10 walks detailed in this book (along with many other suggested walks and variants on the main walks) offer a range of difficulty, length, landscape and culture, presenting the walker with a cross section of this beautiful and varied country. They include an easy three-day hike along the coast in Milne Bay, the relatively easy climb up Mt Wilhelm, PNG's highest mountain, and a more strenuous six-day traverse of the Owen Stanley Ranges along the Kokoda Trail.

Along with notes on each area and its cultures, this book provides maps and all the practical information you'll need, such as where to hire guides and carriers, places to stay before and after each trek, the main features, trail standard, length, climate, equipment required and access to the trails.

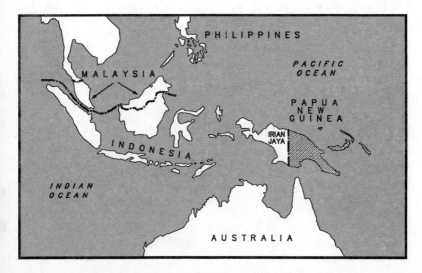

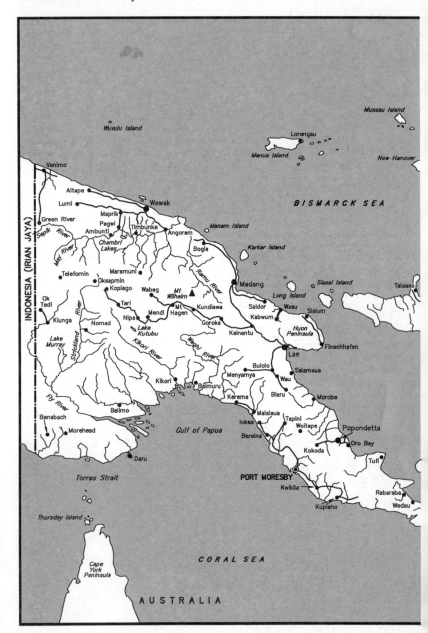

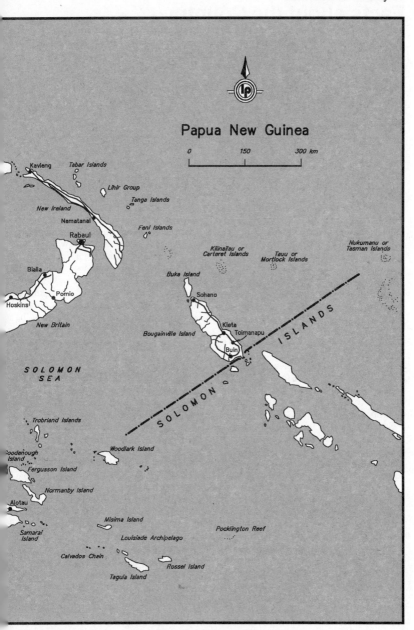

Papua New Guinea

Facts about the Country

HISTORY

The history of Papua New Guinea prior to the arrival of European colonists in the 19th century is only starting to be pieced together. The task is daunting. The highly fragmented indigenous cultures left no written records and the marks they made on the landscape have almost been completely erased by the tropical environment.

The First Arrivals

It is believed that humans reached PNG and then Australia by island-hopping across the Indonesian archipelago from Asia, perhaps more than 50,000 years ago. The migration was probably made easier by a fall in the sea level caused by an ice age.

At no time was PNG completely joined to South-East Asia but it was joined to Australia, probably until about 6000 years ago. As a result PNG shares many species of plants and animals (including marsupials) with Australia, but not with Indonesia. The Wallace Line marks the deep water between Bali and Lombok, and Kalimantan and Sulawesi (in Indonesia) that formed a natural barrier to animals and humans. In order to reach PNG people had to cross open water on canoes or rafts.

Several waves of people have arrived in PNG from Asia, and this may be reflected in the distribution of Austronesian and non-Austronesian languages. The Austronesian languages are scattered along the coast and are spoken throughout Polynesia and Micronesia. The majority of Papua New Guineans speak non-Austronesian languages and, it is believed, arrived before the Austronesian language speakers.

As the world's climate warmed the sea level rose, isolating PNG and submerging the original coastal settlements. Parts of the Huon Peninsula have subsequently risen due to volcanic activity. Evidence of early coastal settlements has been exposed – 40,000 year old stone axes have been found.

People reached the Highlands about 30,000 years ago and most of the valleys were settled over the next 20,000 years. Trade between the Highlands and the coast has been going on for at least 10,000.

Kuk (or Kup) Swamp in the Wahgi Valley (Western Highlands Province) has evidence of human habitation going back 20,000 years, but even more significantly there is evidence of gardening beginning 9000 years ago. This makes Papua New Guineans among the first farmers in the world. The main foods farmed at this stage are likely to have been sago, coconuts, breadfruit, local bananas and yams, sugar cane (which originated in PNG), nuts and edible leaves.

It is still uncertain when the pig and more productive starch crops (yams, taros and bananas) were introduced, but it is known that pigs arrived at least 10,000 years ago. Domesticated pigs – which continue to be incredibly important to ritual and economic life – and these new crops were probably brought to PNG by a later group of colonists from Asia.

Surprisingly, the South Papuan coast seems to have been mainly settled in the last 3000 years, although that's another date that keeps receding with new finds.

The prehistory of the islands has always been assumed to be shorter than that of the mainland, but new evidence shows that New Ireland and Buka (North Solomons) were inhabited around 30,000 years ago. People in New Britain have been trading with other islands for more than 10,000 years, and the first-settlement date for Manus has now been pushed back to 10,000 years ago.

Potatoes & Axes

The first European impact on PNG was indirect but far reaching. The sweet potato was taken to South-East Asia from South America by the Portuguese and Spanish in the 16th century and it is believed Malay traders then brought it to Irian Jaya, from where it was traded to the Highlands. The introduction of the sweet potato must have brought radical change to life in the Highlands. Its high yield and tolerance for poor and cold soils allowed the colonisation of higher altitudes, the domestication of many more pigs, and a major increase in population.

The next development preceding the permanent arrival of Europeans was the arrival of steel axes which were also traded from the coast up into the Highlands. The introduction of these more efficient axes reduced the workload of men (making axes, garden-clearing, canoe-making, etc), increased bride price payments and, because of the increased leisure time, encouraged war – all of which boosted the status and importance of village elders or 'bigmen'.

European Contact

PNG's history of real European contact goes back little more than a century, although the island of New Guinea was known to the European colonial powers long before they came to stay.

The first definite European sighting of the island took place in 1512 when two Portuguese explorers sailed by. The first landing was also Portuguese: Jorge de Meneses landed on the Vogelkop Peninsula, the 'dragon's head' at the north-west corner of the island. He named it 'Ilhas dos Papuas'. In the following centuries various Europeans sailed past the main island and its smaller associated islands, but the spreading tentacles of European colonialism had far richer prizes to grapple with. New Guinea was a big, daunting place, it had no visible wealth to exploit, but it most definitely did have some rather unfriendly inhabitants. It was left pretty much alone.

Only the Dutch made any move to assert European authority over the island and that was mainly to keep other countries from getting a toehold on the eastern end of their fabulously profitable Dutch East Indies empire (Indonesia today). They put their claim in by a round-about method. Indones-

ian and Malay traders had for some time carried on a limited trade with coastal tribes for valuable items like bird of paradise feathers. So the Dutch simply announced that they recognised the Sultan of Tidor's sovereignty over New Guinea. Since in turn, they held power over the island of Tidor, New Guinea was therefore indirectly theirs – without expending any personal effort. That neat little ploy, first put into action in 1660, was sufficient for over 100 years, but during the last century firmer action became necessary.

The British East India Company had a look at parts of western New Guinea back in 1793 and even made a tentative claim on the island, but in 1824 Britain and the Netherlands agreed that Holland's claim to the western half should stand. In 1828 the Dutch made an official statement of their claim and backed it up by establishing a token settlement on the Vogelkop. Nothing much happened for 50 or so years after that, although the coastline was gradually charted and Australia became interested.

A series of British 'claims' followed but these were repudiated by the British government. In 1883 the Queensland premier sent the Thursday Island police magistrate up to lay yet another unsuccessful claim, but the next year Britain finally got around to doing something about their unwanted would-be possession. At the time the British population consisted of a handful of missionaries and a solitary trader.

There were still very little happening over on the Dutch side of the island, but on the north coast of the eastern half a third colonial power – Germany – was taking a definite interest. When Britain announced, in September 1884, that they intended to lay claim to a chunk of New Guinea, the Germans quickly raised the flag on the north coast. A highly arbitrary line was then drawn between German and British New Guinea. At that time no European had ventured inland from the coast and it was nearly 50 years later, when the Germans had long departed, that it was discovered that the line went straight through the most densely populated part of the island.

New Guinea was now divided into three sections – a Dutch half to keep everybody else away from the Dutch East Indies, a British quarter to keep the Germans (and anybody else) away from Australia, and a German quarter because it looked like it could be a damn good investment. The Germans were soon proved wrong; for the next 15 years the mosquitoes were the only things to profit from the German Neuguinea-Kompagnie's presence on the north coast. In 1899 the Germans threw in the towel, shifted to the happier climes of the Bismarck Archipelago and quickly started to make those fat profits they'd wanted all along.

Over in the Dutch half nothing was happening at all and the British were trying to bring law and order to their bit. In 1888 Sir William MacGregor became the administrator of British New Guinea and set out to explore his possession and set up a native police force to spread the benefits of British government. He instituted the policy of 'government by patrol' which continued right through the Australian period. In 1906 British New Guinea became Papua and administration was taken over by newly independent Australia. From 1907 Papua was the personal baby of Sir Hubert Murray who administered it until his death in 1940.

European Exploration

Exploration was one of the most interesting phases of the early European development of PNG. This was almost the last place to be discovered by Europeans and the explorers were only too happy to put their daring deeds down on paper. Gavin Souter's book *The Last Unknown* is one of the best descriptions of these travels.

At first, exploration consisted of short trips in from the coast, often by parties of early mission workers. Later the major rivers were used to travel farther into the forbidding inland region. The next phase was trips upriver on one side, over the central mountains and down a suitable river to the other coast – crossing the tangled central mountains often proved to be the killer in these attempts.

From the time of the Australian take over of British New Guinea, government-by-patrol was the key to both exploration and control. Patrol officers were not only the first Europeans into previously 'uncontacted' areas but were also responsible for making

Children playing on plane wreck

the government's presence felt on a more or less regular basis. The last great phase of exploration took place in the '30s and was notable for the first organised use of support aircraft. This last period included the discovery of the important Highlands region. By '39 even the final unknown area, towards the Dutch New Guinea border, had been at least cursorily explored. Since the war there have been more exploratory patrols and the country is now completely mapped, although previously 'uncontacted' peoples have been found recently and it's possible that there are more Highland clans yet to discover the outside world.

WW I & WW II

Almost as soon as WW I broke out in Europe, New Guinea went through a major upheaval. Australian troops quickly overran the German headquarters at Rabaul in New Britain and for the next seven years German New Guinea was run by the Australian military. In 1920 the League of Nations officially handed it over to Australia as a mandated territory, and it stayed that way right up until WW II.

When WW II arrived, all the northern islands and most of the north coast quickly fell to the Japanese. The Japanese steamrollered their way south and soon Australia only held Port Moresby. The Japanese advance was fast but short-lived and by September 1942, with the Pacific War less than a year old and Port Moresby within sight, they had run out of steam and started their long, slow retreat. It took until 1945 to regain all the mainland from the Japanese, and the islands (New Ireland, New Britain, Bougainville) were not recovered until the final surrender, after the atom bombing of Hiroshima and Nagasaki.

The end of Colonialism

There was no intention to go back to the pre-war situation of separate administrations and in any case Port Moresby was the only major town still intact after the war, so the colony now became the Territory of Papua & New Guinea. The territory entered a new period of major economic development with a large influx of expatriates, mainly Australians. When it peaked in 1971 the expatriate population had expanded from the 1940 total of about 6000 to over 50,000. Since then it has fallen to closer to 20,000 and is still declining.

The post war world had an entirely different attitude towards colonialism and Australia was soon pressured to prepare Papua & New Guinea for independence. A visiting UN mission in 1962 stressed that if the people weren't pushing for independence themselves then it was Australia's responsibility to do the pushing. The previous Australian policy of gradually spreading literacy and education was supplemented by a concentrated effort to produce a small, educated elite to take over the reins of government.

Irian Jaya After WW II, Indonesia gained its independence from Holland, and claimed the west half of the island. The Dutch held out through the '50s, and attempted to prepare the colony for independence. However, they were out-manoeuvred at the UN, and in 1963 the Indonesians, with support from the USA, took over.

Part of the Dutch hand-over agreement was that the people should, after a time, have the right to vote on staying with Indonesia or opting for independence. In 1969 this 'Act of Free Choice' took place. The 'choice' was somewhat restricted by Indonesia's President Suharto stating that: 'There will be an act of self-determination, of free choice, in West Irian but if they vote against Indonesia or betray or harm the Indonesian people, this would be treason.' When 1000 'representative' voters made the act of free choice there was not a treasonable voice to be heard.

Following Indonesia's takeover of Irian Jaya, the indigenous Papuans, who had been sold-out so badly by the rest of the world, organised a guerrilla resistance movement – the Free Papua Movement, widely known as the OPM (Organisasi Papua Merdeka). Since its inception it has fought with varying degrees of success against tremendous odds.

Independence

In PNG the progress towards independence was fairly rapid through the '60s. In 1964 a House of Assembly was formed and internal self-government came into effect in '73, followed in late '75 by full independence. At this time PNG still had a very low rate of literacy and there were parts of the country only just emerging from the stone age, where contact with government officials was still infrequent and bewildering.

A country divided by a huge number of mutually incomprehensible languages, where inter-tribal antipathy is common and where the educated elite accounts for such a small percentage of the total population would hardly seem to provide a firm base for democracy. Yet somehow everything has held together and PNG works fairly well, especially by new-nation standards. Papua New Guineans have generally dealt with the problems of nationhood with a great deal of success.

Bougainville There was a real possibility of PNG falling apart when military action by secessionists on Bougainville closed the giant Panguna mine in 1989. With such a diverse society, PNG struggles to maintain a sense of nationhood at the best of times, and when the Bougainville Revolutionary Army began what amounted to a civil war, there were nervous glances around the rest of the country. That threat seems to have diminished, but the problems on Bougainville remain and the island is off limits.

Law & Order

The most publicised problem that faces PNG today is one that can go under the general heading of 'Law & Order'. The problem encompasses everything from traditional tribal wars and modern corruption, to personal violence. When you hear talk of *rascals* and the 'rascal problem' this is what it is being referred to – not schoolboy pranks.

As you travel around PNG, and especially when you speak to white expats, you will be hard put to keep this problem in perspective. Extreme paranoia is contagious and crime is a favourite topic of conversation. What you

must continue to ask yourself is: How does it compare with home (think of the Sunday newspapers in your home city) and how does it relate to the friendliness and hospitality I meet everywhere I go? (See the Safety section in the Facts for the Bushwalker chapter for more information.)

Perhaps the greatest problem is that PNG is not yet a cohesive state, so rules of behaviour that will be strictly upheld within a community will not necessarily be upheld outside it. A man who would never dream of cheating someone in his village might be proud of robbing someone from a rival tribe and feel similarly free from constraints in a strange city.

Although people rarely starve in PNG and the village or clan can nearly always meet most simple needs, there is a growing cash economy. This demand for cash and the limited opportunity most people have to make money obviously creates pressures.

Young men, even those with minimal educational standards, aspire to the status and material wealth that was achieved by the small elite the Australians developed. These ambitious young men, usually unmarried and between about 18 and 30 years old, are drawn to the cities. Once there they take advantage of relatives who, under Melanesian tradition, are responsible for feeding and housing them. Unfortunately sufficient jobs just do not exist, so these bored young 'have-nots' wander the town, play cards and pool, drink beer and...

GEOGRAPHY

PNG lies barely south of the equator, to the north of Australia. It is the last of the string of islands spilling down from South-East Asia into the Pacific and really forms a transition zone between the two areas. After PNG you're into the Pacific proper – expanses of ocean dotted by tiny islands. PNG occupies the eastern end of the island of New Guinea.

PNG's remote and wild character is very closely tied to its dramatic geography. The place is a mass of superlatives – the mountains tower, the rivers rush, the ravines

Top: Parimeta Bay, near Topura, Milne Bay Province (YP)
Bottom: Kuvira Bay, near Topura, Milne Bay Province (YP)

Top Left: Cassowary (JM)
Top Right: Flowers in the lower montane forest (YP)
Bottom Left: Tree kangaroo (JM)
Bottom Right: Hornbill (AJ)

plunge – name a geographical cliche and PNG has it. These spectacular features have much to do with the country's diverse people and its current state of development. When a mighty mountain range or a wide river separates you from your neighbouring tribe you're unlikely to get to know them very well.

The central spine of PNG is a high range of mountains with peaks over 4000 metres high. It's unlikely that a permanent road across this daunting natural barrier will be completed soon, although temporary tracks were attempted during WW II. Meanwhile, travel between the south and north coasts of PNG still means walking or flying.

Great rivers flow from the mountains down to the sea. The Fly and the Sepik rivers are the two largest: the Sepik flowing into the sea in the north, the Fly in the south. Both are navigable for long distances and both are among the world's mightiest rivers in terms of annual water flow.

In places the central mountains descend right to the sea in a series of diminishing foothills, while in other regions broad expanses of mangrove swamps fringe the coast – gradually extending as more and more material is carried down to the coast by the muddy rivers. In the western region there is an endless expanse of flat grassland, sparsely populated, annually flooded and teeming with wildlife.

PNG is in the Pacific volcano belt but, apart from a few exceptions along the north coast such as Mt Lamington, near Popondetta, which erupted unexpectedly and disastrously in 1951, the live volcanoes are not on the mainland. There are a number of volcanic islands scattered off the north coast and in Milne Bay plus, of course, the active region on the north coast of New Britain. Earthquakes, usually mild, are more widespread.

One of the most interesting features of the geography of PNG is the central highland valleys. As the early explorers pushed inland the general conclusion was that the central spine of mountains was a tangled, virtually uninhabited wilderness. In the '30s, however, the highland valleys were accidentally

discovered and the wilderness turned out to be the most fertile and heavily populated region of the country. The best known valleys are around Goroka and Mt Hagen, but there are other more remote places right across into Irian Jaya.

PNG is endowed with striking coral reefs making it a paradise for scuba divers. There are reefs around much of the mainland coast and, more particularly, among the islands of the Bismarck Sea and Milne Bay areas.

The major offshore islands – New Ireland, New Britain and Bougainville – are almost as mountainous as the mainland with many peaks rising to over 2000 metres.

CLIMATE

The climate is generally hot, humid and wet year round, but there are some exceptions. Officially there's a wet and a dry season, but in practice, in most places, the wet just means it is more likely to rain, the dry that it's less likely. The exception is Port Moresby where the dry is definitely dry – the configuration of the mountains around Moresby accounts for this two season characteristic. The wetter time of the year is from December to March, the drier time May to October. During the two transition months (April and November) it can't make up its mind which way to go and tends to be unpleasantly still and sticky.

There are many variations on this pattern, the most notable being Lae and Alotau, where May to October is the wet season. Some places, such as Wewak and the Trobriand Islands, receive a fairly even spread of rain throughout the year, and others, such as New Britain and New Ireland, have sharply differing rainfall patterns in different areas.

Rainfall, which is generally heavy, nonetheless varies enormously. In dry, often dusty Port Moresby the annual rainfall is about 1000 mm and, like places in northern Australia, it is short and sharp and is then followed by long dry months. Other places can vary from a little over 2000 mm in Rabaul or Goroka, to over 4500 mm in Lae. In extreme rainfall areas, such as West New Britain or the northern areas of the Gulf and

Western Provinces, the annual rainfall can average over six metres a year.

Temperatures on the coast are reasonably stable year round – hovering around 25°C to 30°C, but the humidity and winds can vary widely, changing the way each day feels. As you move inland and up, the temperatures drop fairly dramatically. In the Highlands the daytime temperatures often climb to the high 20°Cs but at night it can get quite cold. During the dry season, when there is little cloud cover to contain the heat, highland mornings can be very chilly. If you keep moving up into the mountains you'll find it colder still. Although snow is rare it can occur on the tops of the highest summits and ice will often form on cold nights.

Gulf & Western
> The Gulf Region is very wet year round – peaking between May and October. The inland Western Region can also be very wet.

Highlands
> In most of the Highlands the rain comes from November to April but is generally not unpleasant. May to October is cooler and drier. In the Southern Highlands the wet begins a little earlier and lasts a bit longer and it is more likely to rain at any time year round.

Lae & Morobe
> In Lae it's hot and humid from November to February, wetter but cooler from May to October with the heaviest rain in June, July and August. In Wau and Bulolo it is the exact opposite.

Madang
> In Madang it is rainy, with frequent thunderstorms from November to May.

Manus
> There is no real wet season in Manus.

Milne Bay
> This maritime province has a wide variation of weather conditions. Alotau is wetter from April to October, with most rain in September. The Trobriand Islands have fairly even rainfall.

New Britain
> November to April on the north side is the wet season (including Rabaul and the Gazelle Peninsula), while on the south side of the island the rain comes May to October and comes much heavier. There is no fixed wet season in the Gazelle Peninsula's mountains.

New Ireland
> Kavieng receives a fairly even spread of rainfall, and the south of the island is wetter from November to May.

Oro
> The wet season in Oro is from October to May with the heaviest rain at the beginning and end of the season.

North Solomons
> January to April is wet but cooler, while November and December are pretty hot in the North Solomons.

Port Moresby & Central
> It is dry, dusty and windy from May to October; it is wetter and cooler inland.

Sepik
> July to November is the dry season and the wettest time is between December and April.

FLORA & FAUNA

Of about 9000 species of plants, over 200 are tree-size. While there is more diversity in the lowland rainforests, a great number of species are only found in the moist montane forests. At these higher altitudes (which are reminiscent of Tasmania or New Zealand) pines and antarctic beech thrive and orchids abound. At around 3900 metres, the forest grades into scrub, then meadows.

Most of PNG is forested, broken by shifting cultivation, even in areas where it is very steep. Commercial logging is generally localised, but is expanding. Clear-felling methods are often used. In the south are extensive savannahs similar to those of northern Australia.

PNG's wealth of wildlife does not include large and spectacular animals, like elephants or tigers, but is interesting in many ways. There are about 250 species of mammals, mostly bats and rats, including about 60 marsupials, notably tree kangaroos. There are also two kinds of echidnas (spiny anteaters).

It is for its 700 or so bird species that PNG's wildlife is most renowned. There is a general similarity to Australian bird life, but PNG's is often more colourful. New Guinea is the home of 38 of the world's 43 spectacular and gaudy species of birds of paradise, with their bizarre displays and mating rituals. The closely related bower birds are also found, and while they lack incredible feathering, they more than make up for it in their skill in building bowers and elaborate gardens, complete with well-kept lawns and flower arrangements.

PNG can boast more parrot, pigeon and kingfisher species than anywhere else in the world. All sizes and colours can be found, from the world's largest pigeon, the crowned pigeon, to the world's smallest parrot, the pygmy parrot, which scurries along small branches and feeds on lichens.

Kingfisher

Perhaps the most notable birds are the giant cassowaries. Related to the Australian emu, they are stockier birds adapted to forest areas and have a large, horny casque for crashing through the undergrowth. Like birds of paradise, cassowaries are of great ceremonial significance to many of PNG's tribal groups.

Also represented in PNG are about 200 species of reptiles, including two species of crocodiles, 13 of turtles and about a hundred different kinds of snakes. Few snakes are dangerous but all are greatly feared by villagers, who regularly burn grassland areas to control them, especially in the Highlands.

There are many thousands of species of weird and wonderful insects, notably a beautiful variety of huge birdwing butterflies, including the world's largest butterfly, the Queen Alexandra's Birdwing. Some insects, such as the brilliant green scarab beetles, are used as body ornaments.

National Parks

Conserving the diversity of PNG's natural resources is complicated by the ancient customs of traditional land ownership. Totally protected areas are few. Prior to independence only two national parks were established, and only two have been established since, but others have been proposed. A compromise concept is Benchmark Reserves protecting small parts of exploited areas.

The National Parks Board also recognises Provincial Parks and Local Parks, better known as Wildlife Management Areas. These are multi-use areas, protecting specific types of wildlife under pressure because of its use for food or ceremonial functions. They encourage communities to prevent over-exploitation and the Wildlife Management Areas are the responsibility of those communities. The rights of the people living in the affected area are given priority if there is to be commercial exploitation.

Also important is the concept of Protected Species, in which all wildlife belongs to the traditional land owners. The list of protected species began in the 1920s to protect the many species of bird of paradise and egret from commercial exploitation for their valuable plumes. Added later were most of the birdwing butterflies, the long-nosed echidna and many others.

There seems to be a growing awareness of the necessity to conserve forests and wildlife, but traditional landowners are often torn between the rich rewards offered by foreign logging and mining companies and the destruction of their environment. The problems on Bougainville can be seen as at least partly due to a new generation choosing the environment over cash. Still, traditional slash-and-burn agriculture is widespread and with a growing population the remaining forests are under threat.

Large scale commercial exploitation is unlikely to be as disastrous in PNG as in neighbouring countries to the west. This is not only because of the recognition of traditional land ownership, but because of the serious social, economic and environmental problems which are resulting right next door. Irian Jaya is now coming under serious exploitation pressures and the same pressures are found in the Solomon Islands. The long-term future in PNG remains uncertain, but the current developments in conservation awareness are very encouraging.

For the latest information on National Parks you can write to the National Parks Service, PO Box 5749, Boroko. For information on Wildlife Management Areas contact the Wildlife Conservation Section, Department Environment & Conservation, PO Box 6601, Boroko.

GOVERNMENT

PNG has a three-tiered system of democratic government (national, provincial and local) based on the Australian and Westminster models. The Governor General (who is the representative of the British monarch – PNG is a member of the Commonwealth) is the largely ceremonial head of state and is elected by parliament. There is an independent judiciary and public service.

The most important political forum is the National Parliament and all citizens can vote in elections, held every four years. The parliament elects the prime minister, who appoints ministers from members of their party or coalition. Provincial government was introduced in 1976, when the nineteen provinces and the National Capital District were proclaimed. Each has an elected provincial assembly, an executive council and premier. The national parliament retains ultimate control and a number of provincial governments have been suspended for mismanagement. Each of these governments has wide powers over education, health and the economy, and the right to levy some taxes and fees.

There are more than 150 local councils.

ECONOMY

Until recently, the economy was based on copper, coffee, cocoa and copra. This ignored the fact that most people lived within a successful subsistence economy, and the contribution made by Australian grants.

Since the mid 1980s, copper has been overtaken by gold as the biggest single export, the value of copra exports and the Australian grant have declined markedly, but at least 85% of the population is basically still subsistence farmers.

PNG is in the enviable position of having a booming and increasingly diversified mineral sector and largely untapped forestry and fishing resources. Further reserves of gold, copper, silver, nickel, oil and gas are being discovered, virtually daily. In most regions there is sufficient arable land to produce agricultural surpluses. The relatively small population and this natural wealth means that PNG has tremendous economic potential and in terms of Pacific island states, it is a giant.

There is very little squalor in PNG, and beggars are effectively nonexistent. There are nutritional problems in some parts of the country (shortage of protein is an age-old difficulty) but virtually everybody is fed and clothed, even if they are unemployed in the cities. This is due in large part to the *wantok* system, a unique Melanesian system of clan responsibility. Wantok literally means 'one talk' or common language and signifies a shared origin. Members of a clan look after one another and share the clan's wealth. This system continues to be tremendously influential and has worked well in situations where only one clan-member earns a wage – a single wage is often distributed among dozens of people.

POPULATION & PEOPLE

The population is approaching four million. Over a third of the people live in the Highlands. Some scholars divide the people into Papuans, descended from the original arrivals, and Melanesians, more closely related to the peoples of the Pacific. Also, particularly in outlying islands, some people are closer to being Polynesian or Micronesian. The dividing line between these definitions is a very hazy one.

Politically, four regional groups, reflecting cultural and historical links, have developed:

Papuans (from the south), Highlanders, New Guineans (from the north) and Islanders.

There is a wide range of physical types, from the dark Buka people of the North Solomons, who are said to have the blackest skins in the world, to the lighter, more Polynesian people of the south Papuan coast. After a spell in PNG you'll soon learn to recognise the shorter, often bearded, highland men and many other distinct groups.

The rugged terrain kept groups from mixing and has meant a huge diversity of languages and cultures.

Grassroots

Grassroots is a slang term which has entered the language, and refers to, roughly, 'the people': a grassroot lives in a village or in town on a low income. Given the enormous diversity of cultures and their mutual suspicion, the development of this unifying concept is a healthy sign for PNG.

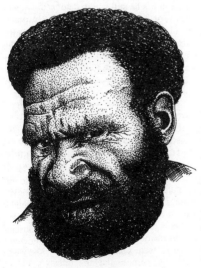

Highland man

Expatriates

There is still a considerable expatriate population, although it has fallen from its 1971 peak of around 50,000 to a current figure closer to 20,000. The expatriate population is made up of a wide variety of nationalities. Although Australians are still in the majority, there are Germans, British, Americans, Chinese and Filipinos, among many others.

More than half the expatriates live in Port Moresby and many of them are in the country on short-term contracts with international companies. Often they lead lives that are totally divorced from reality, commuting between air-conditioned offices, their company-provided houses (invariably surrounded by razor wire) and some sort of club. Partly as a consequence of this isolation their attitudes to, and perceptions of, the country are sometimes quite inaccurate.

You'll also meet expats who have been in PNG since before independence, including ex-*kiaps* (patrol officers), whose attitudes are more realistic. The network of long-term expats can be a handy one to lock into.

Although some mission workers have been criticised for their blinkered attitudes and destructive impact on traditional culture, others have done valuable work in education, health, agriculture and transport. They also work with the hapless people lured by the 'big city' aura of towns like Port Moresby. They continue to have a very strong influence on the country. There's also a large and diverse volunteer contingent including Peace Corps, Cuso and VSO workers among others.

Who's Who

Western residents are almost always known as expats and the indigenous people are frequently referred to as nationals – never ever natives. The term 'national' is increasingly out of favour; many Papua New Guineans prefer, where a label is necessary at all, to be described by their tribal or regional name. In remote areas, Westerners are still occasionally called *masta* or *missus*, but for most people this is offensively colonial. The colonial era is still sometimes referred to as the *taim bilong masta*.

CULTURE

The people of PNG belong to many different cultures and it's difficult to make generalisations. You'll find more information about arts and cultures in the various parts of this book, but understanding even one of the cultures is a lifetime's work – hence the number of anthropologists in the country. However, nearly all Papua New Guineans are Melanesian and have some things in common.

Melanesian Society

PNG is changing fast, but the vast majority of people remain dependent on subsistence agriculture and live in small villages. Many aspects of life are still carried out traditionally, and the social structure and an individual's responsibilities and privileges remain significantly unchanged. Following is a brief overview of pre-contact traditional life.

Despite sophisticated agriculture and, in some areas, extraordinary maritime skills, the main tools and artefacts were made of wood, bone, pottery or stone. There was no metal-working, no domestic animal power and the wheel was unknown. Extensive trading networks existed, especially along the southern coast and among the eastern islands, but also along the navigable rivers and between the coast and the Highlands. Shells were highly valued and in some places were used as a kind of currency. Other trade items included pottery, stone tools, obsidian, dyes, salt and sago.

Women did most of the day-to-day work, growing food and looking after the household. Men cleared the bush for gardening, hunted and undertook trade and warfare. Young men and bachelors sometimes worked for older men.

The social units were generally small, based on family, clan and tribe, the most important being the extended family. Some observers have described these communities as democratic Edens, where ownership was communal and everyone's basic needs were met. In reality, village elders or a bigman could hold virtually dictatorial powers and

in some places, such as Bougainville and the Trobriand Islands, hereditary chiefs and clear-cut classes developed.

In traditional PNG societies individual ownership did not exist in the same way as it does in Western societies, but the accumulation of wealth and its display was often a vital prerequisite for prestige and power. Ownership was vested in the household, which was controlled by a male elder. Within and between the households of the village there were complicated networks of responsibility, which provided a kind of social security.

Fundamental to the society were notions of reciprocity and family obligations: help (whether it be labour, land, food or pigs) was often given out of duty, or in the expectation of some kind of return (perhaps loyalty in time of war, assistance in organising a feast). Surplus wealth was not accumulated for its own sake, but so it could be given away, creating prestige for the giver and placing obligations on the receiver.

In most cases a bigman did not create a dynasty. Although a bigman's son had a head start in life he still had to demonstrate qualities of his own: hard work, bravery, leadership, trading skill, knowledge of magic. Different societies sought different characteristics in their leaders but economic ability was common to all. Wealth was necessary for a man to develop dependents and supporters.

The creation of wealth required hard work, and since women were largely responsible for agricultural production it was essential for a man with any ambition to get married. And it was the big men who monopolised the supply of female labour. Big men decided whether a young man would remain a bachelor and would sometimes 'give' assistance to young men to help them meet the bride price. Polygamy was often a feature of leadership.

In many areas, warfare and ritual cannibalism were commonplace and 'payback' killings perpetuated an endless cycle of feuding. Each small group was virtually an independent nation, so dealings with the next-door tribe were international relations. Although alliances were common, they tended to be shifting and expedient, rarely developing into large, long-term federations.

The world for most Papua New Guineans was closely proscribed: beyond their own clan they were surrounded by hostile or suspicious neighbours who often spoke a completely different language. Although no quarter was ever given in war, and women and children were not in any way exempt from attack, fighting usually occurred in highly ritualised battles, and only after negotiations had failed. Bows and arrows and spears were the weaponry, and there were generally few casualties.

Traditional Wealth

Although the country has shifted to a cash economy to a great extent, traditional forms of wealth are still very important, particularly in the Highlands and on the Milne Bay islands. A wad of banknotes can never have the same impact as kina shells, cassowaries or pigs. A large sow might be worth around K600, but many Papua New Guineans would rather have the pig. Another sign of wealth that is now displayed at paybacks and at ceremonial exchanges in the Highlands is a good stack of beer.

Kina shells are large half-moons cut from the gold-lip pearl shell. They they are often worn on ceremonial occasions in the Highlands. The kina coin has a large hole in the centre, probably with the idea that it too could be worn round the neck.

In the Highlands, another traditional display of wealth is the *aumak*, a chain of tiny bamboo rods worn around the neck. Each rod indicates that the wearer has lent out 10 or so kina shells. A long row of these little lengths of bamboo is an indication of great wealth.

In New Britain, shell money is still commonly used alongside the modern paper version, but only for small purchases: tiny shells strung along a piece of bamboo are worth about K0.10 a dozen. In Milne Bay leaf money or *doba* is made out of a bundle of etched and dried banana leaves and grass

skirts are also negotiable currency (K5 to K10). *Bagi*, the elaborate shell jewellery that is ritually traded around the islands, is the most important mark of prestige and wealth.

Highland man wearing *aumak*

Sport

Rugby is the most popular game, although contact sports are potentially dangerous for people who suffered from chronic malaria in childhood. Soccer is also played and, to a lesser extent, cricket.

Rugby matches sometimes end in teargas, so while it's worth seeing one, you should find out the likelihood of trouble before you go. The season is the same as Australia's winter sport season, roughly May to August.

RELIGION

Traditional religions certainly exist in PNG but drawing a dividing line between traditional beliefs (superstition) and religion is all but impossible. As with all religions, the myriad beliefs in PNG have developed over tens of thousands of years, and are primarily concerned with making sense of the world. For example, people who live in danger of crocodile attacks are likely to give crocodiles an important place in their culture; the weather is important to farming communities (and the people of PNG were perhaps the world's first farmers), which often celebrate fertility and harvest.

Most people, especially in the Highlands, traditionally lived in very small, independent communities, surrounded by communities which spoke different languages and could attack at any time. It isn't surprising that many traditional beliefs revolve around fear of the unknown and suspicion of difference. Placating the spirits of ancestors is a common theme in traditional beliefs, as is a fear of evil influences and of sorcery/witchcraft.

Does a collection of interests, beliefs and rules of conduct (such as the payback requirement of an eye for an eye) constitute a religion? The Christian missionaries certainly didn't think so, and have been responsible for the destruction of much traditional culture. Whether you see this as beneficial (stopping tribal wars and getting a better deal for women) or vandalism (the burning of carvings and spirit houses on the Sepik and elsewhere) depends on your own, foreign, value system.

In most areas of PNG traditional life continues, but all over the country the various arms of the Christian Church are extremely influential. Most people in PNG regard themselves as Christian, but most are also very proud of their cultural heritage. The older Churches seem to be able to cope with this dichotomy, concerning themselves with education, health and development issues, but there are plenty of hell-fire fundamentalists up to who knows what in remote areas.

The largest are the Catholic, Evangelical Lutheran and United churches.

LANGUAGE

It is calculated that there are 740 languages in PNG, a third of all the languages in the world. With this amazing basis for mutual incomprehension it's not surprising that there has long been a search for a common linking language.

During the early days of British New Guinea and then Australian Papua, the local language of the Port Moresby coastal area, Motu, was slightly modified to become 'police Motu', and spread through Papua by the native constabulary. It is still quite widely spoken in the southern Papuan part of PNG, and you can easily pick up a Motu phrasebook in Port Moresby.

In the northern German half of the country the German planters were faced with exactly the same communication difficulties as the British. Their solution was *pisin*, a local word that was corrupted into 'pidgin' – a term used today to define any trade language, a sort of mid-way meeting point between two languages. The PNG version of pidgin is now sometimes known as Neo-Melanesian, but more frequently just as Papua New Guinean pidgin or *tok pisin*. It is very close to the pidgin spoken in Vanuatu and the Solomons.

Tok ples is the term which describes a person's 'home' language.

Tok pisin has taken words from many languages, including German, but it is primarily derived from English.

Many educated people would prefer that you spoke to them in English, as crude pidgin is the hallmark of the bullying expat. Uneducated people are often shy about talking to an English-speaker (especially on the telephone) but even if you don't speak pidgin they often unfreeze if you throw a few pidgin words into an otherwise English sentence.

There are 22 letters in the pidgin alphabet, the letters **c, q, x** and **z** of the English alphabet having been omitted. Consonants are generally pronounced the same as in English. Note that **p** and **f** are pronounced (and often spelled) virtually interchangeably, as are **d** and **t**, and **j** and **z**; **qu** is spelled **kw**. **A** is pronounced as in 'pan', **e** as in 'bed',

i as in 'pit', **o** as in 'pot' and **u** as 'put'. There are three diphthongs: **ai** pronounced almost the same as the English letter 'i', **au** pronounced as the sound 'ow' and **oi** pronounced as in 'boil'. Pronunciation of tok ples words, particularly their vowels and diphthongs, is usually the same as in pidgin.

If your pidgin is less than perfect, it is wise to attach *yu save?* or *nogat?* (you understand or not?) to just about any sentence. *Save* is pronounced 'savvy'.

Finally, some pidgin confusion. A man's brother is his *brata* and my sister is his *susa*, but a woman's brother is her susa and her sister is her brata. In other words your brata is always the same sex as you, your susa always the opposite. Today *sista* is also in common use, however, and that has the same meaning as in English. Note that *kilim* means to hit (but hard), and to kill somebody (or something) you have to *kilim i dai*.

Careful of the sexual phrases – *pusim* means to copulate with, not to push! And while you can *ple tenis* (play tennis), *ple* is also a euphemism for intercourse. A man's trunk or suitcase may be a *bokis*, but a women's bokis is her vagina. And a *blak bokis* is not a black suitcase but a flying fox or bat!

Pronouns

I	*mi*
you (singular)	*yu*
you (plural)	*yupela*
he/she/it	*em* *
they	*ol*
we	*yumi*
(including person spoken to)	
we	*mipela*
(excluding person spoken to)	
everybody	*olgeta* **
all of us	*yumi olgeta*

* Note that *em* is followed by *i* to introduce the verb as in *em i kaikai i stap* or *em i no singsing*. Similarly after they *ol i wokabaut i go*.
** Note that *ol* indicates the plural as *ol haus* (houses) while *olgeta haus* means 'all the houses' – each of them.

Verbs & Tenses

Tenses are all the same except you append *pinis* (finish) to make it past tense: *mi kaikai pinis* means 'I have eaten'. Two common verbs:

bring, give or take	*kisim*
fasten, shut or lock	*fasim* or *pasim*

Useful Words

yes	*yes*
no	*nogat*
please	*plis*
thank you	*tenkyu*
a little	*liklik*
plenty	*planti*
big	*bikpela*
aircraft	*balus*
airport	*ples balus*
bathroom	*rum waswas*
bedroom	*rum slip*
toilet	*liklik haus;*
	haus pekpek
child	*pikinini*
forbidden	*tambu*
man	*man*
woman	*meri*
hospital	*haus sik*
police station	*haus polis*
letter, book, ticket	*pas*
luggage	*kago*
newspaper	*niuspepa*
photo	*poto*
towel	*taul*
relative	*wantok*

Greetings & Civilities

hello	*gude*
good morning	*moning*
good afternoon	*apinun*
see you later	*lukim yu bihain*
how are you?	*yu stap gut/orait?*
I'm fine	*mi stap gut/orait*

Time

yesterday	*asde*
today	*tude*
tomorrow	*tumora*
dawn	*sankamap*
noon	*belo*

midday hours	*biksan*
night	*tudak*
midnight hours	*biknait*
day before yesterday	*hapasde*
day after tomorrow	*haptumora*
two days ago	*tupela de i go pinis*
two days from now	*long tupela de*
last Monday	*long Mande bipo*
in February	*long namba tu mun*
in two months	*long tupela mun*

Food

food	*kaikai*
sweet potato	*kaukau*
taro	*taro*
Singapore taro	*taro kongkong*
'eating' banana	*banana mau*
cooking banana	*banana bilong paia*
cassava	*tapiok*
sago	*saksak*
yam	*yam* or *mami*
breadfruit	*kapiak*
sugar cane	*suga*
edible greens	*kumu*
corn	*kon*
pandanus fruit	*marita* or *karuka*
unripe coconut	*kulau*

game	*abus*
fish	*pis*
betel nut	*buai*
tobacco	*brus*
salt	*sol*

Small Talk

What time is it?
Wanem taim i stap?
Where are you from?
Ples bilong yu we?
I don't understand.
Mi no klia gut.
I don't know.
Mi no save.
Speak slowly.
Tok isi.

In the Village

My pidgin is not good.
Tok pisin bilong mi i no gutpela tumas.
I can understand, but I find it hard to answer back.
Mi ken harim tasol mi hat liklik long bekim.
I don't understand.
Mi no klia gut.
I don't know.
Mi no save.
You must talk slowly.
Yu mas tok isi.
Let's shake hands.
Yumi sekan.
What is this place/village/land called?
Wanem nem bilong dispela ples/viles /graun?
Can I sleep here/in your village)?
Inap mi ken slip long hia/long ples bilong yupela?
You can sleep in the men's house/in my house.
Yu ken slip long haus man/long haus bilong mi.
Did you bring a blanket and everything else?
Yu karim betsit na ol samting bilong yu i kam?
I've got a tent, can I pitch it over there?
Mi gat sel bilong mi, inap mi putim long hap?

Taro plant

Did you come by yourself?
Yu wanpela i kam?
Yes I did.
Mi wanpela.
Are there any more people coming?
Sampela lain moa bai i kam bihain?
I've come with another man and two women.
Mi kam wantaim arapela man na tupela meri.
Where did you walk from?
Yu wokabaut i kam long we?
Which way did you come?
Yu wokabaut i kam olsem wanem?
I've come from Naoro and Menari.
Mi kam long Naoro na Menari.
What brings you here?
Yu raun olsem wanem?
I'm just travelling/looking at places.
Raun nating tasol/lukluk long ples.
What's the real purpose of your trip?
Wanem wok tru bilong yu?
No definite purpose, just travelling.
Nogat wok, raun nating.
Do you live in Port Moresby/in PNG?
Yu save stap long Mosbi/long PNG?
Where are you from?
Yu bilong wanem hap?
Which country are you from?
Yu bilong wanem kantri tru?
Where exactly are you from?
Yu bilong wanem hap stret?
I'm from North America.
Mi bilong Amerika.
I would like to buy some sweet potatoes and greens/firewood.
Mi laik baim sampela kaukau na kumu /paiawut.
How much?
Em i hamas?
Where do you get your drinking water from?
Ples bilong dring wara we?
I would like to fill my bottle up.
Mi laik pulapim botol bilong mi.
Where is the bathing area?
Ples bilong waswas we?
Where is the toilet?
Toilet (haus pekpek) we?
What are you doing?
Yu mekim wanem samting?

Can I take your photo?
Inap mi kisim poto bilong yu?
Will you be able to send us copies?
Yu bai inap salim sampela poto i kam long mipela?
Yes, but you must give me your name and address.
Mi inap, tasol yu mas givim nem na adres bilong yu.

Hiring Guides & Carriers

I would like to go to that place/village/area.
Mi laik go long dispela ples/viles/hap.
I would like to hire a carrier/a guide.
Mi laik baim wanpela kagoboi/man bilong soim rot.
I would like to hire a carrier to go as far as Kagi.
Mi laik baim wanpela kagoboi i go inap long Kagi.
I would like to hire a carrier at 50 toea per hour.
Mi laik baim kagoboi long 50 toea long wan wan aua.
I would like to hire a carrier at K5 a day.
Mi laik baim kagoboi long K5 long wan wan de.
It's all right, we'll send a boy to go with you.
Em i orait, mipela bai salim wanpela manki i go wantaim yu.
Your load (bag) is too big and heavy.
Kago bilong yu i hevi na bikpela tumas.
You must portion your load (gear) out between two men.
Yu mas skelim kago bilong yu i go long tupela man.
We must get up/go/start walking at the crack of dawn.
Yumi mas kirap/go/stap wokabaut long moning tru.
We'll sleep/spend a night on the road/half way.
Yumi slip/lusim wanpela nait long rot/long namel.

On the Trail

Is there a trail going to Kagi?
Em i gat rot i go long Kagi?
Yes there is.
Em i gat.

There is no trail, it's overgrown.
Nogat rot, bus i kamap pinis
The trail is bad/overgrown/wrecked/big
/little /well defined.
*Rot i nogut/pas or bus/bagarap/bikpela
/liklik/klia olgeta*
mountainous area
ples maunten
bad or dangerous spot, place or area
ples nogut
There are lots of houses along the trail.
I gat planti haus long rot.
Are there any large streams or rivers along
this trail?
I gat sampela bikpela wara i stap long rot?
Is there a bridge or a log across?
Bris o diwai i stap?
There is a log.
Diwai i stap.
forest/garden/hunting trail
*rot bilong bus/bilong gaden/bilong
painim abus*
trail to waterplace/to bathing place
rot bilong kisim wara/waswas
footpath used by the ancestors/the government
Rot bilong tumbuna/kiap (gavman)
vehicle road
rot bilong ka
pig/possum/cassowary/animal tracks
rot bilong pik/kapul/muruk/abus
Pigs wrecked the trail.
Pik i bagarapim rot.
landslide; lots of mud
graun i bruk; planti graun i malumalu
to clean/make/cut/find a trail
klinim/wokim/katim/painim rot
secondary path or road
han rot
the beginning of a path or road
maus rot
Which way does the trail go?
Rot i go olsem wanem?
Where is the trail?
Rot we?
Where is the trail going to Kagi?
Rot i go long Kagi i stap we?
Trail or road intersection. Halfway.
Rot bung. Namel long rot.
Follow the trail.
Bihainim rot tasol.

Follow a path/fallen tree or log/ridge or
spur/fence.
Bihainim rot/diwai/kil/banis
Follow a mountain/stream or river/ditch/the
coast.
Bihainim maunten/wara/baret/nambis.
Follow alongside a ridge or a spur/a mountain
/a stream.
Saitim kil/maunten/wara.
I missed the path, trail.
Mi abrusim rot.
I got lost.
Mi lus long rot.
I got lost halfway.
Mi lus long namel.
I lost the trail.
Mi paul long rot.
On (off) the side of the trail or road.
Arere long rot.
I would like to catch my breath a little.
Mi laik kisim win liklik.
Is the village (place) nearby or far away?
Ples i klostu liklik o longwe yet?
It's near/fairly near/very near.
Em i klostu/klostu liklik/klostu tru.
We must walk briskly, the village is a long way.
*Yumi mas wokabaut strong, ples i longwe
yet.*
I'm not a fast walker.
Wokabaut bilong mi i no strong tumas.
Will we be able to get there in daylight?
Yumi bai inap kisim ples long san?
We'll reach the village at night.
Yumi bai kisim ples long tudak.
The fallen tree (or log) is dry/slippery/all
rotten.
Diwai i drai/i wel/i sting pinis.
Eat quickly and we'll go.
Yu kaikai hariap na yumi go.

Streams & Rivers

small/big/very large stream, creek or river
liklik/bikpela/draipela wara
to ford/cross/follow a river, stream or creek
brukim/katim/bihainim or saitim wara
follow a stream down/up
bihainim wara i go daun/i go antap
by the side of the stream, creek or river
arere long wara

What is the name of this stream, creek or river?

Wanem nem bilong dispela wara?

The current is strong.

Wara i strong.

The stream is in flood/is dry.

Wara i tait/i drai.

That stream can rise quickly.

Wara i save tait hariap.

You won't be able to ford it.

Yu no inap brukim.

The current will carry you down.

Wara bai i karim you.

Is there a bridge?

Bris i stap?

a log/vine/rattan bridge

bris diwai/mambu/kanda

Cross a bridge.

Kalapim bris.

headwaters

hetwara

a tributary

han bilong wara

The water is good.

Wara i swit.

cold water

Kol wara tru.

That water is not drinkable, people shit in it.

Wara i nogut, man i save pekpek long em.

The water is clear/dirty/clean.

Wara i klia/i doti/i klin.

Air Travel

Where is the airstrip?

Ples balus i stap we?

Is there an airstrip in that region or area?

I gat ples balus i stap long hap?

What time does the plane land?

Balus i save pundaun long wanem taim?

What day does the plane land?

Balus i save pundaun long wanem de?

How much is the flight?

Pe bilong balus em i hamas?

I would like to catch a plane/buy a plane ticket to Moresby.

Mi laik kisim/baim balus i go long Mosbi.

Numbers

The suffix *-pela* is added to the stem for counting objects. Numbers without *-pela* are used for prices, time and arithmetic.

½	*hap*
1	*wan*
2	*tu*
3	*tri*
4	*foa*
5	*faiv*
6	*sikis*
7	*seven*
8	*et*
9	*nain*
10	*ten*

The numbers 11 to 19 are formed by adding the numbers *wan* to *nain* after *wanpela ten*.

11	*wanpela ten wan*
12	*wanpela ten tu*
13	*wanpela ten tri*
14	*wanpela ten foa*
15	*wanpela ten faiv*
16	*wanpela ten sikis*
17	*wanpela ten seven*
18	*wanpela ten et*
19	*wanpela ten nain*

After 19 tens are formed by using the numbers *tu* onwards with the ending *-pela*.

20	*tupela ten*
25	*tupela ten faiv*
30	*tripela ten*
35	*tripela ten faiv*
40	*fopela ten*
45	*fopela ten faiv*
50	*faivpela ten*
100	*wan handet*
101	*wan handet wan*
1000	*tausen*
10,000	*tenpela tausen*
100,000	*handetpela tausen*
1,000,000	*wan milian*
once	*wanpela*
twice	*tupela*
thrice	*tripela*
four times	*foapela taim*
10 times	*tenpela taim*

Books

Like any language it takes a lot of study to understand pidgin fully, but you can be communicating on at least a basic level with remarkable speed. Lonely Planet publishes a pocket-sized *Language Survival Kit* called *Papua New Guinea phrasebook* that includes grammatical notes, many useful phrases and a vocabulary. There are a number of alternative phrasebooks and dictionaries that are easily available. The best places to look are the Christian Bookshops in PNG; there is usually one in every town and they have all sorts of literature in pidgin, including, needless to say, a pidgin Bible.

It's well worthwhile buying the *Wantok* weekly newspaper, written entirely in pidgin. As well as being a decent newspaper, reading it is a good way to learn the language. There are also comic strips which are easy to follow, even for beginners.

There is no substitute for actually hearing the language and if you want to get a head start before you get to PNG there is an excellent language course that includes two tapes and an exercise book. Unfortunately, it is no longer available outside PNG. For more information contact the Summer Institute of Linguistics (☎ 77 3544), PO Box 413, Ukarumpa via Lae, PNG.

Facts for the Bushwalker

VISAS & EMBASSIES

The story on visas has made a number of abrupt about turns over the years, so it is wise to check the regulations with a PNG consular office before you depart. In countries where there is no PNG consular office apply to the nearest Australian office.

The latest change to the visa system has been the re-instatement of the one-month 'easy visa', granted to tourists on entry. You pay K10 and you must have onward tickets.

However, don't rely on this, it's better to get a visa before you leave home. Your passport must have at least six months validity, even if you plan to visit PNG for only a few weeks.

A tourist visa requires one photo, costs the equivalent of K10 and permits a stay of up to 60 days. Since they seem to give you what you ask for, ask for the maximum time rather than have to face the problem of extending. There are heavy penalties for overstaying your visa. The most lightly you're likely to get off is paying a K250 fee for 'late application for visa extension'.

You may be asked to show your inward and outward ticketing, that you have sufficient funds and that you have made some sort of accommodation arrangements when applying for your visa. Usually you will only have to show tickets.

In Australia there is a PNG High Commission in Canberra, a Consulate-General in Sydney and a Consulate in Brisbane. Although many travellers fly from Cairns in northern Australia visas cannot be obtained there. The Sydney office issues visas only to residents of New South Wales and the Brisbane office only to residents of Queensland. Allow at least a week for the process.

Jayapura in Irian Jaya is another relatively common exit point to PNG and there is now a PNG consul there.

PNG Embassies

Visas can be obtained from PNG consulates in countries around the world.

Australia
  PNG High Commission, Forster Crescent, Yarralumla. PO Box 572, Manuka, ACT 2603 (☎ 273 3322, fax 273 3732)
  PNG Consulate-General, Somare Haus, 100 Clarence St, Sydney. GPO Box 4201, Sydney, 2001 (☎ 299 5151, fax 290 3794)
  PNG Consulate, Estates House, 307 Queen St, Brisbane. PO Box 220, Brisbane, 4001 (☎ 221 7915, fax 229 6084)
Belgium
  PNG Embassy, 17-19 Rue Montoyer 1040 Brussels (☎ 512 3126, fax 512 8643)
Fiji
  PNG Embassy, 6th floor, Ratu Sukuna House, Suva. PO Box 2447, Government Bldgs, Suva (☎ 30 4244, fax 30 0178)
France
  PNG Embassy, Apartment 272, Flatotel International Coenson, 14 Rue du Theatre, 75015 Paris (☎ 45 75 62 20, ext 272; fax 40 58 12 22)
Germany
  PNG Embassy, Gotenstrasse 163, 5300 Bonn 2, Germany (☎ 37 6855/6, fax 37 5103)
Indonesia
  PNG Embassy, 6th floor, Panin Bank Centre, Jalan Jendral Sudirman 1, Jakarta 10270 (☎ 720 1012, fax 73 4562)
  PNG Consulate, Jalan Serui No 8, PO Box 854, Jayapura, Irian Jaya (☎ 31250, fax 31898)
Japan
  PNG Embassy, Mita Kokusai Bldg 3F 313, 4-28 Mita 1-Chome, Minato-Ku, Tokyo (☎ 345 47801/4, fax 345 47275)
Malaysia
  PNG High Commission, 1 Lorong Ru Kedua, off Jalan Ru, Ampang, Kuala Lumpur (☎ 457 4202/4, fax 456 0998)
New Zealand
  PNG High Commission, 11th floor, Princes Towers, 180 Molesworth St, Thorndon, Wellington (☎ 473 1560, fax 471 2942)
Philippines
  PNG Embassy, 2280 Magnolia St, Dasmarinas Village, Makati, Metro Manila (☎ 810 8456/7, fax 817 1080)
Solomon Islands
  PNG High Commission, PO Box 1109 Honiara (☎ 20561, fax 20562)
UK
  PNG High Commission, 14 Waterloo Place, London SW1R 4AR (☎ 930 0922/6, fax 930 0828)

USA

PNG Embassy, 3rd floor, 1615 New Hampshire Ave NW, Washington DC 20009 (☎ 659 0856, fax 745 3679)

PNG Permanent Mission to the UN, Suite 322, 866 United Nations Plaza, New York 10017 (☎ 832 0043, fax 832 0918)

Visa Extensions

Tourist visas can be extended for one month for a fee of K10. The Immigration & Citizenship Office in the Central Government Offices in Waigani, Port Moresby is the only place in the country where you can extend visas. The office is open only from 8 am to noon. Extending a visa takes at least a week, officially, but one fortunate traveller reports managing it in a day.

Travellers who have tried extending their visas by mail from other parts of the country have generally found it impossible, and have had to get back to Port Moresby to retrieve their passports.

Foreign Embassies in PNG

Most embassies are in Port Moresby. It's worth making a phone call if you plan to visit between noon and 2 pm – some, including the Indonesian Embassy, close completely for two hours. Consulates, embassies and high commissions in Moresby include:

Australia

Independence Drive, Waigani, PO Box 9129, Hohola (☎ 25 9333, fax 25 9183)

France

9th floor, Pacific View Bldg, 1/84 Pruth St, Korobosea, PO Box 1155, Port Moresby (☎ 25 3740, fax 25 0861)

Germany

2nd floor, Pacific View Apartments, 1/84 Pruth St, Korobosea, PO Box 3631, Boroko (☎ 25 2988)

Indonesia

1 & 2/410 Sir John Guise Drive, Waigani, PO Box 7165, Boroko (☎ 25 3116)

Consulate in Vanimo (Sandaun Province)

Italy

Spring Gardens Rd, Hohola, PO Box 6330, Boroko (☎ 25 3183)

Japan

4th & 5th floors, ANG House, Cuthbertson St, Port Moresby, PO Box 1040, Port Moresby (☎ 21 1800)

New Zealand

Waigani Crescent, Waigani, PO Box 1144, Boroko (☎ 25 9444, fax 25 0565)

Philippines

Islander Village, Wards Rd, Hohola, PO Box 5916, Boroko (☎ 25 6414)

UK

Kiroki St, Waigani, PO Box 4778, Boroko (☎ 25 1677, fax 25 3547)

USA

Armit St, Paga Hill, Port Moresby, PO Box 1492, Port Moresby (☎ 21 1455, fax 21 3423)

Visas for Neighbouring Countries

Indonesia The visa situation for people travelling to or from Indonesia is tricky. Regulations can change overnight, and the left hand rarely knows what the right hand is doing. We quite regularly receive tales of woe from travellers, so it pays to be flexible in your plans if you want to incorporate both Indonesia and PNG in your itinerary.

If you enter PNG from Indonesia and plan to exit through Indonesia, do not forget to get a new Indonesian visa in PNG – once you have left Indonesia, the original visa or pass is finished whether or not the time has expired.

One-month visas to Indonesia are issued at the Indonesian Embassy in Port Moresby, and at the new Indonesian Consulate in Vanimo (Sandaun Province), a short hop by air from Jayapura. Apparently these can be extended in Indonesia. Check that the Vanimo office is still operating to avoid having to backtrack to Port Moresby.

You'll find more information in Lonely Planet's *Indonesia – a travel survival kit*, *South-East Asia on a shoestring* and *Papua New Guinea – a travel survival kit*.

Australia All nationalities (except New Zealanders) require a visa for Australia which is issued free at consulates and is usually valid for six months. Extensions beyond the six month period seem to be somewhat arbitrary – sometimes they will and sometimes they won't. Some visitors aged between 18 and 26 can be eligible for a 'working holiday' visa, and you should apply for this in your own country.

Menya women with their children, Menyamya, Morobe Province (YP)

Top Left: Whagi Valley near Mt Hagen (JM)
Top Right: Sago making, Karawari, East Sepik Province (JG)
Bottom: Goilala village near Kerau, Central Province (YP)

DOCUMENTS

The only essential document is your passport. You do not need an International Health Certificate in PNG. One or two places to stay give discounts to members of the International Youth Hostels Association. A valid overseas license is all you need to drive a car for up to three months from the day you arrive.

International Student Identity Cards are useful, especially if you're under 26 years old. Air Niugini offers significant student discounts as do some of the smaller airlines but not, unfortunately, Talair. Airlines sometimes require an International Student Concession Form, which should be available from your school or institution.

CUSTOMS

Visitors are allowed to import 200 cigarettes (or equivalent amount of tobacco) and 1 litre of alcoholic drinks duty free. Personal effects that you have owned for a year are also duty free. You won't have any problem with your camera, film and personal stereo.

Some items of cultural and historical significance are prohibited exports, including anything made before 1960, traditional stone tools, some shell valuables from Milne Bay, and any item incorporating human remains or bird of paradise plumes.

If you plan to buy artefacts, check your home country's import and quarantine regulations. Many artefacts incorporate animal skins or bones from protected animals, for instance, and these may be prohibited imports. If you are carrying the artefacts with you, you will also be subject to the regulations of countries you enter on your way home. Australia has particularly strict regulations on the importation of animal products and even wooden items might require treatment.

MONEY
Currency

The unit of currency is the kina which is divided into 100 toea.

Most international currency travellers' cheques are acceptable. Banks can be found in all the big towns, but off the beaten track you may have trouble finding a place to change money. Don't run short. On walks, you'll need plenty of smaller denomination notes and a supply of coins, as villagers won't have change.

You aren't allowed to take out of the country more than K200 in notes and K5 in coins, or more than K250 worth of foreign cash.

Exchange Rates

Australia	A$1	=	K0.69
Britain	UK£1	=	K1.44
Canada	C$1	=	K0.78
France	FF1	=	K0.17
Germany	DM1	=	K0.59
Indonesia	1000 rp	=	K0.47
Japan	Y100	=	K0.84
New Zealand	NZ$1	=	K0.52
Singapore	S$1	=	K0.59
USA	US$1	=	K0.97

Banks

There is one easy way of carrying money around and that is to open a passbook savings

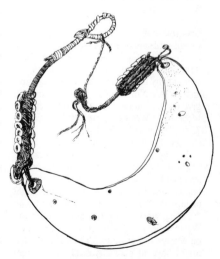

A kina shell necklace –
one form of traditional money

account with a Papua New Guinea Banking Corporation (PNGBC) bank. You can then withdraw money from your account at any branch or agency – found on quite a few of the larger government stations – around the country. It's more convenient than changing traveller's cheques and you get interest on your money.

The PNGBC was once part of Australia's Commonwealth Bank and *might* honour passbook savings accounts (with blacklight signatures) held by customers of the Australian Commonwealth Bank. There is some difference of opinion on this between various officials in PNG and Australia, so don't count on it.

The PNGBC and Westpac (an Australian-based bank) are widely represented. Other banks include the Bank of South Pacific (member of the National Australia Group) and the Australia & New Zealand Banking Group (ANZ).

Banking hours are 9 am to 2 pm (3 pm for the PNGBC) from Monday to Thursday and 9 am to 5 pm on Fridays.

It's relatively simple to have money transferred to a bank (preferably Westpac) in PNG from overseas.

Credit Cards

Credit cards are beginning to take off but are by no means accepted everywhere. Both American Express and Diners Club are accepted by the ritzier hotels and restaurants and by Air Niugini and Talair. Amex will give cash advances from their office in Port Moresby at Westpac Travel (☎ 25 4066, fax 25 1675) in Ori Lavi Haus on Nita St in Boroko, PO Box 1552 Boroko.

The ubiquitous Australian Bankcard is unknown and while Mastercard is becoming acceptable at some of the more expensive hotels, few places take Visa. That might change, as Westpac is now associated with Visa as well as Mastercard. The main Westpac branches will give a cash advance on Mastercard of up to K75 on the spot but might have to phone Australia (for a fee) before they can give larger amounts. ANZ will probably do the same with Visa.

Costs

PNG is very expensive. Budget for Australian prices or higher, *not* Asian prices. Once you get into the villages, however, you move into an almost cashless economy where you can live for much less.

Bargaining & Tipping

Bargaining is not a natural part of most day to day transactions. It is never a game or an integral, enjoyable part of shopping as it is in Asia. Prices in the markets are set and fair (often they are clearly displayed) and prices on Public Motor Vehicles (PMVs) are also set.

The only time you will come across anything approximating bargaining (serious negotiation would be a more appropriate description) is when you are being charged for a photograph, buying artefacts or are hiring a guide or boat. With artefacts you are sometimes offered an outrageous first price and you are expected to ask for the 'second price'. It's very unwise to use bargaining strategies such as belittling the artefact or questioning the vendor's honesty. Remember that if the vendor is selling on behalf of someone else (not unusual) they might not be *able* to lower the price.

Sometimes negotiations will take days. Be low key, not aggressive. This is not an Asian game and you could easily offend someone.

Do not tip, it isn't expected.

WHEN TO GO

The climate is the main consideration in deciding when to visit PNG – see that section of the Facts About the Country chapter. International and domestic flights are heavily booked from before Christmas to early February, with a lull in January.

WHAT TO BRING

The best advice, wherever you go, is to take too little rather than too much. Keep in mind that the domestic airlines have a baggage weight limit of 16 kg, although as a tourist you can usually slip by if your bags weigh around 20 kg.

General

Clothing Most of the time all you will require is lightweight clothing, T-shirts, sandals and swimming gear. Natural fibres, cotton in particular, will be most comfortable in the sticky, lowlands humidity. Sunglasses will also be useful.

Don't come laden with gaudy T-shirts, boardshorts, and other 'beach culture' clothing. Other than the small rich elite, most people dress conservatively and many buy their clothes from second-hand stores. Flaunting your foreignness will make you stand out and could attract thieves.

Women must dress discreetly; the often scanty styles of traditional dress do not apply to foreigners and mission influenced people can be very prudish. From a security point of view, it's not a good idea to call attention to yourself with revealing clothes. A below-the-knee dress is the best solution, although where this is impractical trousers are usually OK, as long as they're not very tight. Shorts are definitely not a good idea – even on men shorts can be too short or tight. A bikini is inappropriate at all but the most Westernised and protected locations.

Other Although most day-to-day requirements are available in PNG's big towns, you won't find many specialist shops. If you take any regular medication, bring a good supply, although chemists in the big towns are reasonably well stocked.

Although they often fog up, glasses are preferable to contact lenses which, due to the high humidity levels, irritate the eyes and are difficult to keep clean. Make sure you carry a spare pair; although glasses can be bought in Lae and Port Moresby, they are very expensive. Sunglasses are useful.

A mask and snorkel is definitely worth having, as hire shops are few and far between, prices are high, and virtually every beach is a snorkeller's delight.

For Walking

The equipment necessary for walking in PNG depends on whether you plan to sleep in village houses or camp out, and the altitude range to be spanned. Remember that PNG is very rugged and you will find it extremely exhausting to carry more than 15 kg. Of course, you can hire carriers.

Clothing The climate is generally warm and trails seldom climb above the tree line, so cold weather gear is not needed unless you plan to climb the higher peaks. Clothing worn at home on a summer weekend hike, along with a sweater and pair of long trousers and rain gear, is basically all you need. Don't venture above the tree line without warmer clothing – it can snow on Mt Wilhelm and other peaks.

A list of clothes to bring might include:

Bush Hat
Indispensable. Bring one that can protect your eyes against the rain, especially if you wear glasses.
Headband
Keeps sweat out of your eyes.
Shorts
For men only. Ideal for most walking in PNG. They are also worn when bathing or swimming so bring two or three pairs. They should be lightweight and cotton.

Long Trousers

Women should always wear long trousers (or a long skirt where feasible). Everyone needs trousers above the tree line, and they give protection anywhere when walking through sharp grasses.

Socks

Long, thick socks protect against scratches and will make you feel less worried about snakes.

T-shirts & shirts

Two or three cotton t-shirts or shirts should be enough. Long-sleeved shirts will give protection against the sun and insects.

Laplap

This is PNG's version of the sarong. It can be used as a dressing gown, a beach towel, a bed sheet and of course a sarong.

Sweater

Essential above 3000 metres and useful elsewhere in the Highlands.

Rain gear

Rain is common and often torrential, and in the mountains it is often too cold to be ignored. A short raincoat and a separate cover for your pack is a good solution. The raincoat should 'breathe', or the humidity will be unbearable.

Cold Weather Gear

Only needed if you plan to go above the tree line. A hat, a pair of gloves and a warm jacket are necessary. A pair of nylon over-trousers add extra comfort in wet weather. Always take along at least one change of clothes in cold areas.

Handkerchiefs

A must if you wear glasses, to wipe off the rain and condensation caused by the high humidity.

Footwear The wet, often muddy and slippery conditions on most trails make even the most hi-tech footwear unsuitable for PNG. Outside towns, Papua New Guineans seldom wear shoes. The toughened skin on their feet and legs enable them to go barefoot and their wide feet and splayed toes (a result of going barefoot) provide the best grip available.

You'll be walking on rock slabs and slippery, sloping moss-covered logs; walking down creeks on slimy rocks and negotiating steep, wet, muddy and slippery trails. Tread and traction are therefore extremely important. Footwear must also be durable, as there is sharp limestone to be negotiated and many of the walks are long.

Don't worry about waterproofing, as no footwear will keep your feet dry.

Leather hiking boots provide excellent ankle support and contribute to a safer walk.

The wet conditions mean that leather boots deteriorate rapidly, maybe totally disintegrating, but as most of the walks described in this book are relatively short, this isn't so much of a problem. Nevertheless, you should dry your boots as often as possible. You won't be able to replace worn-out boots in PNG.

The best walking shoe for PNG is probably just a pair of good running shoes, if you have strong ankles. They don't become heavy when they are wet, and some have excellent tread. Few brands of running shoes are available in PNG, but the excellent Dunlop KT-26 can normally be found in Boroko (Port Moresby) at Apana Sports in the Hugo Mall or the Arcade Discount Shop in Kwila Plaza, for about K50.

'Jungle boots', with rubber soles and canvas uppers, are not the best shoes, but they do remain light when saturated, and they grip fairly well. However, after three weeks of walking they will be worn out. The Taurama Pharmacy and Kim Foon & Sons, both on Tabare Place in Boroko (Port Moresby), usually stock jungle boots. Expect to pay about K30. They can sometimes be found in other towns.

Golf shoes, oddly enough, are worth considering as their spikes provide excellent grip. The type with screw-in spikes is best as they can be replaced when broken and easily removed when not needed. Apparently, they are quite durable. Golf shoes can be found in sport shops in Port Moresby, Lae, Mt Hagen and Rabaul.

Socks, preferably thick, give protection in the unlikely event that you are bitten by a snake. Gaiters prevent seeds from clinging to your socks and also protect against snakes, leeches, nettles and other plants.

No ice or snow climbing equipment is needed.

Bring a pair of thongs (flip-flops) or another pair of sandshoes for use in villages.

Equipment Little specialist outdoor equipment is available in PNG. However, items used regularly by local people, such as bush knives, pocket knives, day packs, mosquito nets, and lightweight cooking pots are available in the towns.

You might be able to hire walking gear from Traditional Travel (☎ 21 3966, fax 21 2849, PO Box 4264, Boroko) in Port Moresby. Contact them well in advance, as all their gear might be in use.

Because of the frequent and heavy rain, pack everything in separate plastic bags. A money belt or pouch is essential in the towns and recommended in the villages. Because of the heat, the pouch or belt and its contents soon become sodden with sweat, so make sure paper items are sealed in plastic.

The following list of equipment should not be regarded as exhaustive. Some items will not be necessary to some walkers.

Pack
Internal frame rucksacks are best for PNG, as there is no frame sticking out to be caught by the dense vegetation.

Pack Cover
Unless you're using a rain poncho, a cover is necessary to keep your gear dry.

Day Pack
Handy for carrying cameras, water bottles, etc, particularly if you plan on hiring local carriers to carry the bulk of you gear, but also if you want to go day tripping.

Tent
Not really necessary unless you walk beyond populated areas or spend some time above the tree line, or are in a group. See the Accommodation section later in this chapter for more information.

Tarp or Plastic Sheet
Not necessary but very useful. It can be used to built a makeshift shelter or to waterproof an existing one. A tent fly works just as well.

Sleeping Bag
Necessary if you plan to spend time above 1000 metres. For sleeping in village houses, a light summer bag is all you'll need; village people always sleep by a warm fire. In a tent, especially above the tree line, a warmer bag is required. PNG's highest mountains commonly experience frost.

Sleeping Sheet
Can be used in the lowlands (below 1000 metres) as a substitute sleeping bag.

Sleeping Mat
The floors of most village houses are very uneven, and many are dirty.

Mosquito Net
Essential if you hope to get any sleep in such places as the Sepik Basin, many parts of the Gulf and Western provinces and the coastal areas of Central and Oro provinces. In mountain areas below 1000 metres a mosquito net isn't usually necessary for comfort, but is still essential to protect you against malaria.

Stove
Not necessary but very useful. Firewood is abundant almost everywhere in the country, but it is often sodden. Dry firewood is always available in villages. Kerosene (paraffin) and gas are sold almost everywhere and methylated spirits can be bought at chemists. Other fuels may be hard to come by.

Cooking Utensils
You'll need some utensils, one or two pots, a plate, a bowl and a mug. Remember that it is your responsibility to look after the guides or carriers you hire – you might need a larger pot and extra plates and utensils.

Pocket Knife
Invaluable for opening tins and for peeling such food items as sweet potatoes, taros, etc. Get one that also has scissors.

Water Bottle
Essential. In the villages, all drinking water is fetched from nearby streams, then carried home. A bottle is also necessary on the trail. A two litre bottle is recommended.

Torch (flashlight)
Essential, as villages are very dark at night. Of the many types of batteries available in PNG, the D size is the most readily available. Bulbs for torches that take batteries other than D size can be hard to come by.

Rope
A 20-metre length of rope is highly recommendable for ensuring safe crossing of rivers, particularly during the rainy season.

Compass
Highly recommended. Remember that compasses bought in the northern hemisphere might not work in the southern hemisphere.

Bush Knife (machete)
Unless you plan to walk off the beaten track, to camp out or to go beyond populated areas, a bush knife (or an axe) is not really necessary.

Miscellaneous
> Carry toiletries, toilet paper, a small plastic bag for holding toilet paper and litter before disposal, a bar of laundry soap, a mirror, sunscreen, insect repellent, a towel, a money belt, safety pins, a sewing kit, a pair of scissors, matches (but preferably a lighter), candles, large needles and fishing line for repairing your gear, spare shoelaces (strong and long ones are hard to come by in PNG), and a basic medical kit (see the Health section later in this chapter).

You might want a mask and a snorkel if you plan coastal walking, a pair of binoculars for bird watching, an altimeter, a small hurricane lamp, and some trade goods and gifts for the people in the villages.

Take 10 and 20 toea coins if you plan on buying food in the villages. Some 50 toea and K1 coins and small denomination notes are necessary for paying guides or carriers. Larger notes will be difficult or impossible to change in villages.

As long as they are correctly stamped, many pilots will post letters for you. Get some stamps and an update on postal rates before you head out for the bush.

TOURIST OFFICES
Local Tourist Offices
There are few outlets for general tourist information in PNG. One of the best sources is Air Niugini. They play a major role in promoting tourism and most offices are helpful and have some printed information.

There is an information office in the international arrivals hall at Jacksons Airport in Port Moresby. Here you can get a visitors' guide and an annual accommodation directory which is useful for fairly up-to-date information on hotel prices.

A number of provincial governments have officials whose responsibilities include tourism, although they don't have a specific department. You would stand a good chance of reaching them if you addressed your query: Tourist Officer, Department of Commerce, (name of province). There are real live Tourist Offices in Madang and Rabaul and a number of other provincial boards,

bureaus and offices, especially in Manus, Milne Bay and New Ireland.

If you're stuck for information the best thing to do is simply ask around. There'll usually be someone who can help. In small places you'll often find an English-speaker at the airstrip.

National The national tourist offices in PNG are:

Air Niugini
> PO Box 7186, Boroko, PNG (☎ 25 9000)

PNG Tourist Office
> PO Box 7144, Boroko, PNG (☎ 25 1269)

Jacksons Airport (☎ 25 8776)

Provincial The provincial tourist offices in PNG are:

East New Britain Tourist Bureau
> PO Box 385, Rabaul, East New Britain, PNG (☎ 92 1813)

Madang Visitors' Bureau
> PO Box 2025, Jomba, Madang, PNG (☎ 82 3302, fax 82 3540)

Manus Tourist Officer
> PO Box 37, Lorengau, Manus Province, PNG (☎ 40 9361, fax 40 9218)

Milne Bay Visitors' Bureau
> PO Box 337, Alotau, Milne Bay Province, PNG (☎ 61 1503, fax 61 1402)

New Ireland Tourist Bureau
> PO Box 103, Kavieng, New Ireland Province, PNG (☎ 94 1449, fax 94 2346)

Overseas Reps
Air Niugini offices are the best sources of information. Embassies can help, as can the tour operators.

USEFUL ORGANISATIONS
There are walking clubs in Port Moresby and Lae. Clubs form in other places from time to time, but the members are mainly transient expats, and the clubs fold when the enthusiasts move on.

The PNG Bushwalkers Association in Port Moresby has regular weekend walks, which would not only give you a chance to see something, but also to meet some nice people. Finding the current contact person might be tricky – Vladek Gontarez, who works in the Roads & Bridges section (☎ 29 2091) of the Department of Works might still be around. If not, someone at the Australian High Commission might know who to contact.

The Lae Explorer's Club is active, with plenty of walks of varying standards, and you can rent some equipment. You can also consult their useful archives, where you'll find a copy of Robin King's *A Bush Walker's Guide to the Huon Peninsula*, which describes many excellent walks throughout the Huon Peninsula near Lae. It was compiled in 1975, so it's out of date but is still a good source of information. Membership is only K5, but you don't have to be a member on your first walk. The current contact person is John Clarke (☎ 42 6510) but that will almost certainly change.

The Yacht Club or Unitech would be a good places to ask for current information, or check the notice boards at Unitech, post offices, Anderson's supermarket in Eriku and the Bali newsagency store in town.

You can also get good walking information from Traditional Travel (☎ 21 3966, fax 21 2849, PO BOX 4264, Boroko, NCD) which offers organised walks and has a reasonably priced information service, as well as excellent contacts throughout the country.

You might be able to find a copy of Helen Pickering's 1987 *Tari Walks of Adventure and Discovery*, which describes many interesting walks throughout the Tari Basin. It was printed by Evangelical Printers in Tari.

Organised Walks

A number of companies offer organised walks. They're not cheap, but they are worth considering if you have limited time. It's hard to guarantee itineraries at the best of times in PNG, but professional companies will probably have a better chance of sticking to them than you will. Some of them also go to places you would be hard pushed to reach yourself, even if you did find out they existed. Most have a range of different tours in addition to walking:

Grassroutes Ecotravel
PO Box 710, Rabaul (☎ 92 1756)
New Rabaul-based organisation encouraging low-budget treks and accommodation in co-operation with villages in New Britain and New Ireland. Worth checking out.

Haus Poroman
PO Box 1182, Mt Hagen, PNG, (☎ 52 2722, fax 52 2207)
Haus Poroman is one of the best places to stay in PNG, and they also offer Sepik canoe trips, Highlands treks and other packages.

Melanesian Tourist Services
PO Box 707, Madang, PNG (☎ 82 2766, fax 82 3543)
Suite 10B, 302 West Grand Ave, El Segundo, CA 90245, USA (☎ (213) 785 0370, fax (213) 785 0314)
32 Mossville Gardens, Morden, Surrey SM44DG, UK (☎ (081) 540 3125, fax (081) 540 5510)
Alt-Schwanheim 50, 6000 Frankfurt am Main 71, Germany (☎ (69) 35 6667, fax (69) 35 0080)
Via Teulie 8, 20136, Milano, Italy (☎ (02) 837 5892)
Air Niugini, Continental or Qantas offices
Operates the luxury cruise boat *Melanesian Discoverer*, the Madang Resort Hotel and a couple of other up-market lodges. Niugini Diving Adventures is based at the Madang Resort Hotel. Also vehicle tours and some treks.

Mountain Travel – Sobek
6420 Fairmont Ave, El Cerrito CA 94530-3606 (☎ 1-800 227 2384, fax 1-510 525 7710)
Sepik and Trobriand tours.

Niugini Tours
100 Clarence St, Sydney 2000, Australia (☎ (02) 290 2055)

Raging Thunder
PO Box 1109, Cairns 4870, Australia (☎ (070) 31 1466, fax (070) 51 4010)
Rafting, sea-kayaking and treks.

Traditional Travel
PO Box 4264, Boroko, NCD, PNG, (☎ 21 3966, 21 2849)
Highly recommended. A variety of tours, including canoeing on the Sepik, trekking, fishing in Gulf Province, sailing canoes in Milne Bay, bicycling on New Ireland. Although their prices are not in the shoestring range, they are lower than some other operators'. The best thing about Traditional Travel, though, is that their tours break out of the tourist cocoon and emphasise meeting (and staying with) villagers.

Trans Niugini Tours
PO Box 371, Mt Hagen, PNG (☎ 52 1438, fax 52 2470)
44B Aplin St, Cairns 4870, Australia (☎ (070) 51 0622, (070) 52 1147)

Suite 105, 850 Colorado Blvd, Los Angeles, CA 90041, USA (☎ toll-free 1-800-621 1633 (CA), 1-800-521 7242 (USA & Canada), fax (213) 256 0647)

Suite 433, 52-54 High Holborn, London WC1V 6RB, UK, (☎ (071) 242 3131, fax (071) 242 2838)

Blumenstrasse 26, 4000 Dusseldorf 1, Germany (☎ (0211) 80127, fax (211) 32 4989)

Via Ferdinando Galani 25/D 00191 Rome, Italy (☎ (06) 329 3697, fax (06) 328 6261)

A large organisation similar to Melanesian Tourist Services. Trans Niugini also operates Sepik cruises (on the *Sepik Spirit)* and has the award-winning Ambua and Karawari lodges and a hotel near Madang. Many tours are offered, including some aimed at those on lower budgets.

Tribal World

PO Box 86, Mt Hagen, PNG (☎ 52 1555, fax 55 1546)

Tribal World operates a chain of hotels and offers some tours, including canoeing, trekking and, sometimes, rafting.

United Touring International

Koyata Bldg 3F, 2-5 Yotsuya 2-Chome, Shinjuku-ku, Tokyo 160, Japan (☎ (03) 335 52391, fax (03) 335 52438)

BUSINESS HOURS & HOLIDAYS
Business Hours

Most offices are open from 7.45 or 8 am to 4 pm. Shops generally stay open later, especially on Friday nights and they're also open on Saturday mornings. Trade stores and snack bars usually have more liberal hours.

Banks are open from 9 am to 2 pm (3 pm for PNGBC), Monday to Thursday and until 5 pm on Friday. At Port Moresby airport there's a bank agency which supposedly opens for the arrival of all international flights – but not necessarily for departures.

Post offices are open from 9 am (sometimes 8 am) to 5 pm weekdays and on Saturday mornings. There's generally not much point in visiting government offices between 12.30 and 2 pm even though lunch officially starts at 1 pm and finishes at 1.30 pm.

Alcohol licensing regulations vary from province to province so the hours publicans can sell beer vary. It's not unusual for a town or even a whole province to be declared 'dry' if there has been trouble.

Holidays, Festivals & Cultural Events

Each of the twenty provinces of PNG has its own provincial government day and these are usually a good opportunity to enjoy *sing-sings* (traditional ceremonies and dances). Generally, however, sing-sings are local affairs with no fixed yearly schedule, so you'll have to depend on word of mouth to find out about them.

Shows and festivals are held on weekends, so the dates change from year to year, usually only by a few days. Similarly, the public holiday associated with a provincial government day will usually be on a Friday or a Monday.

If you want to be certain of a festival date before you arrive, try contacting one of Air Niugini's overseas offices.

1 January
New Year's Day
22 February
New Ireland Provincial Government Day
Kavieng Show (perhaps moving to late July)
Easter
Traditional church services.
20 April
Oro Provincial Government Day
June-August
Yam Harvest Festival (Trobriand Islands)
Mid-June
Queen's Birthday
Port Moresby Show – traditional and modern events.
Central Provincial Government Day
July
Morobe Provincial Government Day
7 July
Milne Bay Government Day
23 July
Remembrance Day (mainly Port Moresby)
Rabaul Frangipani Festival – commemorating the first flowers to blossom after the 1937 eruption of Matupit.
Early August
Madang Provincial Government Day
Maborasa Festival (Madang) – includes dancing, choirs and bamboo bands.
August
Manus Provincial Government Day
Simbu Provincial Government Day
Southern Highlands Provincial Government Day
Late August
Mt Hagen Show – a big gathering of clans with traditional dances and dress.

Early September
Goroka Show – similar but bigger than Mt Hagen Show. This used to occur on even-numbered years, but may become annual.

16 September
Independence Day – a great time to be in PNG with many festivals and sing-sings all around the country.
East Sepik Provincial Government Day
Hiri Moale, Port Moresby. Big festival celebrating the huge Papuan trading canoes.
Malangan Festival (Kavieng or Namatanai, in New Ireland) – the two-week festival includes the famous tree-dancers.
Milne Bay Show

October
Enga Provincial Government Day
West New Britain Provincial Government Day

October or November
Tolai Warwagira (Rabaul) – a two-week festival of sing-sings and other events. Currently celebrated on odd-numbered years.

November
Oro Tapa Festival, Popondetta

1 December
Gulf Provincial Government Day

6 December
Western Provincial Government Day

25 December
Christmas

Man at sing-sing

POST & TELECOMMUNICATIONS
Post
There is no mail delivery service so if you're writing to people within PNG you must address your letters to post office boxes. Box numbers of hotels and useful companies are given throughout the book. Add the name of the relevant town and the province:

Niugini Guest Haus
PO Box 108
Wewak
East Sepik Province

There's a poste restante service at most post offices. Underline the surname and print it clearly if you want the letter to arrive safely. Even then you have to cross your fingers. However, if you have a fixed address, mail usually seems to be quite reliable.

The amount of time a letter takes to be delivered varies radically – it can take from three days to three weeks to travel between Australia and PNG. Allow at least three months for parcel post from PNG to North America. Wrap parcels carefully as surface mail can be very rough. If they're packed in cardboard cartons, with paper packing, masks or other purchases should get back OK.

Postal Rates
Letters within PNG	K0.21
Aerograms	K0.45
Airmail letters (up to 20 grams):	
to Australia, New Zealand	K0.45
to Asia	K0.60
to Europe, North America	K0.90

Note that postcards are charged at the letter rate, so you can send two aerograms to Europe for the price of a stamp for one postcard.

Many of the pilots who land on the 450 or so strips strewn across the country will post letters for you, if they are stamped.

Telephone
The phone system in PNG, although limited

to the main centres, is extremely good. You can direct dial between all the main centres, and there are no area codes to worry about, unless you're ringing a radio phone in which case you dial 019 for the operator. You can also direct dial most of the world, even from payphones.

Payphones charge K0.20 for local calls. For long distance or international calls, feed in more money every time the red light shines. Unused coins are refunded.

Pay phones can be hard to find, however. There are usually a few near the post office. In Port Moresby, Lae, Mt Hagen and perhaps some other larger towns you'll find payphones which take phone cards – post offices and a few shops sell the cards.

Some big hotels may allow you to use their phones but the cost is much higher.

Fax

Kwik piksa leta (fax) has taken off in a big way in PNG. You can send faxes from post offices for a few kina, and they can be a useful way of making accommodation bookings. Fax numbers are listed in the telephone directory.

TIME

The time throughout PNG is the same as Australian Eastern Standard Time, and 10 hours ahead of UTC (GMT). When it's noon in PNG it will also be noon in Sydney, 9 am in Jakarta, 2 am in London, 9 pm the previous day in New York and 6 pm the previous day in Los Angeles.

PNG is close to the equator, so day and night are almost equal in duration and it gets dark quickly. The sun rises about 6 am and sets at about 6 pm. There is no daylight saving (summer time) in PNG.

ELECTRICITY

The electric current on the national grid is 240 volts, AC 50Hz (the same as in Australia). While all the towns have electrical supplies most of PNG does not have power, other than that provided by the occasional privately owned generator.

WEIGHTS & MEASURES

PNG uses the metric system. See the back pages of this book for conversion tables.

MAPS

The *Tourist Guide to Papua New Guinea* (which includes city maps) produced by Shell and the PNG Office of Tourism, and the excellent little map produced by Air Niugini are good general maps.

The whole country is covered by topographic maps down to the 1:100,000 scale; there is not yet a complete series for scales larger than that, eg 1:25 000. The National Mapping Bureau in Waigani (☎ 27 6465, fax 25 9716, PO Box 5665, Boroko, NCD) keeps a complete inventory of the country's 1:100,000 and 1:250,000 topographic map series. They cost about K4 a sheet. In addition to these a wide range of other maps, including the available 1:50,000 and 1:25 000 topographic maps, are available from the Bureau. You can order from overseas.

The contour lines and the position of streams or mountains on the topographic maps are quite reliable but the toponymy (place-naming) leaves much to be desired, with incorrect spellings or even the wrong name altogether. Villages are not always in the right position, or might no longer exist.

The European names of some rivers and mountains on the maps are not always known to the local people. Also, a river might be called different names by the various cultural and linguistic groups living nearby. For instance, the upper Strickland River, as foreigners know it, is called Om by the people living on the western side of it and Lagaip by those living on the eastern side.

In spite of these problems, a topographic map is necessary. Even if the names are wrong, the centres of population are always clearly indicated, and local people can help sort out difficulties.

The toponymy of the maps in this book is more reliable than that of most other maps.

As well as the Mapping Bureau in Port Moresby, maps are sold at some provincial Lands departments, but you're much more likely to find the map you want in Port Moresby.

In Lae, the Cartographic Section of the Department of Surveying and Land Studies at Unitech (☎ 43 4950) sells all the 1:100,000 series. They don't have 1:250,000 maps. Also in Lae, the Lands Department (☎ 42 2879, PO Box 412), in the Morobe provincial government buildings sells the 1:100,000 and 1:250,000 maps for the Momase region (Morobe, Madang and Sepik provinces).

In Mt Hagen, the Department of Lands at the end of Kuri St has the Highlands sheets of the 1:100,000 topographic map series, and many others, plus sheets of the 1:250,000 series.

In Madang, the Lands Department (☎ 82 2795, PO Box 2072, Yomba) is in the provincial government offices and sells the 1:100,000 and 1:250,000 maps for Madang and Sepik provinces, and a few others.

In Rabaul, the Lands Department (☎ 92 1664, PO Box 535) sells the 1:100,000 and 1:250,000 maps for the whole islands area, including Manus, New Britain, New Ireland and Bougainville.

MEDIA
Newspapers
As well as a few skimpy local papers, there is one national daily, the *Post Courier*; it's a tabloid but is more serious than that format usually indicates. If you buy nothing else, it is worth buying *The Times of PNG*, a good-quality weekly review produced by Word Publishing. The same people also publish a good weekly newspaper in pidgin – *Wantok*. Reading the centre-spread of comics is a good way to begin to learn pidgin.

Radio & TV
The National Broadcasting Commission operates an AM and FM radio station in Port Moresby, as well as a number of provincial services, including shortwave. One service which is produced in all regional centres is the Toksave ('talk-savvy' – information) programme. This bulletin-board means that even the remotest villages are in touch with community events.

EMTV is the sole local TV station, but almost everyone can pick up QTV from Australia. CNN, Indonesian and Malaysian programmes are also widely received on satellite dishes.

FILM & PHOTOGRAPHY
PNG is great for photographers and you can easily run through a lot of film, particularly if you happen on some event like a big Highland sing-sing. Film is easily available in the major towns, but it is fairly expensive, even by Australian standards.

Protect your camera and film from the dust, heat and humidity. Humidity damages film and plays havoc with lenses, stimulating the growth of fungi. Keeping gear in an airtight container with silica gel is strongly recommended. You'll find a flash useful, particularly for shots inside village houses. Bring a small cleaning kit and spare batteries.

Allow for the high intensity of the tropical sun when making your settings. Between mid-morning and late afternoon you might want to use a filter to avoid washed-out colour. You'll get the best colour contrasts with 25 and 64 ASA film, and 100 ASA comes in handy on overcast days. The forest canopy is so thick that even on a sunny day little light reaches the ground. You'll need at least 400 ASA film.

Etiquette
Never take a photograph in or of a *haus tambaran* (or any other spirit house) without asking permission. These are holy places and you could quickly find yourself in trouble if you do not respect the feelings of their guardians. It's best to ask several of the male elders first, to make sure you do actually speak to someone who has the authority to grant your request. Even if you just glance through your viewfinder people will assume that you have taken a photo, so be careful.

You'll find people are generally happy to be photographed, even going out of their way to pose for you, particularly at sing-sings. It is absolutely essential to ask permission before you snap. At the very least, remember the standards of privacy you would expect at home – don't, for instance, take a photo of someone washing in their bathroom, even if the bathroom is a jungle stream. Even this is not fail-safe as you cannot assume that your standards are appropriate, so always ask.

You'll rarely have to pay for photographing somebody, but some people, usually men dressed traditionally, do request payment – about K0.50 to K1 is average but it can be a lot more. People are aware that Western photographers can make money out of their exotic photos and see no reason why they shouldn't get some of the action. If you've gone ahead and taken a photo without getting permission and establishing a price, you may well find yourself facing an angry, heavily armed Highlander who is demanding K20 in payment. It would take some nerve to argue.

HEALTH

An International Health Card is not required to enter PNG, and with the exception of malaria, there are no serious health problems. PNG is, however, a rugged country where the environment demands respect and the medical services are often overstretched.

Travel Health Guides

There are a number of books on travel health:

Staying Healthy in Asia, Africa & Latin America, Moon Publications. Probably the best all-round guide to carry, as it's compact but very detailed and well organised.

Travellers' Health, Dr Richard Dawood, Oxford University Press. Comprehensive, easy to read, authoritative and also highly recommended, although it's rather large to lug around.

Where There is No Doctor, David Werner, Hesperian Foundation. A very detailed guide intended for someone, like a Peace Corps worker, going to work in an undeveloped country, rather than for the average traveller.

Pre-Departure Preparations

Health Insurance Get some! You may never need it but if you do it's worth a million. There are lots of travel insurance policies available and any travel agent will be able to recommend one. Get one which will pay for a flight home if you are really sick. Make sure it will cover the money you lose for forfeiting a booked flight, and that it will cover the cost of flying your travelling companion home with you.

Avoid policies which specifically exclude 'dangerous activities' such as scuba diving and even bushwalking.

Medical Kit There are reasonably well-stocked pharmacies in the main centres but it's a good idea to bring most of your medical needs with you, and definitely a supply of any medication you take regularly. A basic kit for any visitor to PNG might include:

- Antihistamine (such as Benadryl) – useful as a decongestant for colds, allergies, to ease the itch from insect bites or stings or to help prevent motion sickness
- Antiseptic – mercurochrome and antibiotic powder or similar 'dry' spray – for cuts and grazes
- Aspirin or Panadol – for pain or fever
- Bandages and Band-aids – for minor injuries
- Calamine lotion – to ease irritation from bites or stings
- Kaolin preparation (Pepto-Bismol), Imodium or Lomotil – for stomach upsets
- Rehydration mixture – for dehydration, especially that caused by severe diarrhoea
- Scissors, tweezers and a thermometer (note that mercury thermometers are prohibited by airlines)
- Sunscreen, insect repellent and water purification tablets.

Walkers will need to give more careful thought to their medical kits. The further you get from the towns the further you will be from medical help. PNG has an impressive system where health workers live in the villages, but there is a shortage of trained people and facilities and drugs are often very limited.

Before you leave home, you must take medical advice and research how to treat yourself. If you have access to a travellers' medical clinic, use it rather than a GP, and buy a good book.

You should have the knowledge, drugs and equipment to treat malaria, dysentery, lacerations, breaks and sprains, insect and snake bites and respiratory diseases (colds and even pneumonia are common in the Highlands). Make sure you have a strong pain-killer.

Health Preparations Make sure you're healthy before you start travelling. If you are embarking on a long trip make sure your teeth are OK. If you wear glasses take a spare pair and your prescription.

If you require a particular medication take an adequate supply, as it may not be available locally. Take the prescription, with the generic rather than the brand name (which may not be locally available), as it will make getting replacements easier. It's a wise idea to have the prescription with you to show you legally use the medication.

Immunisations No vaccinations are required unless you are coming from a country where yellow fever or cholera is a problem. However, you should consider cholera, typhoid and hepatitis vaccinations and make sure that your tetanus cover is up to date.

Plan ahead for getting your vaccinations: some of them require an initial shot followed by a booster, while some vaccinations should not be given together. This also applies to malaria prophylactics, which have to be begun at least a week before you leave home. The period of protection offered by vaccinations differs widely and some are contraindicated if you are pregnant.

Basic Rules
Care in what you eat and drink is the most important health rule; stomach upsets are the most likely travel health problem but the majority of these upsets will be relatively minor. Don't become paranoid, trying the local food is part of the experience of travel after all.

Water Be careful drinking from PNG's countless streams and rivers, as some can be a source of intestinal diseases such as diarrhoea, bacillary and amoebic dysentery, typhoid and paratyphoid fevers, cholera, hepatitis A and schistosomiasis.

Pigs are everywhere, and people use the streams to wash their clothes, bathe, dispose of rubbish and defecate (to prevent sorcerers taking the faeces and using them to cast a spell).

In the mountains and forests water is usually safe, but near settlements and gardens it leaves much to be desired. Near settlements, many people drink only from the smallest streams, often recognisable by the gutter-like devices which give a better flow of water and help people drink. You'll come across various types of these devices, but most are made from hollowed logs, split sections of bamboo, or simply long and rigid leaves.

Water Purification If you doubt the quality of the water, boil it for 10 minutes or use water purification tablets, preferably iodine-based, as the iodine is effective against cysts and other resilient nasties. Alternatively, five drops of tincture of iodine in one litre of water, left for for 30 minutes, should do the trick.

Food Salads and fruit should be washed with purified water or peeled where possible. Thoroughly cooked food is safest but not if it has been left to cool or if it has been reheated. Take great care with shellfish or fish and avoid undercooked meat.

Nutrition If your food is poor or limited in availability, if you're travelling hard and fast and therefore missing meals, or if you simply lose your appetite, you can soon start to lose weight and place your health at risk. If your diet isn't well balanced or if your food intake is insufficient, it's a good idea to take vitamin and iron pills.

Everyday Health A normal body temperature is 98.6°F or 37°C; more than 2°C higher is a 'high' fever. A normal adult pulse rate is 60 to 80 per minute (children 80 to 100, babies 100 to 140). You should know how to take a temperature and a pulse rate. As a general rule the pulse increases about 20 beats per minute for each °C rise in fever.

Respiration (breathing) rate is also an indicator of illness. Count the number of breaths per minute: between 12 and 20 is normal for adults and older children (up to 30 for younger children, 40 for babies). People with a high fever or serious respiratory illness (like pneumonia) breathe more quickly than normal. More than 40 shallow breaths a minute usually means pneumonia.

Many health problems can be avoided by taking care of yourself. Wash your hands frequently – it's quite easy to contaminate your own food. Clean your teeth with purified water rather than straight from the tap. Avoid climatic extremes: keep out of the sun when it's hot, dress warmly when it's cold. Avoid potential diseases by dressing sensibly. You can get worm infections through walking barefoot or dangerous coral cuts by walking over coral without shoes. You can avoid insect bites by covering bare skin when insects are around, by screening windows and beds, and wearing insect repellent. In situations where there is no information, discretion is the better part of valour.

Medical Problems & Treatment

Potential medical problems can be broken down into several areas. First there are the climatic and geographical considerations – problems caused by extremes of temperature, altitude or motion. Then there are diseases and illnesses caused by insanitation, insect bites or stings, and animal or human contact. Simple cuts, bites or scratches can also cause problems.

Self-diagnosis and treatment can be risky, so wherever possible seek qualified help. Although we do give treatment dosages in this section, they are for emergency use only. Medical advice should be sought before administering any drugs.

Climatic & Geographical Considerations

Sunburn Beware of the tropical sun! Wear a hat that is broad enough to shade the back of your neck, try to keep your skin covered and apply liberal quantities of sunscreen.

Even when it is overcast you can still get burnt, and if you are at any decent altitude

(anywhere in the Highlands) you have less atmospheric protection and the fact that you're not hot does not mean you're not cooking.

Prickly Heat You may be unlucky enough to suffer from prickly heat when you first arrive. Sweat droplets are trapped under the skin (because your pores aren't able to cope with the volume of water) forming many tiny blisters. Anything that makes you sweat makes it worse. Calamine lotion or zinc-oxide-based talcum powder will give some relief but, apart from that, all you can do is take it easy for a few days until you acclimatise.

Dehydration & Heat Stroke Make sure you drink enough – don't rely on feeling thirsty to indicate when you should drink. Not needing to urinate or very dark yellow urine are danger signs. Always carry a water bottle with you on long trips. Excessive sweating can lead to loss of salt and therefore muscle cramping, but taking salt tablets is not a good idea – just add some to your food if you think you're not getting enough.

Dehydration or salt deficiency can cause heat exhaustion. Take time to acclimatise to high temperatures and make sure you get sufficient liquids. Drink even when you are not thirsty. Vomiting or diarrhoea further deplete your liquid and salt levels.

Heat stroke is a serious, sometimes fatal, condition which occurs when the body's heat-regulating mechanism breaks down and the body temperature rises to dangerous levels. Long, continuous periods of exposure to high temperatures can leave you vulnerable to heat stroke. Avoid excessive alcohol or strenuous activity when you first arrive.

The symptoms of heat stroke are feeling unwell, not sweating very much or at all and a high body temperature (39°C to 41°C). Where sweating has ceased the skin becomes flushed and red. Severe, throbbing headaches and lack of coordination will also occur, and the sufferer may be confused or aggressive. Eventually the victim will become delirious or convulse. Hospitalisation is essential, but meanwhile get patients out of the sun, remove their clothing, cover them with a wet sheet or towel and then fan continually.

Fungal Infections Fungal infections are most likely to occur on the scalp, between the toes or fingers (athlete's foot), in the groin (jock itch or crotch rot) and on the body (ringworm). You get ringworm (which is a fungal infection, not a worm) from infected animals or by walking on damp areas, like shower floors.

To prevent fungal infections wear loose, comfortable clothes, avoid artificial fibres, wash frequently and dry carefully. If you do get an infection, wash the infected area daily with a disinfectant or medicated soap and water, and rinse and dry well. Apply an antifungal powder. Try to expose the infected area to air or sunlight as much as possible and wash all towels and underwear in hot water as well as changing them often.

Cold Not only do you have to worry about getting too hot, but also about getting too cold! Admittedly hypothermia is only relevant if you plan to climb the mountains, but if you do, you must be prepared to cope with extreme weather conditions. Even snow is possible on Mt Wilhelm, although that might be preferable to the more likely fog and rain.

Hypothermia (otherwise known as exposure) is a quick and effective killer and prevention is better than cure. It's deceptively easy to fall victim to hypothermia through a combination of wind, wet clothing, fatigue and hunger, even if the air temperature is well above freezing. The symptoms of hypothermia include a loss of rationality, so people can fail to recognise their own condition and the seriousness of their predicament.

Symptoms are exhaustion, numb skin (particularly toes and fingers), shivering, slurred speech, irrational or violent behaviour, lethargy, stumbling, dizzy spells, muscle cramps and violent bursts of energy. Anticipate the problem if you're cold and tired, and recognise the symptoms early. Immediate

care is important since hypothermia can kill in as little as two hours.

First, find shelter from the wind and rain, remove wet clothing and replace with warm dry clothing. The patient should drink hot liquids *(not* alcohol, which can quickly kill the hypothermic patient) and eat some high calorie, easily digestible food. These measures will usually correct the problem if symptoms have been recognised early. In more severe cases it may be necessary to place the patient in a sleeping bag insulated from the ground, with another person if possible (both naked) while they are fed warm food and hot drinks.

Do *not* rub the patient, place them near a fire, try to give an unconscious patient food or drink, remove wet clothes in the wind, or give alcohol.

Altitude Sickness Altitude Sickness, Soroche, Mountain Sickness, Acute Mountain Sickness (AMS) – whatever you call it – can in extreme cases be fatal. In all probability however, you will only be lightly affected, although some travellers have experienced real trouble on Mt Wilhelm. You can't predict your susceptibility.

AMS becomes noticeable at around 3000 metres, becomes pronounced at 3700 metres, and then requires adjustments at each 500 metres of additional elevation after that. The summit of Mt Wilhelm is over 4500 metres high, so if you make a sudden ascent from Lae to Kegsugl, by PMV or plane, and then commence the climb without giving your body a couple of days to adjust to the new altitudes you are likely to make the expedition unnecessarily difficult, even dangerous. Your body has to undergo a physiological change to absorb more oxygen from the rarefied air and this takes time.

Mild symptoms to be expected over 3000 metres include headaches and weakness; loss of appetite; shortness of breath; insomnia, often accompanied by irregular breathing; mild nausea; a dry cough; slight loss of coordination; and a puffy face or hands in the morning. If you experience a few of these symptoms you probably have a mild case of altitude sickness which should pass. Rest (perhaps for a day or so) until the symptoms subside but if the symptoms become more severe or do not improve you will have to descend to a lower altitude. Monitor your condition carefully and realistically. Increasing tiredness, confusion, and lack of coordination and balance are real danger signs. Any of these symptoms individually, even just a persistent headache, can be a warning.

The only cure is immediate descent to lower altitudes. When any combination of severe symptoms occur, the afflicted person should descend 300 to 1000 metres *immediately*, the distance required increasing with the severity of the symptoms. Such a descent may even have to take place at night (responding quickly is vital), and the disabled person should be accompanied by someone in good condition. There's no cure except descending to lower altitudes, but a pain-killer for headaches and an anti-emetic for vomiting will help relieve the symptoms.

Diseases of Insanitation

Diarrhoea Although this is not nearly as much of a problem in PNG as it is in some Asian countries, it is likely you'll get some kind of diarrhoea when you first arrive. This is normal for travellers whose bodies are adapting to strange food and water and you'll probably recover quickly.

Food, in the main towns, is generally problem-free and town water is safe.

Avoid rushing off to the pharmacy and filling yourself with antibiotics at the first signs of a problem. The best thing to do is eat nothing and rest, avoid travelling and drink plenty of liquid (black tea or sterile water). About 24 to 48 hours should do the trick. If you really can't cope with starving, keep to a diet of yoghurt, boiled vegetables, apples and apple juice. After a severe bout of diarrhoea or dysentery you will be dehydrated and this often causes painful cramps. Relieve these by drinking fruit juices or tea into which a small spoonful of salt has been dissolved; maintaining a correct balance of salt in your bloodstream is important.

If starving doesn't work or if you really have to move on and can't rest, there is a range of drugs available. Lomotil is probably one of the best, though it has come under fire recently in medical literature. If you can't find Lomotil, try Pesulin or Pesulin-O (the latter includes tincture of opium).

Ordinary traveller's diarrhoea rarely lasts more than about three days. If it lasts for more than a week you must get treatment, move on to antibiotics, or see a doctor.

Giardia This intestinal parasite is present in contaminated water. The symptoms are stomach cramps, nausea, a bloated stomach, watery, foul-smelling diarrhoea and frequent gas. Giardiasis can appear several weeks after you have been exposed to the parasite. The symptoms may disappear for a few days and then return; this can go on for several weeks. Metronidazole (known as Flagyl) is the recommended drug, but it should only be taken under medical supervision. Antibiotics are of no use.

Dysentery Like diarrhoea, dysentery isn't a serious problem in PNG, but it does occur. There are two types of dysentery: bacillary, the most common, which is acute and rarely persists; and amoebic, which is persistent and more difficult to treat. Both are characterised by very liquid stools containing blood and/or excessive amounts of mucus.

Bacillary dysentery attacks suddenly and is accompanied by fever, nausea and painful muscular spasms. Often it responds well to antibiotics or other specific drugs. Amoebic dysentery builds up more slowly, but is more dangerous, so get it treated as soon as possible. Walkers must research the diagnosis and treatment of dysentery before leaving home, and bring the appropriate drugs.

Cholera Cholera vaccination is not very effective. However, outbreaks of cholera are generally widely reported, so you can avoid such problem areas. The disease is characterised by a sudden onset of acute diarrhoea with 'rice water' stools, vomiting, muscular cramps, and extreme weakness.

Top: Djei Valley, near Menyamya, Morobe Province (YP)
Bottom: Village overlooking the Tauri Valley, Kanabea, Gulf Province (YP)

Top: Goilala village near Tapini, Central Province (YP)
Bottom: Looking across the Udabe Valley from Ononge, Central Province (YP)

You need medical help – but treat for dehydration, which can be extreme, and if there is an appreciable delay in getting to hospital then begin taking tetracycline.

Viral Gastroenteritis This is caused not by bacteria but, as the name suggests, by a virus. It is characterised by stomach cramps, diarrhoea, and sometimes by vomiting and/or a slight fever. All you can do is rest and drink lots of fluids.

Hepatitis Hepatitis A is the more common form of this disease and is spread by contaminated food or water. The first symptoms are fever, chills, headache, fatigue, feelings of weakness and aches and pains. This is followed by loss of appetite, nausea, vomiting, abdominal pain, dark urine, light-coloured faeces and jaundiced skin; the whites of the eyes may also turn yellow. In some cases there may just be a feeling of being unwell or tired, accompanied by loss of appetite, aches and pains and the jaundiced effect.

You should seek medical advice, but in general there is not much you can do apart from resting, drinking lots of fluids, eating lightly and avoiding fatty foods. People who have had hepatitis must forego alcohol for six months after the illness, as hepatitis attacks the liver and it needs that amount of time to recover.

Hepatitis B, which used to be called serum hepatitis, is spread through sexual contact or through skin penetration – it could be transmitted via dirty needles or blood transfusions, for instance. Avoid having your ears pierced, tattoos done or injections where you have doubts about the sanitary conditions. The symptoms and treatment of type B are much the same as for type A, but gamma globulin as a prophylactic is effective against type A only.

Typhoid Typhoid is another gut infection that travels the faecal-oral route – ie, contaminated water and food are responsible. Vaccination against typhoid is not totally effective and it is one of the most dangerous infections, so medical help must be sought.

In its early stages typhoid resembles many other illnesses: sufferers may feel like they have a bad cold or flu on the way, as early symptoms are a headache, a sore throat, and a fever which rises a little each day until it is around 40°C or more. The victim's pulse is often slow relative to the degree of fever present and gets slower as the fever rises – unlike a normal fever where the pulse increases. There may also be vomiting, diarrhoea or constipation.

In the second week the high fever and slow pulse continue and a few pink spots may appear on the body; trembling, delirium, weakness, weight loss and dehydration are other symptoms. If there are no further complications, the fever and other symptoms will slowly go during the third week. However you must get medical help before this because pneumonia (acute infection of the lungs) or peritonitis (burst appendix) are common complications, and because typhoid is very infectious.

The fever should be treated by keeping the victim cool and dehydration should also be watched for. Chloramphenicol is the recommended antibiotic but there are fewer side affects with ampicillin. The adult dosage is two 250 mg capsules, four times a day. Children aged between eight and 12 years should have half the adult dose; younger children should have one-third the adult dose.

Patients who are allergic to penicillin should not be given ampicillin.

Worms These parasites are most common in rural, tropical areas and a stool test when you return home is not a bad idea. They can be present on unwashed vegetables or in undercooked meat and you can pick them up through your skin by walking in bare feet. Infestations may not show up for some time, and although they are generally not serious, if left untreated they can cause severe health problems.

Diseases Spread by People & Animals
Tetanus This potentially fatal disease is found in undeveloped tropical areas. It is difficult to treat but is preventable with

immunisation. Tetanus occurs when a wound becomes infected by a germ which lives in the faeces of animals or people, so clean all cuts, punctures or animal bites.

Tetanus is known as lockjaw, and the first symptom may be discomfort in swallowing, or stiffening of the jaw and neck; this is followed by painful convulsions of the jaw and whole body.

Rabies Rabies is present in PNG but is not at all common. Nevertheless, avoid being bitten or even licked by an animal. If you are, wash and sterilise the site, and if there's a possibility that the animal might be rabid, get help fast.

Sexually Transmitted Diseases PNG might be one of the world's last untouched countries, but AIDS and other STDs are present. Take precautions.

Malaria By far the most serious health risk in PNG is malaria. Although it is the isolated villagers who suffer the most, the disease kills quite indiscriminately and, sometimes, in spite of medical care.

You *must* take a malaria prophylactic. However, malaria has shown a frightening capacity to mutate drug-resistant strains. PNG is now host to malarial strains that can cause deadly cerebral malaria and are resistant to Chloroquine, the most popular anti-malarial drug. Make sure your doctor knows where you are going. Lariam is a new drug which is apparently effective against malaria strains in PNG.

Fansidar is not recommended. Aside from being dangerous in its own right (it is banned as a preventive measure in some countries due to its side effects) it is also used as a last-ditch cure. If a Fansidar-resistant strain develops, a prospect that becomes more likely the more indiscriminately it is used, many people will die.

Whatever prophylactic you use, the only sure way to avoid malaria is to avoid being bitten. Repellent, nets, trousers and long sleeves can all help. The most important time to keep covered is in the evenings and early

morning. Dengue fever, also carried by mosquitoes, is another PNG health danger.

Most people who live in PNG for more than a few years come down with malaria, so getting the proper diagnosis and treatment (essential to avoid dangerous – possibly fatal – complications) is not difficult in towns, but walkers who will be out of touch for a while must be able to diagnose and treat malaria, and carry the necessary drugs. Talk to a *knowledgeable* doctor before you leave home.

Prompt diagnosis and treatment could be a problem if you develop headaches and fever after you return home, where you might be told to go away and take a couple of aspirin. If this happens, get a second opinion – fast!

Cuts, Bites & Stings
Cuts & Bites PNG isn't a particularly dirty country but it is in the tropics so you should take care that cuts and insect bites don't become infected, otherwise you risk tropical ulcers. These nasty, weeping sores are very difficult to get rid of once they take hold and you might need a course of penicillin. The main rule is not to scratch insect bites.

Leeches & Ticks Leeches are present in damp rainforest conditions. Walkers often get them on their legs or in their boots. Salt or a lighted cigarette end will make them fall off. Vaseline, alcohol or oil will also persuade ticks to let go. Do not pull them off, as the bite is then more likely to become infected. An insect repellent may keep them away. You should always check your body if you have been walking through a tick-infested area, as they can spread typhus.

Snakes Nearly 100 different species of snakes are found in PNG but very few of them are dangerous, despite the general hysteria which greets the arrival of any snake in a village. Most snakes are regarded as venomous by villagers, probably because puncture wounds from even non-venomous snakes tend to become infected if not cleaned.

In the unlikely event that someone is

bitten, note that the old treatments of sucking the site and applying a tourniquet are now definitely out. A very tight bandage should be wrapped around the bitten limb, and the patient kept as calm and still as possible – don't carry or, worse, walk them to a possible source of medical assistance. It is imperative that the victim should lie in a sleeping position for 24 to 36 hours. However, if respiratory troubles arise, move them into a sitting position. Theoretically, immobilisation slows the entry of the poison into the blood-stream to a rate where the body can cope with it. You're likely to be a little messed up but if you're young and in good health you should survive.

See the Hazards section later in this chapter for tips on avoiding snakes.

Women's Health

Gynaecological Problems Poor diet, lowered resistance due to the use of antibiotics for stomach upsets and even contraceptive pills can lead to vaginal infections when travelling in hot climates. Keeping the genital area clean, and wearing skirts or loose-fitting trousers and cotton underwear will help to prevent infections.

Yeast infections, characterised by a rash, itch and discharge, can be treated with a vinegar or even lemon-juice douche or with yoghurt. Nystatin suppositories are the usual medical prescription. Trichomonas is a more serious infection; symptoms are a discharge and a burning sensation when urinating. Male sexual partners must also be treated, and if a vinegar-water douche is not effective medical attention should be sought. Flagyl is the prescribed drug.

Pregnancy Most miscarriages occur during the first three months of pregnancy, so this is the most risky time to travel. The last three months should also be spent within reasonable distance of good medical care, as quite serious problems can develop at this time. Pregnant women should avoid all unnecessary medication, but vaccinations and malarial prophylactics should still be taken where possible – ask a doctor. Additional care should be taken to prevent illness and particular attention should be paid to diet and nutrition.

WOMEN TRAVELLERS

Women should always dress conservatively, even when swimming. Outside the resorts, even one-piece swimming costumes do not provide sufficient cover, and bikinis will cause big trouble. A laplap can come in handy as a wrap. Take your cue from the local women – sometimes you'll notice them washing *fully* clothed. Whether on a beach or in a city, lone women must restrict their movements to areas where there are other people around and never go off by themselves.

In many ways Papua New Guinean women have a very hard time and this affects the situation for visitors. Except in the cities, women are almost always subservient to men and physical abuse is common – the government feels it necessary to produce brochure entitled 'Wife-beating is illegal'. In many parts of the country a women never initiates a conversation with a man, never talks to a male outside her family, never eats at the same table as men, never even sleeps in the same house as any man, including her father or husband.

A lone, Western woman traveller has no local parallels and, to a certain extent, a special case will be made of her. Virtually throughout the country, however, it will be difficult for women to have a normal conversation with a man without being misinterpreted as a flirt. Similarly, a Western man who attempts to initiate a conversation with a Papua New Guinean woman can cause embarrassment and confusion.

In the villages, foreign women will often be given 'honorary male' status, which allows you to see and do things forbidden to the village women. This means that your trip is more interesting, but it can alienate the village women. It might be safer (and more enjoyable) to forgo this, and associate solely with the women. Show an interest in their gardens and houses and you'll soon be accepted.

Public displays of affection are almost

unknown, and a Western couple making physical contact in public – even holding hands – is regarded as an oddity and, especially in traditional rural societies, may be regarded with contempt. This can put the woman in danger.

Women should *never* drink alcohol with men.

Guides and carriers are usually men, but women can ask for a female guide or carrier – in the villages, it's the women who do most of the carrying.

Despite the obvious difficulties, we have received a number of letters from women who have clearly enjoyed travelling around by themselves. And throughout the country you'll find women working as administrators, entrepreneurs, pilots, teachers, nurses, missionaries, etc, so it definitely can be done! Nevertheless, I would recommend that women do not travel alone in PNG, especially if they haven't travelled before in a highly sexist society.

Many places have women's groups (which sometimes have guesthouses) and these are good places to find out about women's lives in PNG, and to see what is being done to help alleviate their problems. Note that the Country Women's Association (CWA), which also has guesthouses, is a local branch of a venerable Australian institution, not a grassroots PNG organisation.

SAFETY

This section on safety is much larger than is usual in Lonely Planet guides, and is a response to fears generated by the bad press that PNG gets, especially in Australia. It's true that travellers are robbed, occasionally with violence, and there have been rapes, but PNG need not be the acutely dangerous place it is painted as long as you listen to local advice and, above all, make friends with people who live in the area you are visiting.

One big plus about PNG is that the usual third-world nightmare of hurtling along in a totally unroadworthy bus with a maniac at the wheel doesn't apply. Most public transport is in reasonable condition and most drivers are aware of the payback and compensation problems they would have if they hit anything – even a chicken or a dog – or injured one of their passengers.

Another plus is that you don't have to fear corrupt and violent authorities.

Background

On the rare occasions when PNG is featured in the world's news media, it is likely to be a sensationalist report about some kind of violence. As a result of these reports and the foggy, often inaccurate notions many people have of the past (featuring fierce, head-hunting warriors), PNG is often unjustifiably classified as an extremely unsafe country.

You will get your first taste of these attitudes when you tell your friends your planned destination: 'You're going *where*?' You will get your second taste when you get to Port Moresby, where houses are barricaded like you've never seen them before, and start talking to expats. Everyone will have a favourite gruesome story they will want to tell you. Do not be deterred! If you take reasonable care and use a bit of common sense, you are most unlikely to experience anything other than tremendous friendliness and hospitality.

You will certainly not get an arrow in the back or have your head hunted. Even looked at historically, this should be seen in perspective. In the early days of colonisation the local people were fighting White invaders who were often very unsavoury characters. The Highlands were still being opened up in the '50s and until that time there was no indigenous concept of a large Western-style nation; each tribe was, in effect, a sovereign state so its relations with its neighbours or the white invaders were 'foreign affairs'. And foreign affairs often became warfare, although never on a scale to match the conflicts most countries in Europe have witnessed.

Payback squabbles, land disputes and the like, can still develop into full-scale tribal wars, but they are confined to the direct participants. I heard a reliable story of fighting stopping so a tour group could cross a battlefield, and many expats will tell you of battles they have watched from close at hand. These are not exploits I would recommend unless you are very confident that you know what you are doing. Also, locals might feel obliged to go with you, and this will put them in danger.

In common with many other countries, it is usually not safe to wander around at night, especially in towns, and this is doubly the case for women. It should be noted that crime is in no way race related and that relations between different nationalities are remarkably good.

Tips

You have to be careful, but without becoming paranoid! Make friends with Papua New Guineans, don't close yourself off. Not only will this add to your enjoyment, but also to your security – you will be identified with a local and have access to first-hand advice and information. There are few places in the world where a smile and a greeting (*Moning, Apinun*) are so well received.

You cannot afford to be entirely naive about your popularity, however, because you may well be regarded as a potential source of status, or even wealth. How do you judge whether someone is sincere, or up to no good? There's no easy answer, but you do have to be sceptical and you do have to use your brains. Even if you do decide that someone is all right, don't put yourself in a vulnerable position until you have more than a first impression to go on.

It's not worth considering walking around a big town at night. Even in a group you are vulnerable and there's just no point. There is nothing to see or do on the streets. If you plan to go out to a restaurant or club, catch the last PMV, which normally runs sometime between 6 and 6.30 pm, and get a lift (easy to arrange) or a taxi home. It's worth being especially careful on the fortnightly Friday pay nights – things can get pretty wild.

Take precautions such as concealing some emergency cash and making sure your travellers' cheque numbers are written down somewhere safe. One traveller wrote that while his pack was stolen in a PMV hold-up,

a dirty old billum he had wasn't touched. You can insure your camera, but not your precious exposed films, so think about mailing film home or to a secure address within PNG. If you lose anything, especially in rural areas, it's worth hanging around for a few days and letting it be widely known that you will give a reward for the return of your stuff. This probably won't help to get you your personal stereo back, but your passport and tickets might turn up.

Everything is saner and better away from the towns – the people are friendlier and there are considerably fewer problems. If you are staying in villages, stay with a family rather than in an empty haus tambaran or haus kiap. It's safer and more fun. In most cases, you'll also be much better off with a guide who speaks the tok ples (local language). You won't be so likely to get lost, the guide will know when and who to ask for the various permissions you will need (to camp, to cross someone's land, etc) and you'll have automatic introductions to local people. If you are looking for a guide, start by asking around for someone reliable at missions, government offices, schools or trade stores. Whatever your plans, talk to as many people as you can and listen to their advice.

You are most unlikely to have any trouble from other passengers on a PMV – they're more likely to share their food with you. It isn't particularly common, but there are pickpockets and bag snatchers, so be a little cautious in crowded places like PMVs, bus stops and markets. Don't ever leave valuables unattended in any public place.

Problem Areas

The so-called rascal problem is not just one problem and it flares in different areas for different, often predictable, reasons. Port Moresby and Lae are likely to remain dangerous because of the continuing influx of unemployed young men. The same applies to most other large towns.

Mt Hagen is one town which has this problem, with added trouble because it's the main centre of the volatile Highlands region (people go to town to settle paybacks) and workers from the various mines spend their pay cheques there. Most other Highland towns are also edgy.

Don't travel after dark in the Highlands. Catch PMVs early in the morning so you will reach your destination in daylight, with plenty of time to get your bearings and find somewhere to sleep before dark.

PMVs are regularly held-up on the Wewak-Maprik road. The Wau area flared up recently but the situation seems to be settling. Rascals were rampant in Oro Province but in 1992 most of the rascal gangs surrendered in return for some pretty vague promises by politicians. Whether the peace holds remains to be seen.

There is often tribal fighting in Enga Province. This doesn't usually affect outsiders, but check the situation before you go there.

Walkers in much of the Western and Eastern Highlands, some parts of Simbu and the Southern Highlands, around Garaina in Morobe and possibly around Kunimaipa in Central Province could have problems. Hold-ups of course aren't guaranteed, but in many of these places they're frequent. Unless you're accompanied by a local friend or are walking with a group of people, it would be wise to keep out of these areas. The situation changes all the time, so wherever you plan to walk, ask about the current dangers with a knowledgeable local person or the police. Try to get facts, not rumours.

Most problems happen in the towns and along the roads, not on the trails and in the villages. From time to time, there are also problems near government and mission stations. As a rule of thumb, where traditional cultures are in contact with foreign values, there is a greater risk of running into problems; the deeper you go into the remote forests, the safer you are.

The safest areas of the country are Milne Bay Province (although yam festival time in the Trobriands can be hectic), New Britain, New Ireland and Manus. Remember that you can get into trouble anywhere in the world, but that even in the most dangerous areas of PNG most travellers *don't* have trouble.

Rescue

The National Disaster, Surveillance & Emergency Service (☎ 27 6502; ☎ 27 6666 for emergencies), is a government body based in Waigani (Port Moresby). The service was created in 1984, and is setting up a national communication network that will enable walkers to report their comings and goings, and to assist them if they call for help or are overdue.

This communication network might not yet be operational – contact the centre for more up-to-date information.

In case of an emergency, it is imperative that the service be contacted as quickly as possible. For emergencies, phone ☎ 27 6666 and ask to speak to the duty officer. If you can't get through, phone the police. If the emergency is genuine and wasn't caused by taking unnecessary risks, the cost of the rescue is normally borne by the government.

The service can also give walkers up-to-date information on the area they propose to visit.

Unless you tell your friends, your hotel or the service about your plans there is no way that you can be easily located in an emergency. There are two-way radios at government and mission stations in remote areas, although the government radios are often unreliable.

On the trail you have to depend on your own cautiousness and wisdom. It is imperative to be well prepared, to know what to do in an emergency and to know your physical and mental limitations. Even if the service knows that you are in trouble, it's limited resources and the rugged nature of the country mean that help will not be immediate.

It strongly recommended that, unless you are walking along a frequently used trail, you do not walk alone. This is especially important when the route involves a river crossing.

In every village there are people who will guide you for a small fee. A guide will also help you to understand more of the country, the local cultures, and the flora and fauna.

See also the Hazards on the Trail section later in this chapter.

ACCOMMODATION

The one unfortunate generalisation that you can make about formal accommodation in PNG is that it is too expensive. Overall the quality is pretty good, although often not worth the price charged. Staying in villages is much cheaper and much more interesting.

Booking ahead is a good idea, especially for moderately priced hotels and guest-houses. Most are small and fill quickly. Transport between airports and towns is often nonexistent or very expensive, but most hosts will pick you up if they know you're coming.

Staying in Villages

Meeting people in their villages, sharing their house and their meal and swapping tales with them, is likely to be a highlight for many travellers. The smiles, generosity and kindness are unforgettable. A visitor to a village is always looked after, found a place to sleep and, usually, fed. This unique and rewarding experience is not, however, unalloyed bliss. The generally poor hygiene, the basic conditions and the lack of privacy can be uncomfortable.

Remember to pay your way. Two to five kina for a night's accommodation, a kina or some trade store food in exchange for a meal is reasonable. In some areas where they see a lot of travellers you might pay up to K10.

Melanesian hospitality is usually given to foster a long-term relationship and is based on the idea of exchange. As a transient tourist you don't fit into the traditional patterns, but if you give something in exchange for hospitality, you will be meeting your traditional responsibility, helping the village, and hopefully ensuring a welcome for the next traveller who comes along.

In more remote areas, trade goods are much appreciated and can be given instead of money. Clothing and salt are worth considering but lighter things such as matches, lighters, cigarettes, coarse tobacco (with sheets of newspaper to roll it in), balls of colourful wool that can be used to make billums, large needles (commonly referred to as billum needles), 20 to 30-pound fishing line and plenty of hooks, safety pins, needles and thread, pens and pencils, potato peelers (for peeling sweet potatoes and taros), small knives, scissors, mirrors, combs, razor blades, soap, cups, metal files, and a host of other items are welcomed.

On the coast and in areas which have had a long history of government or mission contact, village houses are generally spacious, have windows and are not smoky. There is good hygiene and an effort is usually made to respect the privacy and the undisturbed sleep we foreigners are so fond of. In these areas, walkers are not so much of a curiosity and the living conditions are quite reasonable.

In the remote areas, some travellers may find conditions in villages hard to cope with. The following descriptions are not aimed at discouraging the walker. Despite the hassles, remote areas are definitely worth visiting and remember that standards of hygiene and decent places to sleep along the trails were major factors in selecting the walks in this guide.

Built on the ground or on stilts, the traditional house is usually a windowless, one-room dwelling made of bush materials. There is no furniture and the occupants sleep on the floor, normally around a large fire which radiates warmth but also a thick and irritating cloud of smoke (which in some regions helps to ward off insects).

Sleeping on floors is not always easy. They are often too short, too sloping or too bumpy and can be too crowded with people who, until late in the night, talk, sing and make countless noises before finally dropping off to sleep, when they snore. Floors can also be too infested with fleas or cockroaches, too littered with chewed sugar cane, betel nut husks and a hundred other nameless things.

People constantly get up at night to pee, rekindle the fire, smoke their pipes and quieten the dogs and pigs which seem to take pleasure in fighting underneath the house. Personal hygiene is often very poor. People are often dirty, their hair literally swarming with lice, their skin covered with ringworm, tinea, cuts, ulcers and abscesses, and malnutrition, malaria and other illnesses are common.

Privacy is not a concept dear to people living traditionally, and the more remote the village, the more of a curiosity you will be. As most houses do not have rooms, you'll often have to dress in public (in a laplap) and people will always accompany when you go to the stream for a wash. Groups of people will constantly follow you, touch you, stare at you and comment on you. Villagers have an incredible ability to use every possible inch of floor space; I was once in a house so crammed with curious people eager to see me that it toppled over!

In the larger villages you'll find pastors, school teachers and aid post orderlies whose houses are a haven of cleanliness. These people are usually quite happy to put you up. A donation is still essential.

If you are uncertain of your ability to cope with life in remote villages, go for a short initial visit and return if you enjoyed it. Some government and mission stations can accommodate guests (with advance notice); they make good bases from which nearby villages can be visited.

Some villages have a haus kiap (a house for patrol officers, kiaps), a council house or some other structure where local people might think you will want to stay. Try to resist this, as not only is staying with a family in their traditional house more enjoyable than sleeping by yourself in a decaying colonial-era structure, it's *much* safer. As soon as you are involved with a community you become, to some extent, the responsibility of that community.

See also the Avoiding Offence section later in this chapter.

Camping

A tent is not really necessary unless you plan to sleep far beyond populated areas or spend some time above the tree line. In most places you will be following a reasonably well travelled route and will come across villages or bush shelters at regular intervals. The shelters are built especially for travellers. Some may not be in good repair and carrying a tent

fly, a tarp or a large sheet of plastic can help to waterproof them.

If you're walking with a group, take a tent so as to not strain the limited accommodation in villages. In more remote villages, sleeping in a tent might be more comfortable and private than sleeping in a house.

Villagers won't mind you pitching your tent by the village square if you ask permission first. In the forest though, every square inch of country has a traditional owner whose permission *must* be obtained before you camp. Although it may look like deserted bush to you, there will almost always be people coming and going. If you camped in the forest and couldn't find anyone to give permission, tell someone when you come to the next village. This applies even above the tree line and far beyond populated areas, but if you have a guide, whose clan probably owns the land, he will probably notify the owners for you.

A tent, a tarp or a large sheet of plastic should be carried on at least two of the walks described in this book: the Kokoda Trail and the Sarawaget Massif.

Town Accommodation – bottom end

You can find somewhere inexpensive to stay in most main towns. 'Inexpensive' is a relative term, though – the cheapest bed in Port Moresby is K20 a night, and elsewhere you'll be paying well over K10 a night for shared accommodation, with a few exceptions.

Most of the cheaper places are mission-run guesthouses and hostels which are usually very clean and often offer generous servings of food in their communal dining rooms, after a blessing. Most hostels exist for the benefit of visiting missionaries and church people, but they are usually happy to take travellers if they have room.

Town Accommodation – top end

Most of the top end hotels are relatively recent constructions, often in a motel style with a few carvings tacked on. Prices range from a little to a lot higher than similar places in Australia. Singles range from about K50 to K90 and up. There's quite a wide variety of prices, and you'd be wise to plan ahead carefully. The major centres all have at least one reasonably high-standard (or at least high-price) place.

Some Coral Sea group hotels have set standby rates on rooms still vacant at 5 pm, and many hotels have weekend specials which can be good value.

There are two exceptional luxury hotels, whose nearest equivalents are the famous African safari lodges, and they should not be missed if you have the necessary funds: the Karawari Lodge lies deep in the jungle on a tributary of the Sepik and, best of all, the Ambua Lodge perches at 2000 metres on a ridge in the Southern Highlands overlooking the extraordinary Tari Basin.

FOOD

While the food is generally uninspiring, you should manage to eat reasonably well, most of the time. In the villages you'll have plenty of opportunity to try local food and to see how people gather and cook it. Although the average diet is mostly made up of bland, starchy staples with very little protein, food traditionally played an important part in social, economic and political life.

Western-style PNG food tends to be unimaginative (the roast and three veg category), although if you're prepared to pay top prices, the food in hotels and restaurants can be good.

Those on a budget will want to cook for themselves as much as possible, but as most fresh vegetables are flown from the Highlands or even Australia, they are scarce in markets and expensive in supermarkets – except in the Highlands, of course.

Other than items such as dried peas, beans, instant potatoes and beef jerky, little hiking food is available.

Local Food
Staples In the low-lying swampy areas of the Sepik and Fly rivers, western Papua and the Gulf region, and also in some areas of the Southern Highlands, Simbu and West Sepik (Sandaun Province), sago is the staple food. Called *saksak* in pidgin, this nutritionally poor, rather tasteless starchy extract is washed from the pith of the sago palm. It is high in calories but low in protein and vitamins. Sago grubs are eaten and other protein is obtained by fishing and hunting.

The sweet potato *(kaukau)*, a root crop native to South America, is the staple food of most Highland communities and is cultivated in the intermontane valleys, usually between 1300 and 2800 metres. There are over 350 known varieties. Kaukau is found along most of the length of the central mountainous spine of PNG and also in many coastal areas. It can be planted at any time and is harvested all year round and supplies most of the calories in the diet.

Pig husbandry is overwhelmingly important in the Highlands and hunting is a significant source of protein in remote areas.

Taro has been largely replaced by kaukau in the Highlands but it is still the staple in many other areas, such as New Britain, some areas of the Huon Peninsula, and in Madang, Oro and Sandaun provinces. Though numerous varieties of taro have been recorded, the two most common are the true taro (taro tru) and the Singapore taro (taro kongkong).

Several species of yams are eaten, the two most common being the greater yam (yam) and the lesser yam (mami). Yams are grown in many areas of the country, but in the Maprik area of East Sepik Province and Massim in Milne Bay Province on the Trobriand Islands, yams have a ceremonial function and are grown for size. Here, yams, the only tropical tuber that can be easily stored, are usually kept in special 'yam houses'.

Cassava is a staple food in some coastal areas of Central Province.

Supplements In many areas, cassava is eaten as a supplementary food, particularly when other food is scarce. Breadfruit is also an important supplementary food, as are coconuts in the lowlands. There are numerous varieties of both cooking and 'eating' bananas. Banana is the main crop along most of the coast of Central Province, the Markham Valley and in other areas. Grown to an altitude of over 2000 metres, bananas are an important supplementary food in many parts of the country.

Other supplementary foods include sugar cane, pitpit, peanuts, corn, beans, bamboo shoots, palm hearts, pandanus (marita and karuka), cucumbers, chokos, pumpkins, gourds, watermelons and a wide variety of leafy greens and other European vegetables. *Okari* and *galip* nuts are common at lower altitudes and tropical fruits are common.

Hunting & Fishing Hunting and fishing are very important, as they provide the protein almost entirely lacking in the staple foods. Both the coast and the larger rivers are fished. Most fish, shellfish and molluscs are eaten. The introduced fish *tilapia (makau* in pidgin) has become an important food for riverside people, and most mountain streams yield eels. Turtles, turtle eggs and dugongs are also eaten.

All the larger animals are hunted, along with snakes, crocodiles, birds, bats, lizards, frogs and insects. In the Highlands hunting takes second place to pig husbandry.

Unfortunately, potential game is often scarce, and protein deficiency remains a serious health problem in many parts of the country. Pigs are the main source of meat protein, although they are not generally eaten on a day-to-day basis, but saved for feasts. Chicken is now quite popular although, strangely, eggs are rarely eaten in the villages.

Cooking Food was (and is) traditionally steamed or boiled in clay pots; steamed in sections of green bamboo; roasted or grilled, either on the fire or wrapped in leaves or bark; baked in hot ashes; or steamed-baked in an earth oven commonly called *mumu.* Today, food is often simply boiled in a metal cooking pot.

The mumu is the most interesting cooking style. A pit is dug and hot stones are placed at the bottom. Meat and vegetables, protected by large leaves (often banana or breadfruit), are placed in layers between the stones, with the more delicate, sweeter and greasy foods on top. The whole thing is covered with leaves (sometimes with earth

as well) and left cooking for a couple of hours. At feasts the pits may be hundreds of feet long, and filled with hundreds of whole pigs.

Few if any spices and herbs are used in traditional cooking, and salt has always been a very valuable commodity in the villages.

Eating in Villages Village food is safe to eat but make sure that pork is thoroughly cooked. Walkers who plan to live on village foods should take along salt as well as protein and vitamin supplements.

Small trade stores seldom sell more than rice, tinned fish, tinned meat, biscuits (crackers), tobacco and salt, and should never be depended on. The tinned food can be pretty awful, especially the meat. The tinned '777' brand is supposed to be the best fish. Instant noodles are also becoming popular.

Root crops, greens and fresh fruits can usually be bought in villages. Most food sold in bundles (such as beans and greens) generally costs K0.10. You'll need coins, as few villagers can change notes.

Town Food
In all the big towns you'll be able to eat comparatively well in hotels or restaurants. At these places you'll usually find reasonable Australian-style food, at prices that are quite a lot higher than in Australia. Think in terms of K10 to K15 and up. Chinese restaurants are reasonably widespread but they are also expensive.

One possibility that is always worth checking for an inexpensive meal is The Club. Many towns still have a club – at one time they were havens for colonialists, but today their memberships are completely open and most will sign in visitors.

The fast food available from kai bars ranges from unthinkably awful to OK. It's usually fried – fish, chicken, lamb chops, rice and chips are the staples, along with things like sheep hearts. Many offer rice and stew, which is cheap and nourishing, although very greasy. You'll find kai bars in every town; bear in mind they usually close by 6.30 pm.

Many larger towns have sandwich bars or cafes and the large Steamships chain stores always have a take-away counter with decent sandwiches.

Mission hostels sometimes supply meals to their guests and these tend to be very good value. In general, however, the shoestring traveller or backpacker will discover that attempting to find something cheap and wholesome is a frustrating experience, and that cooking for yourself is the only way to survive. Some of the hostels have cooking facilities, but even if you don't have a stove handy, it's easy to rustle up a breakfast or a lunch.

Markets sell an inexpensive but often limited range of vegies and all the main towns have well-stocked supermarkets. There is no bargaining in the outdoor markets; prices are set and fair and are often clearly displayed.

Vegetarian Food

You might expect a country where protein deficiency is a chronic problem to be a vegetarian's paradise. Wrong. Some of the Chinese restaurants have vegetarian dishes, and you may find reasonable salads at some of the hotel smorgasbords, but in general the pickings are thin.

The big hotels and restaurants can normally put something together, but in the mission hostels it's a bit more awkward. There's no menu; everyone eats whatever happens to have been cooked and that's that. Again it's possible to organise an exception.

In the villages, I guarantee you'll find it tedious eating sago, yams or sweet potato for breakfast, lunch and dinner. Meat is sometimes produced and, since you're a visitor, a special effort will be made to procure some. It is very difficult to explain the concept of vegetarianism in pidgin to someone who belongs to a society that revolves around the killing and eating of pigs! You also run the risk of offending a host who has killed something in your honour.

So, make sure you have got cooking equipment, bring vitamin and mineral tablets and, if you are a less than strict vegetarian, you may consider temporarily relaxing your preference!

ALCOHOL & DRUGS
Alcohol

South Pacific is now the only brewery in PNG, but they produce two beers. The everyday drink, which comes in a small bottle (known as a *stubby* to Australians), is known as SP; the more expensive and stronger Export version comes in a colourful can. Wine and spirits are very costly, partly in an attempt to restrict their use.

Alcohol abuse is a serious problem, and it is worth keeping track of the fortnightly Friday pay nights. If there is going to be trouble, this is the night it is most likely to happen, be it fights, car accidents or robberies. If you're planning to sleep within shouting distance of a bar, forget it!

Betel Nut

All through Asia people chew the nut of the Areca palm known as betel nut or, in pidgin, *buai*. Although it's a (relatively) mild narcotic and digestive stimulant and is widely used in PNG, it's unlikely to attract many Western drug fans.

The betel nut is too acidic and slow acting to chew by itself – in PNG, betel nut users generally chew it with lime and seed stalks from a pepper plant. The reaction between the lime and the nut produces the narcotic effect and the extraordinary red stains you'll see splattered along footpaths everywhere.

You'll see the nuts, lime and mustard stalks for sale in every market; sometimes there'll be virtually nothing else. If you decide to try it, take lessons with a local expert. Nuts vary in potency, it is possible to burn yourself with the lime and nausea is a common side effect for the unpracticed (remember that first cigarette!).

Marijuana

The Highlands of PNG are the source of reputedly potent marijuana, although foreigners are rarely offered any. If you're tempted to look for it, remember that there are heavy penalties for possession and use and that as a foreigner you're much more likely to be busted and harshly punished than a local. Also, some of the people involved in the trade can be pretty heavy. There are persistent rumours that PNG grass is smuggled into Australia in exchange for military hardware.

Tobacco

Tobacco is an important cash crop and, as in many other developing countries, smoking is widespread and guilt-free. International brands are widely available, often in the full-strength version – there's no poring over tar and nicotine ratings in PNG. Locally made cigars are available in many markets. They look crude but they smell very tempting.

The grassroots' smoke was once tobacco rolled in newspaper (the *Sydney Morning Herald* for preference) but now there are ready-made versions. You puff one of these long cigarettes (the 'ettes' is redundant, they're like thin cigars) for a while then put it behind your ear for later use.

TRAILS

The whole of PNG is criss-crossed by a network of trails which link up every village, hamlet, garden and house across the land. There are few places in PNG which cannot be reached by a path of some kind.

Trails have always lead people to their gardens, sago swamps and hunting territories, and have enabled them to contact other villages to trade, feast, court – and fight.

The quality of a trail depends on its use. The more a place is visited, the more likely it is that the trail leading to it will be well defined. Trails linking friendly villages will be more frequently used and so cleaner and clearer. If neighbouring villages aren't on good terms, the trails between them are generally overgrown and difficult to follow. This isn't unusual, as neighbouring villages can have different cultures and languages, and people are traditionally suspicious of such difference.

For locals, the quality of trails doesn't matter much, as they use them as guides rather than paths intended to make walking easier. Clearing overgrown trails isn't a high priority.

For the bushwalker the difficulty of a particular trail will depend on the type of forest it passes through and the use local people make of it. As a rule though, most trails are steep and wet. Rocky outcrops, moss-covered roots and logs are usually slippery, and innocent-looking boulders in creeks are often treacherously unstable and covered with a slimy, near-invisible film. The muddy water in some creeks means that you sometimes can't see where you're walking.

Fording mountain torrents (or, for that matter, small lowland creeks) isn't always easy, but neither is crossing on a bridge. Some bridges are very sturdy, some are made from vines, some are single logs and others are just frail but ingenious structures held in place by God knows what miracle!

Walking is often hampered by fallen logs and branches, unexpected hollows under the tangled surface roots, clinging bamboo, trailing vines and other impediments. Stinging-nettles and leeches also distract the walker from time to time.

BUSHWALKER FITNESS

Most trails in PNG can be walked by any healthy and fairly fit person who stays within their limits. Nevertheless, the going can be very tough.

In the lowlands, the heat, the insects and the broken topography characteristic of most foothill areas make walking that much more gruelling.

People with knee problems should consider walking in the flatter lowland country rather than the mountains, as trails rarely follow the contours; they are usually the most direct route between two points. In the mountains, most villages are still located high on strategic ridges, and a 400-metre climb to a village isn't uncommon. On many walks, the daily gain in elevation can be well over 1500 metres and many descents are steep and long, playing havoc with your knees.

The walks detailed in this book range from relatively easy to very strenuous.

WHERE TO GO

What you want to see will determine where

you walk. Bird life, for instance, is more abundant in the lowlands, but it's in the upper montane zone that you'll see the most birds of paradise. Large birdwing butterflies are usually seen in the lowlands. The lowland rainforests are the most luxuriant but the moist upper montane forests are, I think, the most fascinating. Wherever you go, the scenery is wild, unique and beautiful.

As the whole country is covered with trails, you can go pretty much wherever you please, so long as you avoid walking through areas where there is danger of hold-ups. See the earlier Safety section for more information.

Remember that no matter how far into the forest you go, *all* land in PNG is owned by someone – you are not in a true wilderness – and this should be respected. Neither should you search for untouched cultures; head-hunting, the old burial rites and cannibalism are all things of the past.

The most interesting areas for walking are those farthest away from established government or mission stations. However, many remote areas are now under the influence of missionaries, usually fundamentalists.

PREPARATIONS

There are three approaches to walking in PNG. You can carry your own gear, you can hire someone to carry it for you, and you can go on an organised walk with a tour company.

Carrying your own gear is often so gruelling that it can prevent you from appreciating the walk and the surroundings. Some of the trails are incredibly steep and the environment makes walking difficult – trails are often wet and slippery – and progress through the forest can be slow.

Even if you don't hire a carrier, you'll often have to hire a guide to take you to the next village. As guides and carriers often charge nearly the same fees, and as guides can carry and carriers guide, you might as well hire a carrier in the first place. That is what most walkers do.

Village people are extremely agile in the forest and are not hindered by the many obstacles which make walking so difficult for foreigners.

Organised walks are not cheap but they are worth considering if you have limited time. It's hard to guarantee itineraries at the best of times in PNG, but professional companies will probably have a better chance of sticking to them than you will. Some of them also go to places you would be hard pushed to reach yourself, even if you did find out they existed. See the Useful Organisations section earlier in this chapter.

PLANNING YOUR ITINERARY

Once you've decided which area of the country you want to visit, planning an itinerary is not too difficult. The first step is to find out how you will get there. This is particularly important and some research should be done to locate all the airstrips, roads or coastal ports giving access to the area, so you'll know the quickest way out in an emergency. A good topographic map will show you the names and locations, but you should also find out who flies, drives or sails there, and when.

Next, you have to get to the roadhead, airstrip or coastal port of call nearest to the area you wish to visit, and start walking from there. You will be able to recruit guides or carriers at any village along the way.

You'll need good topographic maps. The contour lines and the position of features such as streams and mountains on these maps is quite reliable but beware that the names of streams, mountains and villages might not be correct, and villages might have moved or be abandoned. (See the Maps section earlier in this chapter for more information on this.)

Asking for directions to the next government or mission station along your route should mitigate this problem, as local people usually know the way to all the stations within three or four day's walk of their village. They'll be able to tell you the names of the villages you'll need to get to, and how many days it'll take you to get there. Remember, though, that most villagers can't read maps.

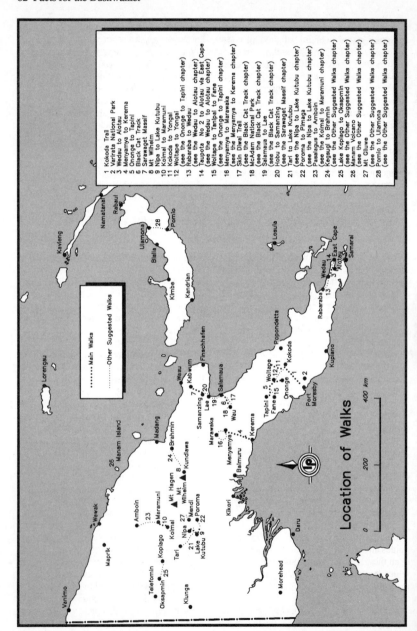

1 Kokoda Trail
2 Varirata National Park
3 Wedau to Alotau
4 Menyamya to Kerema
5 Ononge to Tapini
6 Black Cat Track
7 Sarawaget Massif
8 Mt Wilhelm
9 Nipa to Lake Kutubu
10 Koimal to Maramuni
11 Kokoda to Yongai
12 Woitape to Yongai
   (see the Ononge to Tapini chapter)
13 Rabaraba to Wedau
   (see the Wedau to Alotau chapter)
14 Taupota No 2 to Alotau via East Cape
   (see the Wedau to Alotau chapter)
15 Woitape to Tapini to Fane
   (see the Ononge to Tapini chapter)
16 Menyamya to Marawaka
   (see the Menyamya to Kerema chapter)
17 Skin Diwai Trail
   (see the Black Cat Track chapter)
18 McAdam National Park
   (see the Black Cat Track chapter)
19 Salamaua to Lae
   (see the Black Cat Track chapter)
20 Hobu to Samanzing
   (see the Sarawaget Massif chapter)
21 Tari to Lake Kutubu
   (see the Nipa to Lake Kutubu chapter)
22 Poroma to Pimaga
   (see the Nipa to Lake Kutubu chapter)
23 Pasalaga to Amboin
   (see the Nipa to Lake Kutubu chapter)
24 Kegsugl to Brahmin
   (see the Koimal to Maramuni chapter)
25 Lake Kopiago to Oksapmin
   (see the Other Suggested Walks chapter)
26 Manam Volcano
   (see the Other Suggested Walks chapter)
27 Mt Giluwe
   (see the Other Suggested Walks chapter)
28 Pomio to Ulamona
   (see the Other Suggested Walks chapter)

Location of Walks

Although village councils and committees are good sources of information, it's the *tanim tok* (translator) for the local government authorities that is likely to help you the most. The tanim tok sometimes knows several local languages, and will probably have accompanied patrols through the area. They usually live and work on a government station. District officers and assistant district officers (often still called kiaps) are essentially government clerks these days, and they usually know little about the area they're in charge of.

Some missionaries have an excellent knowledge of their area, but others know nothing except the small valley they live in, as they travel by plane rather than walking.

HIRING GUIDES & CARRIERS

Most people hire carriers, who can usually also act as guides. On at least some sections of most of the walks in this book, you'll need a guide.

Guides and carriers are usually men, and are referred to as male in this book. However, women walkers can ask for a female guide or carrier – in the villages, it's the women who do most of the carrying.

Guides and carriers are usually easy to find, but there might sometimes be problems. Some people might be reluctant to accompany you to the next village for fear of sorcery, especially if the people of that village have a different culture and language. Mountain dwellers commonly see malaria as a sorcery-induced illness and are often reluctant to travel to lower elevations. Local conflicts, work to do in the gardens, the distance to travel and, of course, the wages you offer are other factors that may deter a person from accompanying you.

Because of their fears of sorcery, most guides and carriers are hesitant to go too far from their village and many will not want to return home alone, so they will not accompany you unless another clan member comes along. They like to travel in pairs, and you might be asked to pay for two guides. If so, say that you don't mind a second person

coming along, but you can only afford to pay for the one guide/carrier you've asked for.

The fee is in accordance with the minimum rural wage which is about K5 a day or K0.50 per hour. You might, however, have to pay up to K10 a day, and twice that on the Kokoda Trail. Guides who don't carry should get less, but it not always the case.

In the forest, people are quite trustworthy but on the stations and near roadheads you should arrange a guide or a carrier through a reliable person such as a church leader or school teacher, or through the local government authorities.

It is your responsibility to feed anyone accompanying you and to look after them. If they don't have relatives or friends in a village, you have to make sure that they have somewhere to sleep. In colder areas, you have to provide warm clothes.

ON THE TRAIL
Types of Trails

Following a spur or a ridge (*bihainim kil*), is the easiest and most common way to get around in the mountains. A trail might cross a stream, then follow a spur to the top of a main ridge, follow it for a while, go down a spur to the next stream, and so on. Following contour lines (*saitim kil*) is also common. The trail follows the contour lines along the steep slope of a valley, usually high above a stream but below the main ridge line. In the mountains, little walking is done along valley floors, as the valleys are often too deep and steep-sided.

In the lowlands both valley floors and streams are followed, the latter being necessary when the country consists of low, closely spaced, narrow ridges or spurs. Most lowlands waterways wind a lot, which means there are many crossings to be made to cut across long bends or avoid obstructed ones, or to avoid deep pools of water as you walk in or along the creekbed. Locals call this type of walking *bihainim wara*, although this can also refer to following a stream, a river or even a valley, whether along its bed or high above it.

Small shelters, domestic plants such as

tanget and bamboo, footprints, coals from fires, and animal bones hung on branches, are some signs that can help you locate trails. When walking along less-used trails, villages usually break twigs or cut marks in the bark of trees.

Hazards

There are few hazards on PNG's trails and, with a little care, most of them can be avoided.

Getting lost is the most obvious hazard. There are trails everywhere in the forest, and besides linking villages they may lead to such places as an old village site, an isolated garden plot, a remote pig or garden house, a sago swamp, a hunting ground or an area where there are fruit-bearing trees. The size of a trail indicates only its use – larger trails often go to garden sites rather than to neighbouring villages. Losing your way or taking the wrong path is extremely easy, and you should always have a guide unless you are on a large, well-defined trail linking two nearby villages.

Most trails cross rivers and creeks at shallow fords or over bridges, but it is still important to be extra careful. Fording can be difficult and dangerous, especially if the river is swollen after rain. Mud in the water can hide the bottom, and boulders are often unstable and slippery. Many bridges are unsteady and some, mainly log bridges, are rotten and incredibly slippery. Always use a stick to help cross a river or creek, and on many trails a 20-metre length of rope is needed to ensure safe crossings.

Sharp limestone outcrops, moss-covered and slippery surface roots, steep and slippery clay slopes are a few more hazards encountered on the trail. Concentrating on the path is essential to avoid falls. Assume that each step is unsafe until proven otherwise.

You'll learn to recognise and avoid painful stinging nettles *(salat)* and the lawyer vine *(kanda* or rattan), which has barbs like fishhooks.

Walkers are at risk of being bitten by snakes, but it's very unlikely. Most snakes are neither aggressive nor poisonous, and the sound of you crashing through the bush

should effectively clear the path. Wearing high boots, thick socks (possibly two pairs) and being careful stepping over rocks or logs are wise precautions, however. Grabbing on to stumps when climbing a steep slope is also risky. Don't put your hand into holes and be careful when collecting firewood.

Be extra careful when walking through grasslands, the habitat of the death adder. It's a short, squat, brownish snake. Villagers fear it and this is one reason why a strip of vegetation is often burnt on either side of a grassland trail. This helps travellers spot the snake and, since it prefers taller, cooler, vegetation, keeps it away. If the footpath is overgrown, make lots of noise to scare snakes away.

Death Adder

Bathing Places & Toilets

Men believe they can be defiled by impurities from women's bodies, so men and women usually bathe in different streams. If

Top Left: Lower montane forest at 2600 metres (YP)
Top Right: Cape Girumia from Wamira, Wedau, Milne Bay Province (YP)
Bottom: Finisterre Range, Morobe Province (JM)

Top: The author on his way up to the Pindaunde Lakes, Mt Wilhelm,
     Simbu Province (YP)
Bottom: Looking down on the Pindaunde Lakes, Mt Wilhelm, Simbu Province (YP)

only one stream is available, men always bathe upstream from women. The same applies to toilets. Always ask which toilet or bathing place you should use.

Avoiding Offence

Local View of Foreigners Social, cultural and religious factors shape villagers' attitude to foreigners. Culture shock, sorcery and a fear of strangers are important, but the most common misunderstandings arise when the villagers do not understand why you are there in the first place.

Neighbouring villages are fairly similar, so unless they are trading, going to a feast or other cultural event, most villagers don't feel the need to visit other places and villages. Also, the environment, both physical and cultural, can make travelling seem very hazardous for them. 'Foreign' villages could cast spells on them, there are ghosts and other supernatural beings, and many spirits inhabit the forests and streams.

Rituals are often performed to placate these spirits, and many people travel only if they are accompanied by someone and only if they can stay with friends or relatives along the route.

Because village people generally travel only if they have to, risking many perceived hazards, they find it hard to believe that you are travelling for no real reason. They will often suspect that you have other motives. Could these strangers, who say they are not travelling for work, be spies, rascals or jail escapees? Do they intend to make a fortune out of the photos they take and the notes they write?

These misunderstandings can be resolved if you throw the argument back on the villagers. For instance, ask them if, given the opportunity, they would like to visit Australia. What would they do there? Would they take photos? Would they buy souvenirs? Would they sell them when they returned home? Of course not!

Another source of misunderstanding is the excessive payment some people demand. People in remote areas often have little idea of the value of money, and anyway, many

think that all foreigners are wealthy, or that all will write books, sell photographs or simply be paid thousands of kina by their 'bigman' upon returning to their country.

Most payments are legitimate and traditional, and are part of the system of barter and exchange that subtly governs all aspects of Melanesian society. If money is demanded from you, for access to a mountain, for crossing a bridge or whatever, you must pay without quibbling. All land, all bridges, all trails belong to someone and they have every right to charge for their use. If the amount asked seems excessive, try to agree on a sum that is acceptable to both parties. This does *not* mean bargaining in the Asian sense.

You & the Local People The arrival of a visitor in a village, particularly a Caucasian, always creates lots of curiosity, commotion and some fear. Children become noisy, mischievous and restless; younger children and many women become more reserved and timid. Don't approach anyone who seems afraid, and men should avoid speaking or making eye contact with women. Women walkers, on the other hand, might want to immediately meet with village women, although you shouldn't force yourself onto someone who is nervous.

Shaking hands is greatly appreciated, and shows goodwill and friendly intentions. Your behaviour governs the way you are perceived and treated by the people. You must be both sociable and generous.

Never pass judgement on the people and their customs, particularly their beliefs about sorcery. When you are followed to a nearby stream for a wash, for instance, it is only partly out of curiosity – in many areas, people feel it their duty to protect you against *sanguma*, sorcery-related attacks occurring particularly on people alone at night and near streams.

You must be patient and tolerant. Groups will constantly follow you, touch you, stare at you, comment on you. They'll like to know everything about you, your family, your gardens, your pigs, etc. Ask about their lives and they'll be very pleased.

You will also be questioned about your country. People in remote areas have a very hazy idea of what the rest of the world is all about and often know only four countries: theirs, Australia, Indonesia or Irian Jaya, and America. America tends to include everything that's left over.

Foreign units of time and distance are not used by many villagers, so answer questions in terms they can understand. For instance, instead of saying 'I left my country six months ago', say that such a child was still in his mother's womb when you left your home. Along the same lines, instead of saying 'my sister is so many years older that me', say that she was as big as a certain village girl when your mother gave birth to you. The same applies to your own age; after having told it in years, compare yourself with another person in the village. Instead of saying that your country is 8000 km away, say that it is so many dugout-days, so many PMV-days or so many plane-days (in a small aircraft such as Talair's, of course) away from PNG.

Whatever the quality of your pidgin, it is critically important that you are sociable. Mix with the people. Independent attitudes are very bad form, and can cause your hosts to feel guilty that they have done something to upset you. This causes fear and tension in the community and can even jeopardise your journey, depriving you of help to get to the next village.

Remember the standards which govern the relationship between hosts and guests in your own country. Would it be appropriate to ignore a person who gives you a bed and meal? Talk, sing, smoke if you're a smoker, and always be good company. Take photos, but always ask permission first. Try not to pay for photographs, instead say that you'll send copies – *do* send them, or you could jeopardise the welcome of future visitors.

You must be generous. Papua New Guineans always share their food with you and you should do the same; it's a sign of friendship. If you bring and cook your own food, prepare an extra portion for your host. You'll have to ignore all the curious people watching, but your host might choose to share his plate with them; this should be left to his discretion.

If you have anything stolen in a village, first inform your host who will in turn inform the local council or committee, or the village elders. Don't alarm the village. The people will do their very best to both retrieve the stolen goods and punish the culprit. Thefts are not frequent in the forest and though you should be careful there is no need to be over-worried or paranoid.

See also Staying in Villages in the Accommodation section earlier in this chapter.

Getting There & Away

Although there are some wild and wonderful ways of getting to PNG, almost everybody comes by air. And the vast majority come by air from Australia to Port Moresby, although there are also direct connections with Singapore, Manila, Honiara (Solomon Islands), Jayapura (Irian Jaya, Indonesia) and Guam. Otherwise, there are a few visiting yachts and the occasional cruise ship.

AIR

Air fares and routes are particularly vulnerable to change. The details given in this section should be regarded as pointers only, and you should do plenty of research before buying a ticket.

Air Niugini, the national airline, operates between Australia and Asia (in conjunction with Singapore and Philippines airlines). Australian connections are also made by Qantas, Australia's international airline. Continental flies from the USA via Guam. Garuda, Indonesia's national carrier, will get you to Jayapura in Irian Jaya (via Biak), from where you can fly to Vanimo in PNG.

Port Moresby is by far the largest international gateway. From Vanimo you can fly to Indonesia, and there have been direct flights between Mt Hagen and Cairns in Australia, but not currently. There has been talk of opening another international airport in PNG and various local lobby groups are arguing for international airports on Manus Island, at Wewak, Madang, Lae, Rabaul, Alotau...

Air Niugini has offices in Australia, in Sydney (☎ (02) 232 3100, fax (02) 290 2026), Brisbane (☎ (07) 229 5844, fax (07) 220 0040) and Cairns (☎ (070) 51 4177, fax (070) 31 3402). You can phone toll-free on (☎ (008) 221 742. Other overseas Air Niugini offices include:

Germany
    Raidmannstrasse 45, 6000 Frankfurt 70
    (☎(069) 63 40 95; fax (069) 63 13 32)

Hong Kong
    Room 705, Century Square, 1-13 Daguilar St, Central (☎ (5) 24 2151; fax 8255267291)
Japan
    No 2F Ogikubo Kangyo Bldg, 3-2-2 Amanuma Suginami-ku, Tokyo (☎ (03) 539-70678; fax (03) 539-70677)
Malaysia
    3rd floor, Pelancongan Abadi Sdn Bhd 79, Jalan Bukit Bintang 55100, Kuala Lumpur (☎ (03) 242 6360; fax (03) 242 1361)
Philippines
    G/F Fortune Office Bldg, 160 Legaspi St, Legaspi Village, Makati, Metro Manila (☎810 1846; fax 817 9826)
Singapore
    No 01-05/06/58 United Square, 101 Thomson Rd (☎250 4868; fax 652533425)
USA
    Suite 3000, 5000 Birch St, Newport Beach, Los Angeles, CA 92660 (☎ (714) 752 5440; fax (714) 752 2160)

To/From Australia

Air Niugini's Airbus flies between Sydney and Port Moresby three times each week, via Brisbane. The flight time from Sydney is about three hours, plus an hour's wait in Brisbane. There's a weekly flight between Cairns and Port Moresby on the Airbus and several others on a Fokker F28. Qantas fly to Port Moresby three times a week from Sydney via Brisbane. Currently there are no direct flights between Cairns and Mt Hagen.

One-way economy fares and low/high season APEX return fares between Australia and Port Moresby are:

Departure point	Fare (one way)	Fare (APEX return) low/high
Sydney	A$778	A$940/1085
Brisbane	A$634	A$796/940
Cairns	A$378	A$489/536

The maximum validity of APEX tickets on this route is 45 days. The APEX seasons are complicated, but basically the high season is most of January, mid-April, mid-June to mid-July, mid-September to early October and most of December. As you might have guessed, Australian school holidays are a nice little earner for the airlines!

There isn't much discounting of tickets between Australia and PNG, but ask around and you might find something. STA and Flight Centres International are major dealers in cheap air fares, and it's worth contacting Air Niugini direct.

To/From the Pacific

Solomon Airlines sometimes offers an interesting circle fare between Brisbane, Honiara (Solomon Islands) and Port Moresby, but it's fairly pricey unless you can find a travel agent offering a special deal. Their direct flights from Honiara to Port Moresby costs about A$480 one way but there are sometimes specials. There is increasing bad-feeling between the governments of the Solomon Islands and PNG (due to Bougainville), so don't count on this route remaining open.

Island-hopping all the way from the USA requires careful planning as some connections only operate once or twice a week. Possibilities include: Honolulu – Marshall Islands – Nauru – Honiara – Port Moresby; Honolulu – Guam – Nauru – Honiara – Port Moresby; Honolulu – Carolinas – Nauru – Honiara – Port Moresby; Honolulu – Nandi (Fiji) – Honiara – Port Moresby. The tiny island state of Nauru is the focal point for a lot of these routes and Air Nauru has an interesting network to its Pacific neighbours.

Air fares on these Pacific routes are a bit of a puzzle since Guam – Honolulu and other routes between the USA and Micronesia are treated like US domestic routes, with nice low fares.

To/From Asia

Indonesia The short flight from Jayapura (K60) to Vanimo in PNG is currently the only air route between PNG and Indonesia, but there is talk of direct flights from Vanimo to Biak. This would be much more convenient, as from Biak you can fly to the USA.

Most other international flights out of Indonesia depart from Jakarta. There are flights from Jayapura to Jakarta most days

for about US$440 (cheaper in Indonesia). You have to change planes twice, but you can do the trip in a day.

The only reliable place in PNG to get rupiah (Indonesian currency) is in Port Moresby but don't get too much, you'll get a better price in Jayapura, but not at the airport. See Lonely Planet's *South-East Asia on a Shoestring* or *Indonesia – a travel survival kit* for more information.

Elsewhere in Asia Air Niugini, in conjunction with Singapore Airlines, has weekly flights from Port Moresby to Hong Kong, and two or three to Singapore. Unless you particularly want to visit Hong Kong, that routing is usually expensive. A Singapore to Port Moresby low-season Excursion return fare, valid for 45 days costs around US$1000. From from Manila to Port Moresby on Air Niugini, in conjunction with Philippine Airlines, a 90-day Excursion return fare costs US$950. Both these fares are probably cheaper if bought in Singapore or Manila.

To/From Europe

You can put together a ticket taking you from Europe to Hong Kong, Manila or Singapore and connecting with an Air Niugini (see above) flight to Port Moresby there. A more complicated route would be to fly to Jakarta (Indonesia) and from there to Biak and Jayapura, from where it's a short hop to Vanimo in PNG.

Many people combine a visit to PNG with a holiday in Australasia or the Pacific. A cheap ticket to Australia (possibly a Round-the-World ticket) plus an APEX return ticket between Cairns and Port Moresby might be the cheapest way to get to PNG from Europe.

There are a million-and-one deals on tickets from Europe to Australia and Asia, but check whether there are any good deals on flights all the way to PNG. Singapore Airlines flies from Europe to Port Moresby, and a low-season Excursion fare from London, valid for a year and with a stopover in Singapore might cost under £1100. Philippine Airlines (which flies from Manila to

Port Moresby) doesn't seem to have particularly good deals on direct flights between Europe and Port Moresby, but it's worth checking out their specials between Europe and Australasia.

UK Trailfinders in west London produce a lavishly illustrated brochure which includes air fare details. STA also has branches in the UK. Look in the listings magazines *Time Out* and *City Limits* plus the Sunday papers and *Exchange & Mart* for ads. Also look out for the free magazines widely available in London – start by looking outside the main railway stations.

The Globetrotters Club (BCM Roving, London WC1N 3XX) publishes a newsletter called *Globe* which covers obscure destinations and can help in finding travelling companions.

To/From North America

There are four major alternatives: fly to Australia, then on to Port Moresby, fly to Port Moresby via Guam with Continental, fly to Biak with Garuda then on to Jayapura and Vanimo in PNG, fly to Manila or Singapore then on to Port Moresby.

A return Excursion fare from LA to Sydney costs around US$1500 but there are often specials for less than US$1000. There is a lot of discounting on this route, so ask around. See the To/From Australia section for fares between Australia and Port Moresby.

Continental flies from LA to Port Moresby via Guam. The standard fare is US$995 one way, but there are various specials on return fares, such as US$1750 for a high-season APEX ticket and US$1500 in the low season.

You can fly with Garuda from LA to Biak on Wednesday, Friday and Sunday for about US$770 (cheaper in Indonesia and some LA travel agents offer excellent return fares). There are daily Garuda flights from Biak to Jayapura (US$77, probably cheaper in Indonesia). The Sunday Jayapura to Vanimo flight costs about US$60. This is the easiest way into the Sepik region, but check connections carefully, and remember

that the international date line will affect your calculations.

A one-way Excursion fare on Philippine Airlines from LA to Manila might cost under US$550, but the Manila to Port Moresby sector is expensive, especially if you buy it outside the Philippines.

The *New York Times*, the *LA Times*, the *Chicago Tribune* and the *San Francisco Examiner* all produce weekly travel sections in which you'll find any number of travel agents' ads. Council Travel and STA Travel have offices in major cities nationwide.

The magazine *Travel Unlimited* (PO Box 1058, Allston, Mass 02134) publishes details of the cheapest air fares and courier possibilities for destinations all over the world from the USA.

Travel CUTS has offices in all major Canadian cities. The *Toronto Globe & Mail* and the *Vancouver Sun* carry travel agents' ads. The magazine *Great Expeditions* (PO Box 8000-411, Abbotsford BC V2S 6H1) is useful.

Round-the-World Tickets & Circle Pacific Fares

Round-the-World (RTW) tickets are often real bargains, and can work out no more expensive or even cheaper than an ordinary return ticket. The official airline RTW tickets are usually put together by a combination of two or more airlines, and permit you to fly anywhere you want on their route systems so long as you do not backtrack.

Other restrictions are that you (usually) must book the first sector in advance and cancellation penalties then apply. There may be restrictions on how many stops you are permitted and usually the tickets are valid for 90 days up to a year.

An alternative type of RTW ticket is one put together by a travel agent using a combination of discounted tickets.

Circle Pacific tickets use a combination of airlines to circle the Pacific – combining Australia, New Zealand, North America and Asia. As with RTW tickets there are advance purchase restrictions and limits to how many stopovers you can take.

You might not be able to include PNG on an RTW or Circle Pacific ticket but you can certainly get close, to Australia, Asia or the Pacific. Even adding on the sectors to/from PNG, an RTW ticket might work out cheaper than a direct fare. Flying into Australia, making you way through PNG and picking up the homeward leg in Indonesia, Singapore or elsewhere in Asia is possible on some tickets.

SEA

Basically, entering PNG by sea is now difficult or impossible, unless you're on a yacht or a cruise ship.

To/From Australia

Unless you are a Torres Strait Islander, it is illegal to island-hop between Thursday Island (known as TI to locals) and PNG. You can exit Australia from TI but you must go directly to PNG, usually Daru. There are plenty of fishing boast doing the trip, but no regular direct flights. You are allowed to island-hop as far as Saibai Island, just off the PNG coast, but from there you cannot exit Australia and enter PNG – you must return to Australia.

These rules were once much flaunted but Australian patrols of the area have tightened up and you're likely to be caught if you try to bend them. Non-Australians who enter Australia this way can be charged with illegal entry.

To/From the Solomon Islands

There was once a very interesting 'back door' route into Papua New Guinea from the Solomons to Bougainville. This route is now used by the Bougainville Revolutionary Army to smuggle in supplies and by the PNG army on reprisal raids, so it's definitely out for the non-military traveller!

To/From Indonesia

It is possible but not legal to travel between Irian Jaya and PNG by sea, even the tempting little trip between Vanimo and Jayapura. If you do manage it you'll have problems with immigration.

Yacht

PNG is a popular stopping point for cruising yachties, either heading through Asia or the Pacific. If you ask around it's often possible to get a berth on a yacht heading off somewhere interesting. Often yachties depend upon picking up crew to help them sail and to help cover some of the day to day costs. The best places to try would be Port Moresby, Madang and Rabaul and Milne Bay, although you can quite possibly find yachts visiting at almost any port around the country.

LEAVING PNG

There's a departure tax of K15 (this changes from time to time, both up and down). You have to buy a special stamp at a post office. If you've overstayed your visa, expect to pay a very hefty fine before they let you on the plane.

People on yachts might be hit for a K100 per person 'customs clearance fee', especially at Samarai in Milne Bay.

Getting Around

AIR

Civil aviation was pioneered in PNG and there is no country that was more dependent on flying for its development. Even today, when a sketchy road network is beginning to creep across parts of the country, an enormous proportion of passengers and freight travel by air. Geographic realities continue to dictate this situation: the population is small and scattered, often isolated in mountain valleys and on tiny islands. Unfortunately, these factors also mean that flying is expensive. And, if you have limited time, it's virtually unavoidable.

Airlines

There are two main carriers on domestic routes and numerous small operations, some only for charter but some running scheduled passenger routes. The main outfits are Air Niugini (the national carrier) and Talair, with MAF (Missionary Aviation Fellowship – known to some as the Missionaries' Air Force!) the major small operator.

Air Niugini operates half a dozen Fokker F28s (jets), and De Havilland Dash 7s (big turbo-props) on its domestic routes. Talair once had a huge fleet of small planes but now operates only the slightly larger Twin Otters and Bandeirantes. The MAF fleet is dominated by small aircraft. MAF, because it essentially supplies and transports missionaries rather than carrying passengers, has frequent and fairly regular flights but you'll have to hope there is room for you to go along. There usually is.

You may come across the distinction between first-level, second-level and third-level airlines the first time when you visit PNG. First-level describes a carrier that operates internationally (Air Niugini), second-level covers airlines that make the major domestic connections (Air Niugini and Talair) and third-level means an airline that operates between all the tiny towns and villages (MAF, Talair and many others).

Unfortunately the airline situation in PNG is more complicated than it once was. Air Niugini doesn't fly everywhere (its planes are too big for many strips) and Douglas, once one of the main third-level operators, has folded. To make matters worse, Talair has decided to concentrate on being an interprovincial airline, has sold most of its smaller planes and has drastically cut the number of smaller strips it services.

Air travel is the lifeline of PNG so other operators are taking over the Douglas and Talair routes but some of them are shoestring outfits which might not last long, and getting firm timetables in much advance could be tricky. Many fly charters rather than scheduled passenger routes, and while you can often pay to go along on someone else's charter, this can take time (and beers) to arrange and isn't always possible. Most third-level operators are very approachable, though.

For the addresses of Air Niugini's overseas offices see the Getting There chapter. Head-office addresses are:

Air Niugini
  PO Box 7186, Boroko, Port Moresby (☎ 27 3555)
MAF
  PO Box 273, Mt Hagen, Western Highlands (☎ 55 1506)
Talair
  PO Box 108, Goroka, Eastern Highlands (☎ 72 1240)

Air Niugini logo

Some of the third-level carriers running passenger routes or regularly taking passengers along on charters are:

Islands Aviation (☎ 92 2900, fax 92 2812, PO Box 717, Rabaul)
Flights in New Britain, New Ireland and North Solomons

Airlink (☎ 92 1712, fax 92 1917, PO Box 1930, Rabaul)
Flights in New Britain, New Ireland, North Solomons and Lae

TransNiugini Airways (☎ 25 6183, fax 25 4791, PO Box 3779, Boroko)
Flights in Central Province (including Kokoda Trail strips), and might expand into Simbu Province

Milne Bay Air (MBA) (☎ 25 2011, fax 25 2219, PO Box 170, Port Moresby)
Currently purely charter but expects to get a passenger licence and will be one of the larger operators.

Dovair (☎ 87 1056, PO Box 205, Vanimo)
Mainly Sepik area

Sandaun Air Services (SAS) (☎ 87 1268/79, fax 87 1089, PO Box 206, Vanimo)
Mainly Sepik area

Tarangau Airways (☎ 86 2203, fax 86 2820, PO Box 292, Wewak)
Mainly Sepik area

Northcoast Aviation (☎ 29 7219, PO Box 12, Popondetta)
Mainly Oro Province

MAF has bases (which operate fairly autonomously; not all have phones) in Anguganak, Goroka (☎ 72 1080), Mt Hagen (☎ 55 1317) (head office), Kawito, Madang (☎ 82 2229), Mendi (☎ 59 1091), Nadzab (Lae) (☎ 42 3804), Tari (☎ 50 8014), Telefomin, Vanimo (☎ 87 1091), Wewak (☎ 86 2500) and Port Moresby (☎ 25 2668).

Air Niugini and Talair (along with some of the smaller companies under Talair's wing) have computerised booking systems so bookings are usually quite efficient and can be made from anywhere in the world. Talair is linked to the Qantas system, so you can make bookings at any Qantas office. This level of sophistication does not apply to every PNG airport – some terminals can be more accurately described as sheds.

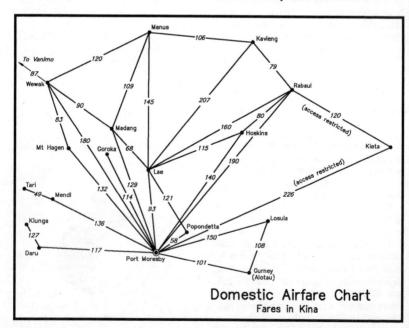

Domestic Airfare Chart
Fares in Kina

Note that Talair and some of the smaller companies do not fly on Sundays.

Warning You have to check-in on Air Niugini's domestic flights an hour in advance of departure time. Take this seriously – half an hour before flight-time they start giving seats to waitlisted passengers.

Aircraft

The planes are small and fill quickly – many Air Niugini flights leave behind a long line of disappointed waitlisted passengers. Book ahead and always reconfirm. If you're told a flight is full, it's often worth trying again – they don't always seem to end up that way. Travel can be more difficult during the Australian school holidays. Many expats bring their children up from their boarding schools and flights are heavily booked around Christmas, early February, late June and late September.

Remember that you may have to fly in *light* aircraft. If you do, flying out with a two-metre *garamut* drum tucked under your arm might be difficult. Not only is your baggage weighed (16 kg is the limit but 20 kg is usually accepted) – so are you.

Unpredictable weather combined with mechanical problems and complex schedules can frequently lead to delays. If one plane is late at one airport the whole schedule can be thrown out. Considering the terrain, the airstrips and the weather, reliability is fair and the safety record is very good. The pilots are extremely skilful – keep telling yourself this as you approach flat-topped ridges masquerading as airports! Many young pilots are intent on building up their command experience so they can move on to a first-level airline, but others stay on because 'PNG has the best flying in the world'.

Discounts & Special Fares

Talair no longer offers any discounts. MAF and some other third-level outfits offer student discounts, but they don't really get into fancy discount structures. MAF also offers discounts of 25% to overseas volunteers with ID.

Air Niugini has a number of special deals. Given the high cost of air travel in the country, even travellers who don't usually pre-book air tickets might want to investigate them. These deals can and do change from time to time, so check before you leave home.

Student Discounts
Full-time students under 25 years old get 25% off domestic fares (50% off if you're under 19). If you're making a booking outside PNG you need to have an International Student Concession Form, signed by the institution. You're also supposed to have one for booking flights within PNG.
Visit PNG
This must be booked outside PNG. You get four domestic flights for US$300, plus additional flights for US$50. This could be a huge saving but tickets can only be bought in conjunction with a tour. There are other conditions – see a travel agent.
See Niugini
These are booked outside PNG, in conjunction with certain advance purchase tickets to/from PNG (including Apex fares). You get 20% off domestic flights, and while you have to book flights before you arrive (well in advance), changes are permitted, with certain conditions. People seem to have no trouble getting the discount on tickets bought within PNG. Maximum stay 45 days.
Weekend Excursion Fares
These round-trip tickets cost only 50% of the standard fare. You have to fly out on Friday or Saturday and back on Sunday or Monday. Unfortunately, only a certain number of discount seats are allocated to any one flight, and they're often booked out long in advance. These fare might apply only at certain times of the year. There are also good-value weekend packages which include accommodation.
Nambawan Fares
These are probably the most useful fares for walkers, as they offer round-trip tickets at 50% discount. You have to stay a minimum of 14 and a maximum of 30 days at your domestic destination, which allows plenty of time to explore. You have to fly midweek. Like the weekend fares, these can be booked out, but it's less likely. You have to buy these tickets in PNG, from the town you'll fly from/to, in person. These fares might apply only at certain times of the year.
Hamamas fares
Offers 30% off round-trip fares, maximum 30 days, minimum seven days. Other conditions similar to Nambawan fares.

SEA

There is a wide variety of interesting sea transport, from ocean-going vessels to canoes. You can plan your trip around Lutheran Shipping's passenger boats or you can just wait under a palm tree and see what comes along.

The main ways of getting around by sea are: large boats, small boats, charters and yacht crewing.

Large Boats

Basically there are boats taking passengers along the north coast between Oro Bay (near Popondetta) and Vanimo, and to the main islands off the north coast. There are no passenger vessels linking the north and south coasts or running along the south coast.

Most of the main cargo lines are reluctant to take passengers on their freighters. However, if you make the right connections, usually via an expat in the shipping office or directly with a crew member at the docks, you'll often manage to get a berth or deck space. The major companies list their schedules in the Shipping Notes section of the *Post Courier*, so you'll at least have an idea of when and where to look for a boat.

Conditions on many freighters can be grim and their schedules are unreliable. Luckily, Lutheran Shipping runs a reliable, inexpensive and reasonably comfortable passenger-only service between Oro Bay and Wewak, with services out to New Britain.

Although there are a number of other smaller operations, some of the main shipping companies and their head offices are:

Coastal Shipping Company
  PO Box 423, Rabaul, East New Britain (☎ 92 2399, fax 92 2090)
Consort Express Lines
  PO Box 1690, Port Moresby (☎ 21 1288, fax 21 1279)
Lutheran Shipping
  PO Box 1459, Lae, Morobe Province (☎ 42 2066, fax 42 5806)
Pacific New Guinea Line
  PO Box 1764, Rabaul, East New Britain (☎ 92 3055, fax 92 3084)

PNG Shipping Corporation
  PO Box 634, Port Moresby (☎ 22 0420, fax 21 2815)

North Coast Lutheran Shipping has a virtual monopoly on passenger shipping along the north coast and services Oro Bay, Lae, Finschhafen, Madang, Wewak, Aitape, Vanimo and intermediate ports.

There are two passenger-only boats, the *Mamose Express* and the *Rita*, which run between Oro Bay and Wewak, with services from Lae to New Britain. The tourist class on these boats consists of air-conditioned seats and berths, and deck class has air-vented seats and berths. If you miss the boat you'll get a 50% refund on your ticket up to 48 hours after sailing, and nothing after that. Booking ahead might be necessary around Christmas.

See the following page for the schedule of Lutheran Shipping passenger-only boats along the north coast. Remember that it can change. Note that some boats go on to New Britain from Lae, so you might have to change if you're going further east or west along the coast. Students are entitled to discounts, although whether this is 50% or 25% differs between booking offices.

Lutheran Shipping's passenger-carrying freighters run unpredictably between Oro Bay and Vanimo (and out to the islands), at fares slightly lower than those on the passenger-only boats.

Islands Lutheran Shipping has a weekly passenger-only boat sailing from Lae to Kimbe and Rabaul (New Britain) on Monday afternoon, arriving on Tuesday. To Rabaul deck class costs K34 and cabin K54.

Coastal Shipping has the *Lae Express*, a passenger boat, running once a week between Lae and Rabaul via Kimbe. Coastal's *Kimbe Express* also sails to Rabaul via Kimbe, with deck class accommodation only. Coastal's *Astro I* departs for Rabaul on Wednesday, running via the south coast of New Britain and stopping at Kandrian, among other places. This is not a passenger

Lutheran Shipping Schedule

Westbound

Port	Depart	Deck	Tourist	Arrive	Port
Oro Bay	1 pm (Tuesday)	K21.50	K32.50	7 am (Wednesday)	Lae
Lae	9 am (Wednesday)	K21.50	K32.50	6 am (Thursday)	Madang
Madang	5 pm (Friday)	K22.40	K33.80	9 am (Saturday)	Wewak

Eastbound

Port	Depart	Deck	Tourist	Arrive	Port
Wewak	noon (Saturday)	K22.40	K33.80	6 am (Sunday)	Madang
Madang	9 am (Sunday)	K21.50	K32.50	7 am (Monday)	Lae
Lae	7 pm (Monday)	K21.50	K32.50	11 am (Tuesday)	Oro Bay

Through Rates

Port	Deck	Tourist
Lae-Wewak	K36.40	K54.60
Wewak-Oro Bay	K58.80	K88.40

boat but there are a few cabins in which you can sometimes travel, for K80 to Rabaul.

Coastal also has unscheduled freighters, running approximately fortnightly, sailing from Rabaul to Kavieng (New Ireland). The 18-hour trip costs about K35/50 in deck/cabin class.

See Lonely Planet's *Papua New Guinea – a travel survival kit* for other routes.

South Coast No freighters officially take passengers on the south coast. For unofficial berths try the shipping offices and docks in Port Moresby, where you'll also find small boats running to Gulf Province. Rambu Shipping is a small line which is reportedly worth approaching.

Small Boats

Local boats and canoes go literally everywhere. For these you have to be in the right place at the right time, but with patience you could travel the whole coastline by village-hopping in small boats.

Work boats (small, wooden boats with thumping diesel engines) ply the coast supplying trade stores on an irregular but fairly frequent basis. They also act as ferries and travelling on one will get you to some very off-the-track places. They aren't very com-fortable and can be noisy and smelly, but for the adventurous there's no better way to travel.

Fares are low – for example, a two-day trip from Alotau in Milne Bay to the Trobriand Islands (overnighting on a tropical beach) will cost about K20. If you're in a major centre ask at the big stores, as they might have a fairly set schedule for delivering supplies to the area's trade stores. Take your own food and water on these boats.

Around New Britain and other places there are slightly more regular coastal services in small freighters, and in some places mission boats run set schedules and will take passengers.

For shorter distances there are dinghies with outboard motors, often known as speed-ies or banana boats. These are usually long, fibreglass boats which are surprisingly sea-worthy despite their bronco-like mode of travel, leaping through the waves. The cost

of running outboard motors makes them very expensive if you have to charter one, but there will often be a speedie acting as a ferry (taking people to church or market) and the fares are reasonable. There are still canoes with outboards around, and you might even get to make a voyage in a sailing canoe on the south coast.

Charter

Many dive operators charter their boats, some for extended cruises. A cheaper alternative, if you're not looking for comfort and the chance to dive, is to try to charter a work boat. Chartering is definitely possible in Milne Bay and probably elsewhere, and between a group, say five or six, isn't ruinously expensive.

Yacht

There are thriving yacht clubs in Port Moresby, Lae, Rabaul and Wewak and it is possible that you might be able to find a berth, if you have some experience. Yachts often clear PNG customs at Samarai Island in Milne Bay.

RIVER

There are a number of rivers that villagers use as 'highways'. These include the Sepik and some of its tributaries (including the April, May and Keram), the Ramu, the Fly and a number of other rivers that flow into the Gulf of Papua.

If you are prepared to rough it and live in the villages, it possible to get around on inter-village canoes. The problem with this is that although they are relatively cheap they only run according to demand – there are no schedules. Traffic builds up from Wednesday through to Saturday because of people moving around for markets, but can be very quiet early in the week and non-existent on Sundays.

If you are short of time, you can charter a motorised village canoe or boat, with a guide/driver. However, this is expensive: probably somewhere between K10 and K20 per hour of running time (this is due to the high cost of operating two-stroke engines)

plus a hire fee. On the Sepik some village guides will quote you an all-up daily rate for tours, including village accommodation, and this can be about K70 a day.

There are also several tour boats cruising the Sepik.

Paddling your own canoe (a dugout bought from a village) is most popular on the Sepik – see Lonely Planet's *Papua New Guinea – a travel survival kit* for detailed information on canoeing down the mighty Sepik.

PUBLIC MOTOR VEHICLE

There is still a very limited network of roads around the country. The most important is the Highlands Highway, which is sealed from Lae to Mt Hagen, unsealed from Mt Hagen to Tari, and a 4WD track between Tari and Lake Kopiago where it ends. Madang is also connected to the highway.

Branching off the Highlands Highway are also a large number of secondary roads that go to numerous smaller places, such as Obura and Okapa in the Eastern Highlands; Chuave, Kegsugl, Kerowagi and Gumine in Simbu; Minj, Banz, Tabibuga and Baiyer River in the Western Highlands; Wabag, Porgera, Kompiam and Kandep in Enga and Ialibu, Erave and Tambul in the Southern Highlands.

There are reasonable roads east and west along the coast from Port Moresby, along the north coast east and west of Madang, into the Sepik basin from Wewak, and the Germans bequeathed excellent roads on New Britain and New Ireland. There is no road between Moresby and the Highlands or between Moresby and the north coast.

Wherever there are roads there will be Public Motor Vehicles (PMVs). Most PMVs are comfortable Japanese minibuses, but they can be trucks with wooden benches, or even small, bare pick-up trucks.

Rural PMVs pick-up and drop-off people at any point along a pre-established route. You can more or less assume that anything with lots of people in it is a rural PMV, although officially they have a blue number plate beginning with P. In the urban areas there are established PMV stops (often indicated by a yellow pole or a crowd of waiting people). The destination will be indicated by a sign inside the windscreen or called out by the driver's assistant.

Stick your hand out and wave downwards and they will generally stop. PMVs have a crew of two: the driver, who usually maintains an aloof distance from the passengers; and the 'conductor', who takes fares. The conductor sits up front next to the passenger-side window, so when the PMV stops, he's the man to ask about the PMV's destination. If it's heading in the right direction and there's a centimetre or two of spare space, you're on. You don't pay – yet.

There are standard fares for PMVs. Ask other passengers if you want to be certain what they are. In the towns you pay the conductor at the end of the trip after you've disembarked. If you tell the conductor where you want to go when you start, he'll let the driver know when to stop. If you make your mind up as you go, just yell 'Stop driver'.

In the country they quite frequently collect the fare either midway through the journey or 15 minutes or so before your final destination. It seems too many passengers were escaping into the bush without paying!

Some expats say that PMVs are unsafe. Ignore these comments. You'll find that the people who are most hysterical about the dangers of riding on PMVs are the people who've never set foot in one. If the vehicle looks in pretty good shape and the driver does too, you are most unlikely to have any problems. Most drivers are very careful. They simply cannot afford to hit a stray person or pig (think of the compensation and the paybacks) let alone injure one of their passengers. You are not immune to armed hold-ups when you travel on PMVs in the Highlands but if you travel during the day and avoid pay afternoons (every second Friday) you're safer in a PMV than in a private car.

Make sure you get to your destination before dark and if you don't, ask the driver to deliver you to wherever you plan to stay. If you're looking for long-distance PMVs

always start at the markets *early* in the morning. PMVs leave town when they're full so if you're the first on board you can spend a very frustrating hour or two circling around looking for more passengers. Market days (usually Friday and Saturday) are the best days for finding a ride. On secondary roads, traffic can be thin, especially early in the week.

CAR

Any valid overseas license is OK for the first three months you're in PNG. Cars drive on the left side of the road. The speed limit is 50 km per hour in towns and 100 km per hour in the country.

Bear in mind the tourist office's recommendations if you are involved in an accident: Don't stop; keep driving and report the accident at the nearest police station. This applies regardless of who was at fault or how serious the accident is (whether you've run over a pig or hit a person). Tribal concepts of payback apply to car accidents. You may have insurance and you may be willing to pay, but the local citizenry may well prefer to take more immediate and satisfying revenge. There have been a number of instances where drivers who have been involved in fatal accidents have been killed or injured by the accident victim's relatives. A serious accident can mean 'pack up and leave the country' for an expatriate.

Car Rental

It is possible to hire cars in most main centres but because of the limited road network (with the exception of the Highlands) you usually won't be able to get far. The major car rental organisations are Avis, Budget and Hertz. One or other of them will have cars in every major town, including on the islands of Manus, New Britain and New Ireland. There are also a few smaller, local firms that are sometimes cheaper than the internationals. Check the yellow pages.

Costs are high, partly because the cars have such a hard life and spend so much time on unsealed roads. All rental rates with the big operators are made up of a daily or weekly charge plus a certain charge per km. In addition you should budget for insurance at around K15 a day. Typical costs and cars are:

Car	per day	per km
Mitsubishi Lancer	K54	K0.45
Mitsubishi Magna	K79	K0.55
Honda Accord	K84	K0.64
Mitsubishi Pajero (4WD)	K88	K0.65

In addition, remote area surcharges of around K15 a day may apply. The Highlands are regarded as remote. The three main operators all have desks at Jacksons Airport, Port Moresby:

Avis
    PO Box 1533, Port Moresby (☎ 25 8429, fax 25 3767)
Budget
    PO Box 1215, Boroko (☎ 25 4111, fax 25 7853)
Hertz
    PO Box 4126, Boroko (☎ 25 4999, fax 25 6985)

BICYCLE

The Highlands Highway is probably out for cycling, because of the danger of robbery. Still, a mountain bike would be very handy on the Trobriand Islands, around the Gazelle Peninsula (near Rabaul) and, best of all, on idyllic New Ireland where there are two long, flat coast roads with little traffic. A couple of companies offer bike tours of New Ireland, and it might be possible to hire bikes in Kavieng.

HITCHING

It is possible to hitchhike, although you'll often be expected to pay the equivalent of a PMV fare. In some places any passing vehicle is likely to offer you a ride. That is, *if* there is a passing vehicle. You're wisest to wave them down, however, otherwise it's possible they'll think you're a mad tourist walking for the fun of it. If your bag is light, it's also sometimes possible to hitch flights from small airports.

WALKING

The best and cheapest way to come to grips with PNG is to walk. With a judicious mix of walks, canoes, PMVs, coastal ships and third-level planes, PNG can change from a very expensive country to a relatively reasonable one.

The Kokoda Trail

The Kokoda Trail crosses the Owen Stanley Ranges between Owers' Corner, 50 km east of Port Moresby, and Kokoda, a large government station west of Popondetta in Oro Province. Walking the trail is very popular with residents and visitors, although the terrain it crosses is some of the most rugged in PNG. Sharp, timbered ridges, steep-sided valleys and fast-flowing rivers all provide the walker with an unequalled opportunity to discover PNG's unique wilderness.

In addition to linking numerous Koiari villages and providing walkers with a practical link between the north and south coasts, this walk introduces the visitor to the richness of the country's rainforests and the grandeur of its landscape. It also gives an insight into the reason for PNG's cultural and linguistic diversity: the startling ruggedness and inaccessibility of much of the country.

HISTORY

Linking the north and south coasts, the trail was first used by miners struggling north to the Yodda Kokoda goldfields of the 1890s, but it was WW II that brought it to the attention of the world.

Following their attack on Pearl Harbor in December '41, the Japanese made a rapid advance down the South-East Asian archipelago and across the Pacific, capturing New Britain and the north coast of New Guinea. Their navy's advance on Port Moresby and Australia was dramatically halted by the Battle of the Coral Sea, and this led to a different plan of attack.

The new strategy was to take Port Moresby by a totally unexpected 'back door' assault. The plan was to land on the north coast near Popondetta, travel to Kokoda and then march up and over the Owen Stanley Ranges to Sogeri and down to Port Moresby.

The Japanese made one serious miscalculation: the Kokoda Trail was not a rough track that could be upgraded for vehicles, it was a switchback footpath through some of the most rugged country in the world, endlessly climbing and plunging down, infested by leeches and hopelessly muddy during the wet season.

The Japanese landed on 21 July '42 and stormed down the trail, overcoming the increasingly desperate Australian opposition. The Allies planned a last-ditch battle for Imita Ridge, within spitting distance of Port Moresby. However, before they reached the ridge, the Japanese forces stopped at Ioribaiwa on the 16 September, their supply lines hopelessly over-stretched. They had failed to supply their troops by air, their plan to make the trail suitable for vehicles had proved to be unrealistic, and a soldier could barely carry sufficient food to get himself down the trail and back, let alone carry extra supplies for the front-line soldiers. At the same time, the Japanese were being stretched to the limit at Guadalcanal in the Solomons, so they withdrew, with Port Moresby virtually in sight.

The campaign to dislodge the Japanese from Buna on the north coast was one of the most bitter and bloody of the Pacific War. The fighting was desperate and the terrain and climate were unbelievably hard. Disease and starvation were as deadly as bullets and bombs.

It is almost impossible to comprehend the courage and suffering of the people who fought here, and it is no wonder the horrors of the Kokoda Trail and the Buna campaign have not been forgotten by either side. Never again did the Allied forces meet the Japanese head-on during WW II. The policy for the rest of the war was to advance towards Tokyo, bypassing the intervening Japanese strongholds. Rabaul in New Britain, for instance, was left alone and isolated while the front moved towards Japan.

The turn-off to the start of the trail, just before Sogeri, is marked by a memorial stone. At McDonald's Corner there is a strange metal sculpture of a soldier; this is

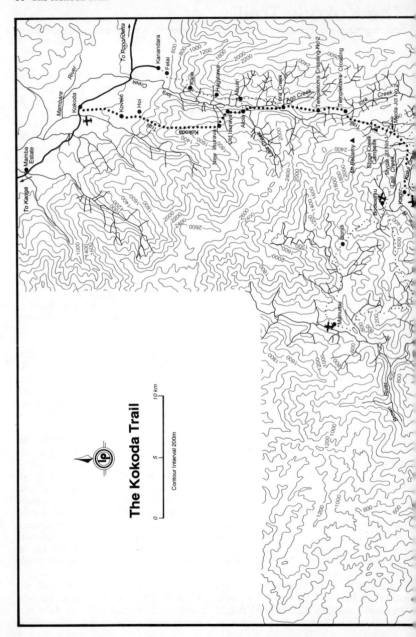

The Kokoda Trail

Contour interval 200m

0   5   10 km

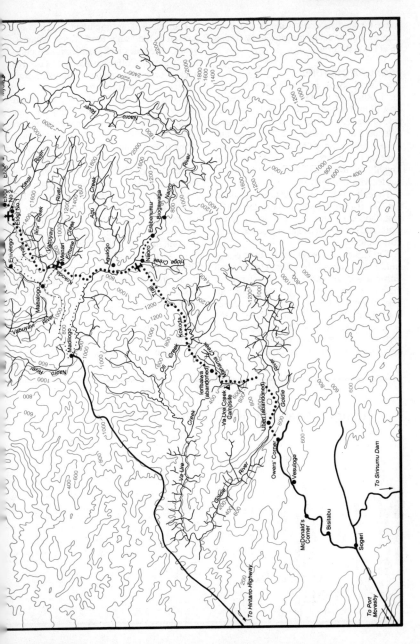

where the road once ended and the trail commenced, but the actual trail now starts further on at Owers' Corner.

PEOPLE & CULTURE

The Koiari people inhabit the area between the foothills of the Owen Stanleys east of Port Moresby, and Kokoda on the northern side of the range. To the west, their territory extends into the valleys of the Agure and Dala rivers, both tributaries of the upper Vanapa. To the east, their territorial border is roughly the top of the range as it forms the border with Oro Province.

The cultural groups whose territory border the Koiari's are the Orokaiva to the north-east, the Fuyuge to the north-west, and the Koita and Motu who live along the coast near Port Moresby.

The Koiari once built houses in tree-tops and, at the time of their first contact with Europeans in the 1880s, were renowned for their fierceness. Nowadays, the people all wear Western clothes, many live in houses built of galvanised iron, and all belong to the Seventh Day Adventist Church. Being converts of that church, they do not raise or eat pigs, chew betel nut or smoke tobacco.

Gardening is an important activity, and kaukau is the staple food. Taros, bananas, yams, vegetables and greens are also commonly grown. Coffee has been introduced as a cash crop and oranges and okari nuts abound throughout the area.

You'll meet the Koiari people in their villages and along the trails. They are very friendly, although not as spontaneous as people from other parts of PNG. This attitude stems from the number of visitors they've seen over the years. Usually, the ice is quickly broken if you show some interest in the place. Young women, however, are particularly shy and reserved and you should respect their wishes if they do not want to talk to you. Male bushwalkers should give women the right of way on the trail – step off the trail, the further the better.

Be aware that men and women bathe in different places; usually the women downstream from the men. The same can apply to toilets, so ask first. Be sensitive, as this is of great importance to the people.

INFORMATION
Features

The Owen Stanley Ranges are the eastern-

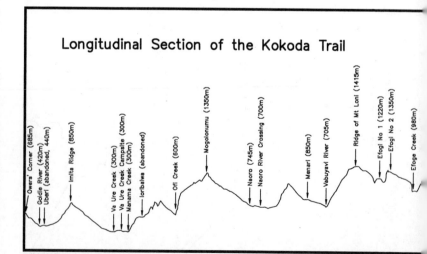

Longitudinal Section of the Kokoda Trail

most part of the central cordillera that runs the length of the country, roughly through the middle. To the west of the area bisected by the trail is Mt Victoria, which at 4040 metres is PNG's fifth-highest mountain.

The area traversed by the trail is more than characteristic of PNG's notorious ruggedness. The slopes are long and very steep and are slippery at the best of times, often treacherous in the wet. Crystal-clear brooks and small streams flow over moss-covered boulders, tumbling down the steep slopes of the mountains before being lost in the thick vegetation. Torrents hurtle down the valleys in their race to the sea; some are crossed on log bridges, others are simply forded.

The area offers diverse forest ranges and rewards the walker with some of PNG's most varied and beautiful rainforest. The rich and luxuriant vegetation along the trail more than makes up for the colour the local culture lacks.

Standard

As the crow flies, Kokoda is about 60 km from Owers' Corner. However, for the walker, the Kokoda Trail is a difficult 94-km

trail where steep, exhausting and seemingly endless ups are followed by similar downs, slippery at best of time, often treacherous in the wet. If you total all the uphill climbing along the trail, it comes to more than 5500 metres of elevation gain.

The trail can be walked by any healthy and physically fit person so long as they stay within their limits. The best section is between Menari and Kagi, although the nicest forests are found at the higher elevations between Kagi Gap and Templeton's Crossing.

The walk can be done in either direction; some people claim it is a little easier walking from Popondetta to Port Moresby.

The trail is usually reasonably clear and well defined except perhaps for the section around the site of the old village of Ioribaiwa, where dense *kunai* grass makes the trail more difficult to follow.

Each of the 20 crossings of the Va Ure and Manama creeks are described here – some with maps – and should pose no undue problems for the walker. Most rivers are bridged but a few must be forded. Crossing is usually easy, but can become difficult and hazardous with heavy rains.

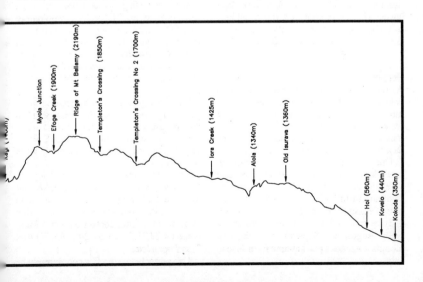

Days Required

Five or six days are needed to complete this walk. The itinerary suggested here requires six, but this could easily be spread over eight or more if you take time to explore, swim in the creeks and visit the Myola grasslands.

There are airstrips at Naoro, Menari, Efogi No 1 and Kagi, as well as in Bodinumu and Naduli, two villages close to Kagi. Myola has an airstrip but only chartered planes land there. For those who can't spare the time to walk the whole trail, an alternative is to fly in to one of these strips, walk a section, then fly out. For such a trip, I would recommend that you fly in at Kagi and walk back to Menari (one day) or Naoro (two days). You could, of course, fly in to one of these strips then walk all the way to Port Moresby or Kokoda.

Another option is to get a PMV from Port Moresby to the village of Madilogo. This avoids two hard days (possibly the hardest) of walking from Owers' Corner to Naoro. It takes about two hours to reach the Kokoda Trail from Madilogo; from there it's another 1½ hours to Naoro and a further 1¾ hours to Menari.

Walking times in this chapter are minimum times – unless you're very fit or are carrying a very light load, you're unlikely to travel much faster than the times given here and might travel more slowly.

Season

As the elevation along the trail ranges from near sea level to 2190 metres, the temperature varies a lot. At the start and end of the walk it is quite hot and very humid. In the mountains it is cool and pleasant during the day, but it can be quite chilly at night.

During the wet season (early December to mid-March) the trail can be very wet and slippery, and some of the rivers may be swollen and difficult to cross. Sunny days are more frequent between June and September, and the trail is drier and more pleasant to walk. August and September are the best months. Oranges ripen anytime from June to July.

Useful Organisations

Traditional Travel (☎ 21 3966) is likely to have the best up-to-date information on the state of the trail. The rangers at the Port Moresby or Kokoda ends of the trail don't have much information.

Before you start out contact the National Disaster, Surveillance & Emergency Service (☎ 27 6502; ☎ 27 6666 for emergencies) to inform them of your party's plans and get up-to-date information on the trail. The office is in Waigani, on the third floor of Morauta House – turn left out of the lift. Don't forget to report in at the District Office at Kokoda.

There are health centres and two-way radios in Efogi No 1 and Kokoda. The Trans-Niugini Airways agents at Kagi and Menari also have radios.

There is a guesthouse in Myola and rest houses in Naoro, Menari, Efogi No 1, Kagi, Alola and Kokoda. Lean-to shelters can be found at Efoge Creek, Templeton's Crossing No 2 and Iora Creek.

Guides & Carriers

A guide might not be necessary, but you're strongly advised to take one, because of the dangers of getting lost and because of the dangers of rascals. The best way would be to take different guides for different sections of the trail, so you always have someone with you who knows local people, but this might not be feasible. At least try to make sure that your guide comes from *somewhere* along the trail.

That said, you'll be hard-pressed to find guides or carriers among the Koiari people – they're just not keen on doing that kind of work. As most people in the area are Seventh Day Adventists, your guide might not work on Saturday.

Traditional Travel (☎ 21 3966) in Port Moresby, besides running a twelve-day tour over the trail, might be able to assist in finding guides and carriers. If you're starting from the other end, contact the Oro Guesthouse (☎ 29 7127, fax c/- 29 7193, PO Box 2) in Popondetta.

One porter between a few people might be

a good compromise. Expect to pay a guide at least K15 to K25 a day (possibly a lot more), and a porter about K10 a day. You have to provide them with food and perhaps some equipment.

People do walk the trail alone, but you're strongly advised not to, as sections are quite isolated. Three people is the safest minimum (too many might mean problems with accommodation), as this allows one person to stay with an injured walker and one to go for help. Ask around the hostels in Moresby to see if you can meet other people planning to walk the trail.

Equipment

Although some locally grown produce can usually be bought in the villages, it is recommended walkers carry their own food. TransNiugini Airways (☎ 25 2211) flies twice-weekly to most strips along the trail and walkers can arrange for supplies to be flown in. Small trade stores at Naoro, Menari, Efogi No 1, Kagi and Kokoda sell the usual tinned meat, tinned fish and rice, but they are poorly stocked and very unreliable.

You'll need a comfortable pair of boots or else a strong pair of running shoes. Good grip is important on the muddy trail. A tent, or a tarp or a large sheet of plastic, is necessary as you will need to spend at least one night out in the forest (remember that lean-to shelters may be occupied by other people). A camping stove is also recommended. Bring a bottle, as you'll need to carry water along certain sections of the trail. Do not forget your sleeping bag and some kind of wet-weather gear (even in the dry season) and good maps and a compass are vital. Finally, remember that your pack shouldn't weigh more than 15 kg.

Maps

Maps are essential. The Efogi (8479) and Kokoda (8480) sheets of the 1:100,000 topographic map series cover the area described by the walk. The very beginning of the trail (only as far as Uberi), however, appears on the Port Moresby (8379) sheet. The same area is also covered by the Buna (SC 55-3) and Port Moresby (SC 55-7) sheets of the 1:250,000 map series. A longitudinal map of the trail, like the one in this chapter, is also available from the National Mapping Bureau.

Warning

At both ends of the trail there has been a lot of rascal activity, and lone bushwalkers have had trouble on the trail itself, although this is unusual. The way to minimise risks is to talk to local people and become known to them. A guide will help, and a guide from the local area is even better. Rascals almost always rob only the bushwalkers they have had advance warning about. If walking from south to north, it's vital that you arrive at Owers' Corner early and walk a fair distance that day. Similarly, make a long day's walk all the way into Kokoda rather than stopping for the night just short of the station.

Port Moresby is extremely dangerous after dark, and you should be careful during the day. See Lonely Planet's *Papua New Guinea – a travel survival kit* for more information.

PLACES TO STAY

There is a wide range of accommodation in Port Moresby, one of the cheapest places being the *Salvation Army* (☎ 21 7683) PO Box 245, Port Moresby. The two-bed rooms cost K25 per person sharing, K40 for a couple or K30 if you want the room to yourself.

In Popondetta, you'll find one of PNG's few accommodation highlights. The *Oro Guest House* (☎ 29 7127, fax c/- 29 7193, PO Box 2, Popondetta) is well managed, very clean and excellent value. Single/double rooms are K30/40, and walkers pay just K8 for a dorm bed and students K5. You can cook your own food but for a few kina they provide excellent breakfasts and dinners.

ACCESS

PMVs run from Moresby to the start of the trail at Owers' Corner. They are infrequent and leave Gordons Market early in the morning. The two-hour trip costs about K3. It might be worth taking a taxi to Gordons to ensure that you get there in time for the PMV.

If you miss the early PMV, you could take one running out the Sogeri road and get off at the Owers' Corner turn-off (K1.50). This means a long walk, although you could hitch. There's also an afternoon PMV to Owers' Corner, but if you take this one you'll have to overnight there. Neither of these options are a good idea, however, as hanging around at the start of the trail puts you at risk of robbery.

PMVs from Gordons Market to the village of Madilogo leave twice a week, on Thursday and Sunday mornings, and return to Port Moresby the same day in the afternoon. The trip costs about K10.

Traditional Travel can arrange transfers to the start of the trail at Owers' Corner, but this is expensive.

Daily except Sunday, PMVs run between Kokoda and Popondetta. The trip takes about three hours and costs K5. PMVs leave Kokoda between 6 and 7 am and return in the afternoon after 2.30 pm. Check at the trade stores if you want a ride out of Kokoda; a few of the store owners also own PMVs.

There are airstrips at Naoro, Menari, Efogi No 1 and Kagi, as well as in Bodinumu and Naduli, two villages near Kagi.

TransNiugini Airways (☎ 25 2211) flies from Port Moresby to most of these strips on Monday and Thursday, departing Jacksons Airport (Port Moresby) early in the morning. To Kagi or Menari the fare is K42.

Northcoast Aviation (☎ 29 7219 in Popondetta) has taken over some of the Talair routes in this area but you can book through Talair offices and agents. Northcoast flies from Port Moresby to Popondetta via Kokoda on Monday, Friday and Saturday. Port Moresby to Kokoda costs K51 and Kokoda to Popondetta is K42.

Air Niugini flies from Port Moresby direct to Popondetta for K58 on Tuesday and Friday, and Talair charges the same for its direct flights on Tuesday, Thursday and Friday.

STAGE 1: OWERS' CORNER TO VA URE CREEK CAMPSITE

Walking time: 4½ to five hours, 10 km
Overnight: camping

Owers' Corner to Goldie River

Walking time: 45 minutes
As tomorrow's Stage 2 of the walk requires a full day to cover, you must ensure an early departure from Port Moresby in order to reach the Va Ure Creek Campsite before nightfall.

From the signpost at Owers' Corner the trail descends, steeply at first then more gently, 265 metres to the Goldie River. Before you enter the forest, there are views in the general direction of Imita Ridge to the north. A bit further on you cross a first stream and reach a convenient rock shelter (see Alternative Places to Stay).

Roughly 20 minutes later the trail then brings you to the Goldie River, which is 12 metres wide and about half a metre deep at this point. Continue straight ahead to the main ford, a little further on. The riverbed can be slippery near the opposite bank, so take care.

Goldie River to Imita Ridge

Walking time: 2¼ hours
A short distance up from the river you reach a large clearing that was Uberi's village square. Except for a few families who have resettled upstream along the Goldie River, most of the villagers now live along the road to Owers' Corner. Some of the house-posts still stand and a sign shows you the way. Camping here is possible (see Alternative Places to Stay).

Mild ups and downs characterise the next section of the trail to Kuile Creek. Shortly past the old square, along the site of the wartime Golden Stairway (4000 steps up the side of the mountain), the trail begins an often steep 380-metre climb to the top of Imita Ridge.

At the beginning of the climb, the path forks as it comes to a hairpin bend. Follow either way, but the smaller path is best as it takes you to a gap in the forest from where there are views back across the Goldie River. It rejoins the main trail at a large resting place used by the local people. A couple of streams are passed on the way up, the last one 10 minutes or so before you reach the top of the ridge. There are no views from Imita Ridge itself.

Imita Ridge to Va Ure Creek Campsite
Walking time: 1½ hours

A tiring descent from the top of the ridge brings you first to Va Ure Creek and from here, after crossing the creek 10 times, down to the campsite. The many crossings are caused by the windings of the creek, and they cut short longer bends, bypass obstructed ones, or avoid deep pools of water as you walk in or along the creekbed. As some of these crossings confuse walkers, I have described them thoroughly and separately. The creek is small and shallow and only three to seven metres wide.

Coming down from Imita Ridge, a short distance from the top and past yet another small stream, a second rock shelter is reached (see Alternative Places to Stay). From here, the trail continues down to the Va Ure and, after running alongside it for a while, comes to the first crossing. There, right across the creek, a poor but possible campsite can be found.

From the first crossing the trail continues slightly above the left-hand side of the creek until it comes to the second crossing. This is well defined and is marked by two arrows painted on boulders in the creekbed. As it carries on towards the third crossing, the trail runs above and alongside the right-hand side of the creek.

Ford the third crossing, then walk along the creekbed for some 20 metres to the fourth crossing, which is well defined and marked with painted arrows. The trail still continues

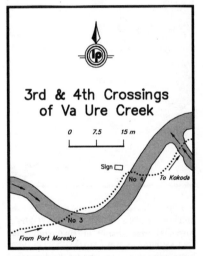

alongside the creek, and the fifth crossing is soon reached. Ford, then walk along the creekbed, around a bend until, on the left-hand side of the creek and where a small tributary meets it, the sixth crossing clearly comes into sight. Check the signs on the trees to know which crossing you're at.

Ford again, then walk for a couple of minutes along the right-hand side of the creekbed, up to the big boulder marked with a painted arrow. This is the seventh crossing. If you look diagonally across the creek, you'll see the trail begin again beside a pandanus palm.

Once across, a sign on a tree tells you to either follow the creek down, or go via the short cut. Take the short cut and when you reach the creek again follow it down for eight metres or so to the eighth crossing. Ignore the signs on a nearby tree as you reach the creek, they're for walkers coming from Kokoda.

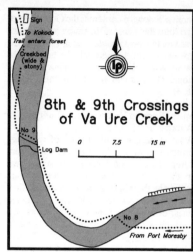

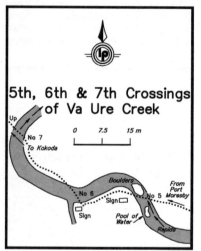

Ford at the eighth crossing, then follow the creekbed down some 30 metres to the large log dam. There, below the dam, ford again for the ninth crossing. Arrows show the way, but they're faint. Once across, continue first along the edge of the forest for about 30 metres, then through it, and you immediately come to a small stream. Follow this up for about 40 metres until another stream joins it. Then, walk about five metres up the stream on the right, and continue up the small hill in front of you. Arrows show the way, but again they're very faint.

On the hill, you come to a large clearing. Look for the trail on the ground. Roughly, it goes north-east for about 10 metres, then north until it enters the forest again. A little

further on, a second clearing is reached. Follow along the right-hand side of it until you re-enter the forest. Continue on down, through a third clearing, to the Va Ure Creek. You're at the tenth crossing but you don't need to ford the creek until tomorrow morning when you depart for Naoro.

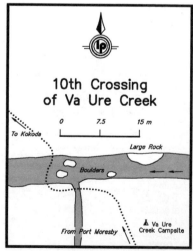

You'll see the Va Ure Creek campsite on the right-hand side of the trail. There is space for two big tents, or four small ones.

Tomorrow's Stage 2 of the walk to Naoro is very long and takes a minimum of 8¾ hours. Make sure you rise at the crack of dawn to ensure an early departure and arrival at the village before nightfall.

Alternative Places to Stay
First Rock Shelter The first rock shelter, only 20 minutes from the start of the trail, can be used as an overnight site by anyone reaching Owers' Corner on a late afternoon PMV from Port Moresby. Walkers coming from Kokoda can also bivouac here and, at the crack of dawn the next day, bc on the road to catch the first Moresby-bound PMV. It is spacious and can sleep four or five people. There is water is nearby.

Old Uberi Village Campsite Uberi is 10 minutes from the Goldie River, one hour from Owers' Corner. The site is large and spacious. You can get water along the trail in the direction of Imita Ridge, four minutes away from the old Uberi village campsite.

Second Rock Shelter The second rock shelter is 10 minutes from Imita Ridge as you go down towards Va Ure Creek. Walkers coming from Kokoda can use this shelter as a possible overnight site. It isn't convenient if you're walking from Port Moresby as it makes the second stage of the walk to Naoro hard and very long. There is water near the shelter and it can sleep four people.

STAGE 2: VA URE CREEK CAMPSITE TO NAORO
Walking time: 8¾ hours, 17 km
Overnight: rest house

Va Ure Creek to Tenth Crossing of Manama Creek
Walking time: 45 minutes
Ford at the campsite in the tenth crossing of Va Ure Creek and carry on as the trail takes you first above Va Ure Creek then down to the first of the 10 crossings of Manama

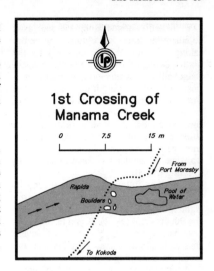

Creek. The Manama is slightly smaller than the Va Ure and, being one of its tributaries, it must be followed up stream.

For some reason, Va Ure Creek crossings are numbered one to 10, but the Manama crossings are numbered 10 to one – this first crossing is signposted No 10.

From the ford, the trail runs beside the creek and, a couple of minutes later, comes to the second crossing (No 9). On the other side, diagonally opposite, it continues to follow the creek up. Soon you come to the third crossing (No 8).

On the other side, through forest, the trail climbs a little and then, a short distance on, goes back down to the creek. Don't cross here but continue along the creekbed for some 25 metres then follow the trail through forest until, a little further on, it takes you back to the creek. As it does, walk to the large boulder marked with a painted arrow and, next to it, you'll see the fourth crossing (No 7).

Ford, and diagonally across from you, on the left-hand side of the large rock and the small stream, see the trail re-enter the forest. Continue for a short way until the trail takes you back to the creek again for the fifth crossing (No 6).

Ford and continue along the trail as it re-enters the forest and climbs a bit before taking you back down to the creek for the sixth crossing (No 5). At the crossing, again diagonally across from you, the trail continues only a little before it once again brings you back to the creek. This is the seventh crossing (No 4). Ford and, opposite you on the other side, continue a short distance through forest until you find yourself once more back at the creek. As you do, follow it up some 10 metres and come to the eighth crossing (No 3).

Ford, then follow the creek up some 10 metres until you reach a sign on a tree on the right. Most walkers will have by then located the 9th crossing (No 2). If you haven't, put your back against the sign and you'll see the trail as it climbs a short spur between the creek and a merging tributary.

A little further, before it goes back down to the creek, the trail takes you through a small clearing. Walk along the forest edge on the right-hand side then, as you near the far side of the clearing, go a little to the left. Here you will see the trail go through a wall of vegetation as it continues on down to the creek for the tenth (No 1) and final crossing.

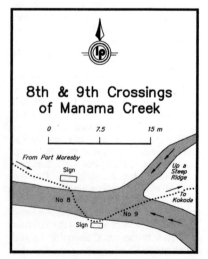

8th & 9th Crossings of Manama Creek

Tenth Crossing of Manama Creek to Ofi Creek

Walking time: 3¼ hours

This section of the walk is one of the hardest. It takes you from Manama Creek, over Mt Tahonumu and down to Ofi Creek. The 650-metre, 2¾-hour climb to the top of the ridge, through the grasslands of the abandoned village of Ioribaiwa, is quite unrelenting. The old village area begins roughly half an hour up from Manama Creek and extends most of the way to the top of the mountain. The people from the village now live along Ofi Creek to the north.

The climb follows the spur up. Very steep and steady, it alternates between sections of grassland and forest. You'll have to watch the trail closely as the grass is dense and it's easy to lose sight of it.

There are several false crests, and the further you climb the better the views of Imita Ridge and the surrounding ranges. Past a stand of betel nut palms, say three-quarters of the way up, the climb eases up a little and continues to the top of the ridge, bypassing the actual summit.

The grasslands that now cover most of the length of the spur result from human activity. The main grass is kunai. Its sharp blades can cut your skin which, as a result of sweating, can become very itchy. You might want to wear long trousers through this section. Other plants, including tanget, wild cardamom, bamboo, okari and breadfruit trees, betel nut and marita, also show that people once lived here.

The descent down to Ofi Creek takes half an hour and is rather steep. As you go down you can hear the creek on your right. On reaching the valley floor, you first come to a small stream; follow it down for a couple of minutes to the main creek. There is a possible but poor campsite on the opposite side of the creek. See Alternative Place to Stay.

Ofi Creek to Naoro

Walking time: 4¾ hours

The ford across Ofi Creek, which is 10 metres wide and about a third of a metre deep, is easy. This is the last water until

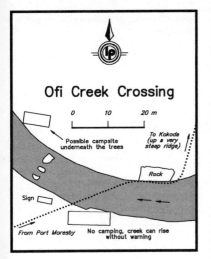

Ofi Creek Crossing

0   10   20 m

Possible campsite
underneath the trees

To Kokoda
(up a very
steep ridge)

Rock

Sign

From Port Moresby   No camping, creek can rise
without warning

Naoro. The trail continues on the other side of the creek, diagonally across from you and on the right of the large boulder.

This section of the walk takes you from Ofi Creek, over the Maguli Range, down to the village of Naoro. First a 3½-hour, 750-metre climb takes you from the creek to the top of the range. There are many false crests followed by short, relatively flat sections, and the climb is quite steep and unrelenting. Finally, at the end of yet another steep clamber, you reach the top of the ridge at a place called Mogolonumu. The top is flat and grassy, and people have planted a casuarina and tanget. There is also a sign which tells you that Naoro is still another 1¼ hours away.

From here on you are near population centres and the trail is usually cleaner and clearer, making the walk to Kokoda much easier.

From Mogolonumu the trail descends, generally gently but at times more steeply, down to the Naoro Valley. A grassland is eventually reached. From here, in addition to the ranges to the north, you can see the hamlet of Agulogo on a ridge in front of you.

From that grassland the trail continues

steeply down to the village. Soon the airstrip comes into sight and, a bit further, past some gardens, you reach the upper part of the village. From the bottom left corner of the square the trail continues to the rest house and Menari.

It's a few minutes from the upper village square to the rest house, which you'll find along the main trail near the airstrip. It can sleep many people, has an hearth and costs about K5. The caretaker provides the firewood. Hoge Creek is the village watering place and bathing area; drinking water is collected upstream from the bathing area. Ask people to show you the right place.

The people of Naoro used to live in Biogawaga, a now-abandoned village further up the Naoro Valley. Some time after WW II, they moved to present-day Naoro. However, following some deaths attributed to sorcery, most people later moved to Erebenumu, also further up the Naoro Valley, downstream from Biogawaga. Erebenumu is about 30 minutes' walk along a flat path from Naoro.

Alternative Place to Stay
There is a poor but possible campsite underneath the trees on the north side of Ofi Creek, downstream from the ford. Although reasonable during the dry season, it can be rather damp and sometimes muddy during the wetter time of the year. Do not camp on the grassy area by the creek; it can flood without warning.

STAGE 3: NAORO TO EFOGI NO 1
Walking time: 6¾ hours, 19 km
Overnight: rest house

Naoro to Menari
Walking time: 3¼ hours
After a walk of 1¾ hours along the Naoro River flats, the trail brings you to the foot of the next range. From there it climbs steeply to the top of the ridge then drops steeply into the Vabuyavi Valley to reach the village of Menari.

From Naoro the trail follows the airstrip until, about three-quarters of the way down,

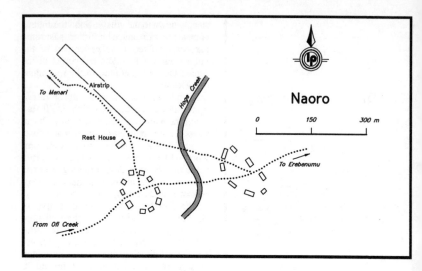

it swings sharply to the left and enters the forest. From here, crossing several streams and some swampy ground, it continues along the Naoro River flats to reach, within an hour, the bridge over the 15-metre-wide Naoro River.

Across the river the trail continues to a small bush-material rest house, right by the turn-off to Agulogo. Before you leave Naoro, ask whether this is still operating.

Shortly past the turn-off, the trail brings you to Agu Creek, a large stream crossed by a log bridge. *Logo* means 'flat place', so Agulogo means something like 'the flat place around Agu Creek'. A little way past the creek, after climbing up and over a small hill, the trail forks. The left path leads to Madilogo; take the right for Menari. The foot of the range is now a short distance away. You'll pass three small streams on the way; fill up your bottle at one of them, as this is the last water until Menari.

It takes 1¼ hours to reach Ladavi, the top of the range, from the valley floor. Again, the climb is very steep and unrelenting. From Ladavi there are views of Menari, and if the weather is fine Mt Victoria (called Mata by the Koiari) can be seen in the distance to the

north-east. Menari is now 35 minutes away. Just before reaching the village you'll come to a large creek, the Emune. It's a good spot to have a rest. On reaching the first houses of Menari, the trail forks. Go either way. The left path takes you straight to the village square; the right leads to the square via a watering place – the small Tutui Creek.

Menari is a large village with two trade stores, a community school and a rest house (see Alternative Places to Stay). Several coconut palms, as well as numerous orange and okari nut trees, surround the village square.

Menari to Efogi No 1
Walking time: 3½ hours

After leaving Menari and crossing the Vabuyavi River the trail climbs steeply up to the top of the next ridge from where it descends down a gentle grade, to Efogi No 1.

The trail leaves Menari from the rest house and continues down the right-hand side of the airstrip until, roughly 40 metres from its lower end, it swings sharply to the right and drops down to the side of it. A short distance away, as the trail continues down towards the Vabuyavi River, it passes on the left the

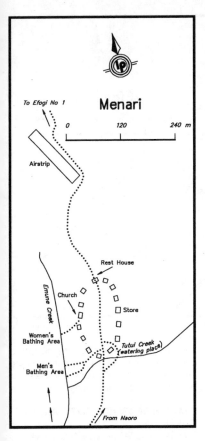

Menari

To Efogi No 1

0   120   240 m

Airstrip

Emune Creek

Church

Women's Bathing Area

Men's Bathing Area

Rest House

Store

Tutui Creek (watering place)

From Naoro

to a large lookout area called Tabunumu. From here you can see the whole country you've walked through: the Ilini, Vabuyavi and Emune valleys; followed by Mt Ladavi, the Naoro Valley and Mt Mogolonumu. Hombrum Bluff and the Varirata Plateau near Port Moresby can also be seen to the south-west on a clear day.

From the lookout the trail continues steeply for a short way to the very top of the ridge, bypassing the summit of Mt Loni. The summit is accessible by a small path that branches off behind the sign at the top of the ridge.

From the top, a gentle downhill grade soon brings you to a gap. Kagi village can be seen from here, and two airstrips: Kagi on the right and Bodinumu on the left.

Along the trail look for coffee trees, taros, marita and a fleshy, entirely red-purple plant from which a red dye can be extracted. In many areas it is used to dye billum rope. To extract the dye, hold a leaf 15 cm or so from a source of mild heat but do not dry it. When the leaf is soft and malleable squeeze the dye out and rub it onto your skin or a piece of wood.

As you continue through old and new gardens, along and over fences, Efogi No 1 and its airstrip, then the school compound, soon come into sight. Near the village, at the end of a steep but short descent, the trail brings you to a small stream, the Elome. If you want to take water, do it here; the next stream, the nearby Batali, is polluted by people bathing in it upstream.

From here you carry on to the airstrip, then the DPI station, and finally the village square. Built on a short, sandy plateau, Efogi No 1 is quite large, and is surrounded by a thick wall of bamboo, tamarillos, bananas, coffee bushes and orange trees.

The first large building you come to is the old church; to its right, a wide track takes you to the new church and, opposite, the rest house. The rest house costs about K5, has no verandah, and is rather unattractive. A sign on the door says, 'We don't allow such hard drinks commonly named as beer SP and smokes'.

Batali Creek is used as a bathing and

turn-off leading to the schoolhouse and the village of Manalogo.

A little further on, at the end of a steep but short descent, the log bridge over the rushing, seven-metre-wide Vabuyavi River comes into sight. This river really is the Vabuyavi, not the Kaival as the sign says.

From the river a two-hour, 710-metre climb along a switchback footpath brings you to the top of the next ridge. The trail is again steep and unrelenting. On your way up, on the left-hand side of the path, you'll pass a turn-off leading to the village of Enivilogo. A little below the top of the ridge you'll come

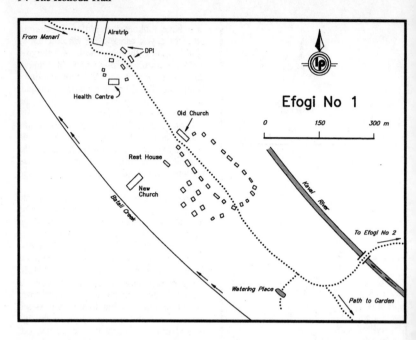

Efogi No 1

watering place; drinking water is collected upstream of the bathing area. A spring on the right-hand side of the track as you leave the village towards Efogi No 2 also provides good, cool water.

Alternative Place to Stay
The *Menari Rest House* is a large, comfortable bush-material rest house with a verandah. It costs about K5 per night. Both sexes bathe in Emune Creek. Women follow a path which starts by the far end of the

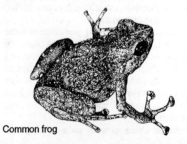

Common frog

church; men follow one that branches off to the right of the Kokoda Trail, at the very top end of the square. The men's path forks as it nears the creek; go either way.

STAGE 4: EFOGI NO 1 TO EFOGE CREEK
Walking time: 5½ hours, 12 km
Overnight: camping

Efogi No 1 to Efogi No 2
Walking time: one hour
After a short descent to the Kavai River the trail climbs steeply to Efogi No 2, also called Launumu.

You'll pass two watering points on your way down to the river. Fill up your bottle at either one; it's a hard 200-metre climb up to Efogi No 2. Shortly past the second spring the log bridge over the eight-metre-wide Kavai River comes into sight.

Across the river a steep climb brings you to the top of the next ridge, then you walk

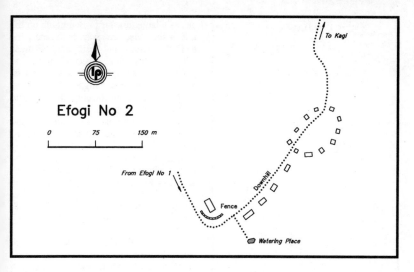

Efogi No 2

down to the village square. You'll see a small path branching off to the right of the trail as you come to the first group of houses; it leads to the village watering place. There is no rest house in Efogi No 2 but a tiny house, if not occupied by visiting relatives, is sometimes used to accommodate visitors. It is not recommended, but if you do stay there, contribute some money or goods.

Efogi No 2 to Kagi
Walking time: 1½ hours
After a steep descent to Efoge Creek the trail climbs steeply to reach Kagi. The trail to Kagi leaves Efogi No 2 from the bottom left corner of the village square and continues down, pleasantly through gardens at first then more steeply, to the Efoge Creek (seven metres wide, half a metre deep). This creek is not the Kolui as the sign says but the Efoge – neither is it the Efogi. The Kolui is a small tributary of the Efoge, and it flows in the valley between Kagi and Naduli.

Ford above the rapids. The trail continues to the left of the large flat rock covered with vegetation. It switches back and forth up a very steep grade to the airstrip and its bush-material passenger terminal. The whole

Vahume Valley can be seen from the airstrip, and Efogi No 1 and No 2 can be seen from behind the terminal. All three rivers, the Vahume, the Vabuyavi and the Naoro, feed into Brown River, which flows into the sea some 50 km north-west of Port Moresby.

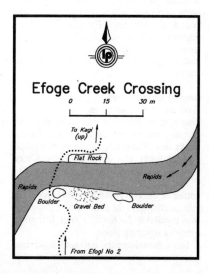

Efoge Creek Crossing

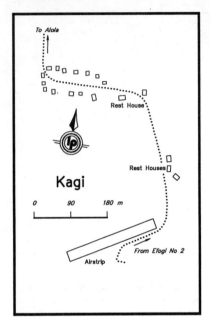

Kagi is now only 10 minutes away. As you continue past the airstrip, the first group of houses on your right is the rest house compound (see Alternative Places to Stay). Kagi resembles the villages visited earlier, but its location on a ridge-top rewards the visitor with magnificent views over the Vahume Valley.

Kagi to Efoge Creek

Walking time: three hours

This next section of the trail leaves Kagi and climbs some 500 metres and 2¼ hours along a spur-line to Kagi Gap. From there, a gentle descent takes you down to Efoge Creek which you'll cross for the second time.

The trail leaves Kagi from the top right corner of the village square. On leaving the village, disregard the path on the right which runs parallel to the Kokoda Trail. It leads to a nearby watering place.

From the village the trail runs down into a hollow then, as it starts to climb out of it,

passes a large turn-off to Bodinumu on the left. A short distance away, as you near the end of the climb and beside two tall trees with a whitish bark, a second turn-off is passed on the right. Also fairly large, it first leads down to the community school then, after crossing the small Kolui Creek, goes up to the village of Naduli.

From here the route is well defined and continues up the spur, towards the ridge of Mt Bellamy. The ascent, though mostly gradual, gets quite steep as you near the forest. Roughly halfway between the forest and the village, after passing many old and new gardens and running along and over several fences, the trail comes to a small stream. This is the last water until you reach Kagi Gap.

Further on, the climb continues through forest. At one point, at the foot of a very steep climb, the trail forks. Go either way, as both routes take you up to a nearby lookout. The right arm goes straight up; the left is a switchback footpath. The whole Vahume Valley, including Kagi, Naduli and their common schoolhouse, can be seen from the lookout. On a clear day the coast around Port Moresby can also be seen.

From here the climb continues until, a short distance from Kagi Gap, it finally eases then levels off. Near the end of that section you'll see on the right-hand side of the trail a well-defined path leading to a nearby stream. A little further, after a couple of steep sections, a small, grassy area is reached. It marks the top of the spur and is known as Kagi Gap. At the gap itself, on the right, a small path branches off to eventually join with the trail linking Naduli and Myola.

A gentle slope now takes you down, past the first and second Myola turn-offs, towards Efoge Creek. The first Myola turn-off is reached within 10 minutes, the second within 30 minutes. Both branch off to the right. The second is the main one and a sign by the trail, along with a bunch of wild pandanus palms and flowering shrubs strewn over a grassy area, clearly identifies it. For more details on a side trip to Myola see the following section.

Efoge Creek, the proposed overnight site, is only 10 minutes on from the second Myola turn-off. Beside the creek are several campsites and a lean-to shelter that can sleep up to six people.

Alternative Places to Stay

The Kagi Rest House is a lovely bush-material rest house with many sleeping platforms, a nice verandah, running water and a large outdoor kitchen. It overlooks the Vahume Valley and costs about K8 a night.

There is another rest house by the village square. Though you'll also find running water and an outdoor kitchen, this place is much noisier and not as nice. Expect to pay about K5. Make yourself at home at either place; the caretakers will drop in later when they find out you're there. There are a couple of trade stores in Kagi.

Side Trip to Myola

Walking time: two hours one way
Overnight: Myola Guesthouse
Tall mountains surround the large area of grassland known as Myola. Used during WW II as a drop-off point for supplies, this beautiful spot is now the site of the pleasant *Myola Guest House*. The nightly charge of K25 includes a hot shower, a woven cane bed, linen, and plenty of food. You're served hot bread for breakfast and tea in the afternoon. Being Seventh Day Adventists, the caretakers don't cook breakfast or lunch on Saturday, but they will provide food for you to prepare. They do, however, cook your dinner at the end of the Sabbath. You should book, as there might not be anyone around if you aren't expected. Contact Traditional Travel (☎ 21 3966) in Port Moresby.

Some interesting trips can be made from Myola. They include a four-hour return trip to the two waterfalls (tall Iora and wide Edate) which can be seen from the airstrip; a 4½-hour return trip to some lovely tree fern colonies; and a 1½-hour excursion to a Ford Trimotor which crashed during the war. In June and July you can see different species of bird of paradise displaying. Guides for any of these walks are available.

Myola can be reached from two different points along the Kokoda Trail. Both routes are fairly level. I call them Myola Junction No 1 and Myola Junction No 2. It takes two hours to walk to Myola from the Junction No 1, 1½ hours from No 2 Junction.

Although the second turn-off is the main route in, walkers bound for Kokoda will find it more interesting to walk in from Junction No 1, and out by way of No 2. Bear in mind that the second route is no shorter than the first; the junctions are about half an hour apart. See the preceding Stage 4 for information on getting to the junctions.

Junction No 1 Trail The path is small at first, but becomes much larger soon after it crosses a stream, when it merges with the trail coming in from Naduli. Shortly after crossing Efoge Creek on a small log bridge, the path joins with the Junction No 2 trail, which comes in on the left. At this intersection, you'll see a sign showing you the way, engraved on a dead tree lying by the side of the trail.

From the intersection, at the top of a small ridge that forms the watershed between the north and south coasts, Myola Gap is reached. There are beautiful views over the whole grassland area, including the guesthouse, still an hour's walk away. The route now is fairly straightforward: after first descending to the grassland, it crosses Iora Creek on a log bridge and finally heads for the guesthouse.

The grassland can be very wet during the rainy season; some parts may be waterlogged, and the whole place changes into a swampy area covered with grassy vegetation.

Junction No 2 Trail From the Kokoda Trail it's a 20-minute walk along a mainly level grade to the intersection between the first and second junction trails. From here the trail is the same as for Junction No 1.

Myola back to the Kokoda Trail Walkers continuing on to Alola and Kokoda must go right at the first trail junction, then right again at the Kokoda Trail, to enter it at Junction No 2. Those heading for Kagi and Port

Moresby must go straight at the first trail junction, right at the second, and left at the Kokoda Trail.

STAGE 5: EFOGE CREEK TO ALOLA
Walking time: 5½ hours, 17 km
Overnight: rest house

Efoge Creek to Templeton's Crossing
Walking time: 1½ hours
Following an easy climb up to Kokoda Gap, the trail drops down into the Iora Valley at Templeton's Crossing.

After an easy climb from Efoge Creek the route levels off as it reaches Kokoda Gap, at 2190 metres the highest point along the trail. From here the path continues along a mainly level grade until it opens onto a small grassy area. From here, high above Templeton's Crossing, there are nice views down the Iora Valley.

A short descent into the valley follows which is steep at first then more gentle. It brings you to a log bridge over the vigorous, six-metre-wide Iora Creek at Templeton's Crossing. The trail takes you past two possible campsites (see Alternative Places to Stay) just before you reach the river.

Templeton's Crossing to Iora Creek
Walking time: 2¼ hours
A short walk takes you first from Templeton's Crossing to Templeton's Crossing No 2. From there, after a steady climb that takes you high above the river, the trail descends to the second and last crossing of the Iora at Iora Creek.

After first running beside a tiny stream to the left of the bridge at Templeton's Crossing, the trail swings sharply to the left and climbs a little above Iora Creek. Levelling off at the end of the climb, it continues along the contours for a while past several sparkling streams and an equal number of mild ups and downs, until it eventually drops back to the creek at Templeton's No 2.

There is neither a village nor a crossing at Templeton's No 2. There is, however, a lean-to shelter as well as several possible campsites (see Alternative Places to Stay).

The second log bridge over the Iora, at Iora Creek, is now 1¾ hours away. Continuing through the grassy vegetation in front of the Templeton's No 2 shelter, the trail runs along the creek until, a little further along and past a couple of possible campsites, it turns left and starts to go up the eastern wall of the valley. A short but steady climb follows, which ultimately brings you to a well-defined spur running between the Iora and a merging tributary, Ago Creek. At the end of the climb, upon reaching the top of the spur, a gentle downhill grade takes you back down to the river.

The second crossing of Iora Creek is much like the first – logs join the boulders in the creekbed. Just before the crossing, the trail brings you to another lean-to shelter and a large grassy area which, if cleaned a little, can be made into a large campsite (see Alternative Places to Stay).

The Iora is a large mountain torrent and after heavy rains the bridge can be washed away, making the stream impossible to cross. There is an alternative route which leads to Kokoda and the lowlands without crossing the river. See Alternative Route to the Lowlands for more information.

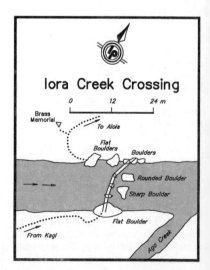

Iora Creek Crossing

Iora Creek to Alola

Walking time: 1¾ hours

This section of the walk takes you up, across Lala Creek, to the village of Alola.

After leaving Iora Creek from the small gravel bed to the left of the bridge, the path continues beside the creek for a while. Avoid the dense salat growing along this section of the trail.

From here, after many scrambles in and out of numerous small streams, the trail eventually brings you to a small log bridge over the four-metre-wide Lala Creek. A short climb to Alola follows. The path is steep at first but then more gentle, and takes you past many old gardens and through secondary growth to a large grassy area just below the village. As you reach it, you will see a large trail branching off on your right; it leads to Abuari, a neighbouring village situated high above and across the Iora. Alola is now a couple of minutes away, up on the hill on your left.

There is a small rest house at the far end of the village. Built of sawn timber and topped with a galvanised-iron roof, it has a verandah and costs about K5. Kaeledaba Creek, a small stream some 50 metres down the trail towards Kokoda, is the village watering place and bathing area.

Alternative Places to Stay

There are two possible campsites at Templeton's Crossing, just above the creek as you come down from Kokoda Gap. At Templeton's No 2 Crossing, a permanent lean-to shelter that sleeps up to six people is right next to the creek. As well, scattered above and below the shelter, there are several campsites.

At Iora Creek, as well as a permanent lean-to shelter, there is a large grassy area that can be used as a campsite.

Alternative Route to the Lowlands

Walking time: 2¼ hours to Abuari, six hours to Kanandara.

This section describes an alternative route from Iora Creek to the lowlands. It runs roughly parallel to the Kokoda Trail on the opposite side of the Iora Valley. This route takes you from Iora Creek, by way of the Koiari villages of Abuari, Hagutawa, Kaile and Felai, down to the Orokaiva village of Kanandara.

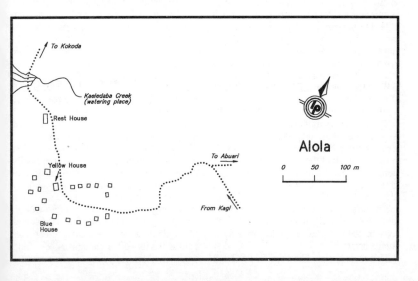

It enables you to bypass Iora Creek if the log bridge there has been washed away, and it gives you the opportunity, at the village of Abuari, to either return to the Kokoda Trail or to continue on down to Kanandara and the lowlands.

There is a bridge spanning the Iora between Abuari and Alola, two villages on opposite sides of the Iora Valley. It is therefore possible to return to the Kokoda Trail at Alola and continue on down to Kokoda station. The bridge is maintained by the people of both villages and to get from one side of the valley to the other takes little more than an hour if you're fit, but it is very steep.

You could continue from Abuari down to the lowlands at Kanandara. The trail between the two villages is large and well maintained, and takes roughly 3½ to four hours to walk. PMVs going to Kokoda and Popondetta can be found in Kanandara. No PMVs run on Saturday and most vehicles, especially those going to Popondetta, leave the village fairly early in the morning.

The turn-off to Abuari, about 10 minutes from the lean-to shelter at Iora Creek, is not well marked and can be difficult to find. First, walk back up the Kokoda Trail, past a small grass and fern clearing. Soon after re-entering the forest, the trail levels off a little. On the left you'll see a stump, then another about seven metres along, and two more a further 10 metres away, near a tall casuarina. These last two, standing by each other as if to form a gate, indicate the turn-off to the village of Abuari. Look for the bunch of tangled roots growing between the two stumps.

The route now is fairly straightforward. After a short but steep descent to a ford across Ago Creek, the trail climbs steeply up the eastern wall of the valley then continues along the contours and over many small streams to the first gardens of Abuari. The Ago Creek, which is six metres wide and about half a metre deep, is relatively easy to ford, and it's only a few minutes' walk between the first gardens of Abuari and the village itself.

This route is more like a typical PNG trail

than the main Kokoda Trail: many fallen trees hamper your progress and the path, generally narrow but well defined, is often strewn with slippery stones and colonies of salat. The trail between Abuari and Kanandara is busier and so is much wider and cleaner.

STAGE 6: ALOLA TO KOKODA
Walking time: 5¼ hours, 19 km
Overnight: rest house

This section of the trail runs down from Alola to the lowlands at Hoi. From there, along a large and mainly levelled track, the route continues for another 1¼ hours to Kokoda.

After crossing the small Kaeledaba Creek, Alola's watering place, the trail climbs to the top of a small hill behind the village. From here there are good views of the village and the Iora valley. The next half-hour's walk takes you over a couple of small streams and across a deep gully, to the aid post. This is next to the turn-off to Uama, a hamlet about 10 minutes away on the left, and is easily recognisable to the lovely hedges surrounding it.

Many mild ups and downs characterise the next section of the trail which, within an hour, takes you from the aid post to the old village site of Isurava. Camping at Old Isurava is possible, but let the people at New Isurava know that you did.

The route continues for about 15 minutes along the contours and over many small streams to New Isurava. It is not particularly attractive and there is no rest house.

From the village a short descent first brings you down to two small streams, the Etumu and the Ilole. From here, after first going up another small hill, the trail finally drops down to the lowlands. This last descent is steady and unrelenting, as well as fairly steep in places. The route passes through many old gardens sites, now overgrown with choko creepers. Commonly found in gardens throughout the country, this creeper is valued for its edible cucumber-like fruit, tendrils, shoots and young leaves.

Immediately on reaching the lowlands the trail comes to an intersection. The right-hand path leads to the nearby hamlet of Hoi; take the left to Kokoda. There is no rest house at Hoi, nor is there any place to sleep until you reach Kokoda, although if you ask, villagers will certainly allow you to camp on their land.

Shortly after the intersection, the trail brings you to two small streams; fill up your bottle as water from here on is scarce or of poor quality. The route to Kokoda is now fairly straightforward: always keep to your left – disregard any trail or track branching off to your right.

Kokoda is now 1¼ hours away. After first reaching the main village of Hoi the route continues, along a fairly level grade and past the hamlet of Ebole, to the large village of Kovelo. This is where the Kokoda Trail ends.

Kokoda is still half an hour away, down a large vehicle track and through several large rubber and cocoa plantations. If you arrive at Kokoda station hungry, the first trade store on your left has the biggest selection of goodies.

There is a large rest house in Kokoda, with four beds, a flush toilet, a shower and a kerosene (paraffin) stove. A night's accommodation costs about K5, and the key is available from either the National Parks ranger or the district officer. If advised beforehand the ranger can also arrange accommodation for larger groups. Contact him through the district office: dial 019 then ask the VHF operator to put you through to Kokoda station. The ranger also has the key to the Kokoda Memorial Museum, worth a visit if you can spare the time.

There have been several robberies, some involving guns, from the rest house. The ranger strongly recommends that you keep your door locked at night, and that you do not open it to anyone under any circumstances. Some bushwalkers have felt more secure staying at the police station.

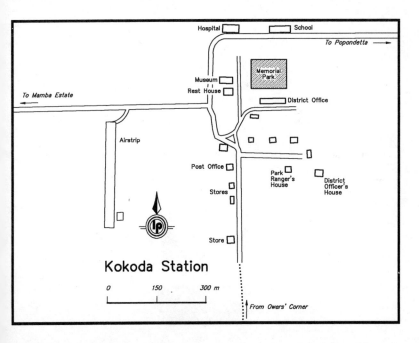

Kokoda Station

OTHER SUGGESTED WALKS
Kokoda to Yongai

Though it can be walked either way, this hike is best done from Yongai down to the lowlands at Kokoda. If used in conjunction with the Kokoda Trail and some of the walks described in the Ononge to Tapini chapter, this route can be included in an 11 or 12-day walk from Owers' Corner, near Port Moresby, to Tapini in Central Province.

After completing the Kokoda Trail you could, for instance, walk up to Yongai and then continue over Murray Pass and the Central Range to Woitape and the Udabe Valley. From there, Tapini is three days away. At Tapini you can catch a PMV or a flight back to the coast and Port Moresby (see the Ononge to Tapini chapter).

The walk down from Yongai to Kokoda can be done in two or three days. It takes about five hours to walk from Yongai to the village of Kafano and a further three hours to get from there down to the Buri River. A two-hour walk from the Buri River takes you to Asimba, a large village with a community school and an aid post. Another two hours is needed to reach Kainilong from Asimba and, finally, a four-hour walk brings you from Kainilong to the Kanga River and the village of Kanga. Soon after, you reach the village of Towe and the road linking it with Kokoda. If the road is passable you'll soon find a vehicle going to Kokoda. If not, you'll have to walk another couple of hours to Mamba Estate.

Maps to consult for this walk are the Wasa (8380) and Kokoda (8480) sheets in 1:100,000 topographic map series, or the Buna sheet (SC 55-3) of the 1:250,000 map series.

Varirata National Park

Opened in 1973, Varirata National Park is the oldest national park in PNG. Its easy access and proximity to Port Moresby make it a popular weekend destination for Moresby-ites who come in great numbers to enjoy a picnic or to trade the dry, dusty city for the cool park.

HISTORY

The park is on the traditional hunting grounds of the Koiari people and is known by them as Wodobonumu. It was first reserved in February 1963 and in December 1969 it was committed to the care and control of the National Parks Board which, on the 8th of October 1973, officially opened it as a park. The land on which the park lies was acquired by the government in October 1986.

PEOPLE & CULTURE

Varirata National Park used to be a traditional Koiari hunting ground but since the acquisition of the park by the National Parks Board hunting and gardening have been prohibited.

There was once a traditional Koiari tree house on the trail from the Welcome House to Gare's Lookout, but it has now been dismantled. For more information on the Koiari people, see the People & Culture section of the Kokoda Trail chapter.

INFORMATION

Features

Varirata National Park is on the Varirata Plateau and its south-western boundaries follow the escarpment of the Astrolabe Range. This location, high above the coastal strip, gives some excellent views towards the coast, from four lookouts.

Despite its proximity to dry Port Moresby, the park has an average rainfall of 5000 mm a year. As a result, more than half of its area is covered with rainforest. Other types of vegetation consist mostly of eucalypt savannah, gallery forest and secondary growth.

The park's birdlife is rich and abundant. The Raggiana bird of paradise lives here and in the early morning and evening from June to November, it is possible to see the birds at a marked display tree along one of the trails. Other birds include cockatoos, wild fowl, doves, pigeons, kites and kingfishers. Wallabies are common, and wild pigs, bandicoots, possums, bush rats and different species of pythons can also be found.

Standard

None of the trails is difficult and all are clearly marked. It takes about three hours to walk all the trails. More time can be spent picnicking or at the lookouts.

Season

At some 800 metres above sea level, the park enjoys pleasant daily temperatures of about 26°C. Most of the park's annual 5000 mm of rain falls from December to April. As the walks are short, and as most of the rain falls in the afternoon, it is certainly possible to visit during the rainy season.

Useful Organisations

Information on the park can be obtained by writing to the National Parks Service, PO Box 5749, Boroko (☎ 25 4247), or contact the ranger (☎ 25 9340).

When you arrive you're given a leaflet describing the park and the walks.

Equipment

Water from Narirogo Creek is not safe to drink, so bring your own. Runners or very light boots are ideal footwear.

Maps

If you want more detailed information on the area surrounding the park, see the 1:50,000 Sogeri sheet, the 1:100,000 Port Moresby

(8379) sheet and the 1:250,000 Port Moresby (SC 55-7) sheet.

There's a Welcome House at the Park but it's rather run-down and few exhibits remain. There is a K1 per adult entry fee to the park.

PLACES TO STAY

Although it's possible to camp in the park your belongings aren't secure. There is, however, the *Varirata National Park Lodge*. The accommodation costs K40, whether there is one of you or a group. Bedding and cooking facilities are provided, but bring your own food and utensils. For more information phone the ranger (☎ 95 9340).

ACCESS

Varirata National Park is 37 km from Boroko (Port Moresby). Follow the Sogeri road and branch off to the right 32 km from Boroko, just after the No 2 hydro station. A small sign indicates the intersection; from here the toll-gate is five km away, the Welcome House six km and Varirata Lookout eight km.

PMVs leave Port Moresby from Gordons Market, but only operate along the Sogeri road. From the turn-off (K1.50 from

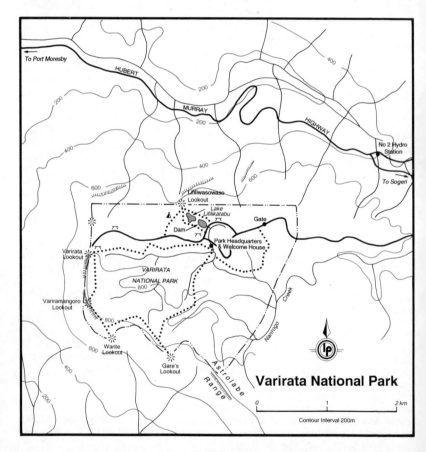

Varirata National Park

Contour Interval 200m

0   1   2 km

Gordons), walk to the park or hitch a lift – preferably on weekends, as there is hardly any weekday traffic.

LIFILIWASOWASO LOOKOUT
Walking time: 10 minutes

This walk is the shortest of the four in Varirata. It goes from the Welcome House, past the small Lake Lifilikatabu, to the Lifiliwasowaso Lookout and back to the road by way of the camping ground.

Various types of savannah plants and shrubs, along with some kunai, dominate the plant communities found along this short trail. Water plants and a variety of tall pitpit are also found by the edge of the lake.

Both Hombrum Bluff and Rouna No 1 power station can be seen from the lookout.

VARIRATA CIRCUIT TRAIL
Walking time: 35 minutes

Beginning on the main road near the tollgate, this trail runs by a small creek to the main picnic area near the Welcome House.

The vegetation along this trail is interesting, as the route wanders through eucalypt savannah (at the beginning of the walk near the main road) and tropical rainforest.

From June to November, the Raggiana bird of paradise can be seen displaying on a signposted display tree halfway along the trail between 6 and 7 am and at around 4 pm.

VARIRATA LOOKOUT TRAIL
Walking time: 30 minutes

Beginning at the Welcome House, this trail runs along a small creek all the way to Varirata Lookout. Rainforest predominates along most of the trail, except close to the lookout where you'll find eucalypt savannah.

The lookout offers good views of Port Moresby.

Raggiana bird of paradise

GARE'S LOOKOUT CIRCUIT TRAIL
Walking time: one hour

Beginning at the Welcome House, this trail takes you first to Gare's Lookout then along the escarpment of the Astrolabe Range to Varirata Lookout. There are four lookouts, each overlooking the coast from a different angle.

Rainforest predominates along most of this trail, although there is eucalypt savannah at the beginning and end.

There are good views of the coast between Taurama and the village of Tubuseria from Gare's and Warite lookouts. On clear days the Rigo coastline, including the villages of Gaire and Kapa Kapa, can also be seen.

Wedau to Alotau

The rugged and magnificent coastline stretching from the village of Wedau to East Cape, the easternmost tip of the PNG mainland, is one of the most beautiful in the country. Dolphins sometimes swim close to shore, outriggers drift around bays and hospitable people live in well-kept hamlets nestling idyllically in groves of coconut palms. This superb walk is a perfect choice for anyone wanting to discover PNG's coastal areas and their people.

HISTORY

In 1890, the Reverend Maclaren, the first Anglican missionary in the country, made a trip up the north-east coast to reconnoitre the region allotted to his mission. The following year, joined by Reverend King, he made a second trip and, on 10 August 1891, purchased land on the Dogura Plateau from the Wedau people for the erection of a mission station.

The two enthusiastic missionaries immediately built a small chapel but, with sickness soon taking its toll on the two men, further extension of the mission was slow. Maclaren died at the end of 1891 and King had to withdraw to Australia. He was able to return to Dogura and, in 1896, in a stream near the village of Wedau, he baptised the first converts to the new religion.

By 1905, the area had boarding schools for boys and girls and a training college for teachers and evangelists.

In 1934, work began on a cathedral on the Dogura Plateau, both to serve the ever-increasing congregation, and to mark the area as the centre of the country's Anglican diocese. The cathedral, like the chapels it replaced, was called St Peter & St Paul. During the five years it took to build, some 170 men from all parts of the diocese (speaking a total of 35 languages) worked on the cathedral, each giving three months free labour. At the time, it was was the largest permanent building in PNG and was built, under the guidance of Robert Jones, of reinforced concrete and local timber, at a total cost of £4000.

However, in spite of the cathedral, the importance of Dogura as the base of the Anglican Church in PNG has greatly declined. Due to its easier accessibility, Popondetta is now the Anglican headquarters.

Today, little of Dogura's former grandeur remains. The cathedral is still there and a large school and a good hospital serve the community, but the people of Wedau feel that somewhere along the line their part in the making of the Anglican Church in PNG has been forgotten.

St Peter & St Paul Cathedral

PEOPLE & CULTURE

With nearly a century of contact and close association with the Anglican Church behind them, the Wedau people have kept little of their original culture.

The people were once cannibals, and frequent wars were fought with neighbouring tribes from the mountains. Ironically, the Dogura Plateau, the site of the cathedral, was once a traditional fighting ground.

The Anglicans provided some of the best education to be found anywhere in PNG, and it is not uncommon to find Wedau people holding important and prestigious offices around the country. Sir Kingford Dibela, a Wedau man, was once governor general.

At the village level, fishing and gardening, particularly of taro, remain important.

Wedau is an Austronesian language spoken

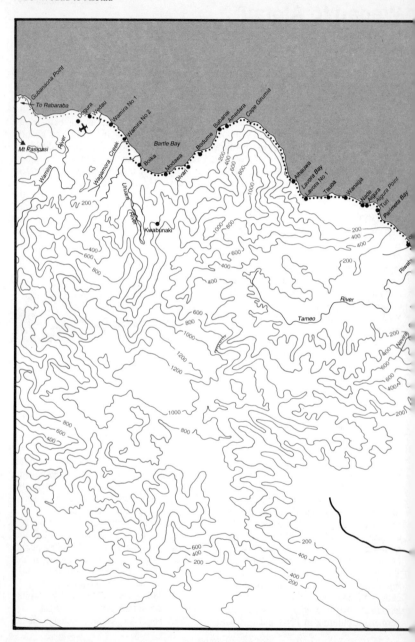

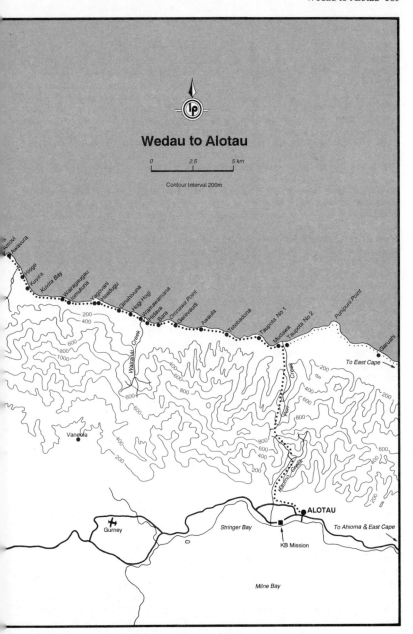

Wedau to Alotau

0   2.5   5 km

Contour Interval 200m

by people along the north-east coast from Dogura in the west to Awaiama and Cape Ducie (near East Cape) in the east. Before the late 1950s, when the government decided that English should be the country's language of education, Wedau was widely used by the Anglicans to spread the Word and to educate students. Wedau is still commonly used as a regional lingua franca from Cape Vogel to Cape Ducie , but English and pidgin are also understood and spoken by most people.

INFORMATION

Features

Dramatic, kunai-covered mountains drop steeply down to a narrow coastal strip all along Milne Bay Province's north-east coast. Cut by numerous streams and tumbling waterfalls, these mountains constitute the southern extension of PNG's central cordillera.

Many small bays and narrow, pebbled beaches fringed with coconut palms and galip trees line the coast, and there are views of Cape Girumia, an impressive promontory that plunges into the sea near Wedau. Standing out against the sky to the north are the rugged d'Entrecasteaux Islands. Cape Vogel can be seen to the west, and to the east East Cape.

A small path, running along the shoreline at the foot of the mountains, links the villages along this part of the coast with Alotau, the capital of Milne Bay Province.

Standard

The first part of this walk, from Wedau to Taupota No 2, is easy and pleasant, closely following the shoreline. The trail is well defined and frequently used by the local people, and anyone can walk it. The Wamira River can be swift, but you can easily find help to ford it.

The second part of the walk involves a low crossing of the central range. The route follows a small stream up from Taupota No 2 to the top of the range, then another down to Alotau. Although not strenuous, this part of the walk is a little more difficult, particularly along Haumo Creek as you descend towards Milne Bay. In addition to being fairly steep, the descent occasionally involves a little rock-scrambling and a narrow ledge overlooking the creek must be negotiated. A guide is recommended for this last stage of the walk, if only to help you through that difficult section along the creek.

Although this walk can be done in either direction I recommend walking from Wedau to Alotau. Not only is a reliable guide easier to find in Taupota than in Alotau but the trail along Haumo Creek is harder to locate when followed up rather than down.

As a last point, never ever sit directly underneath a coconut palm, as nuts, green or brown, fall without notice.

Days Required

The itinerary suggested here requires four days to walk and allows some time to enjoy the views, swim or snorkel. It can be walked in three longer days if time is short. An interesting variation to this trip is to walk to Alotau via East Cape. See the Other Suggested Walks section at the end of this chapter.

Season

The daytime temperatures expected along the coast are in the order of 27 to 30°C. At night, temperatures can be two or three degrees cooler.

The rainy season is from the end of November to the end of April and the area averages between 1500 and 2000 mm of rainfall a year. June, July and August are the best months for walking, although May and September can also be nice.

Mango trees are literally all over the place and they bear fruit in August and September and again in December and January.

Useful Organisations

There is a good hospital and a two-way radio in Dogura. There's a small Talair ticket agency, in the same building as the Anglican Diocese's office. There is a small aid post in Topura and a health centre in Taupota No 1.

There are trade stores in Wedau, Topura

and Taupota but they are poorly stocked and very unreliable. There is a small market in Wedau on Wednesday and Saturday between 7 and 7.30 am. Bring some small change. Most villagers are happy to sell you green coconuts to drink if they can find someone to climb for them. Mangoes are available in season.

Guides & Carriers

A guide is not necessary along the coastal part of this walk, and carrying your own gear is highly recommendable as it will allow you to linger as long as you want.

A guide is recommended between Taupota to Alotau, for the walk over the central range. Not only is there some rock-scrambling involved along upper Haumo Creek, but the path is at times difficult to follow, especially once you reach the lowlands. Ask around in Taupota. Make sure your guide understands that he must take you at least as far as the first houses on the outskirts of Alotau. Expect to pay about K5.

Equipment

Runners or very light boots are ideal footwear. Sunscreen and a wide-brimmed hat are advisable. Don't forget your snorkelling gear. Swimmers should dress appropriately – shorts are much more appropriate than a skimpy costume for men, and women should wear a T-shirt as well as a wraparound. Bikinis and even one-piece swimming costumes are definitely not acceptable.

Maps

Additional information on this walk can be found on the Alotau sheet (8977) of the 1:100,000 topographic map series. The Samarai sheet (SC 56-9) of the 1:250,000 map series covers the entire area from Rabaraba to East Cape.

PLACES TO STAY

In Wedau, stay at the *Women's Guesthouse*. It has 12 beds, flush toilets and showers, and it's particularly clean and spacious. It's a nice place to have a day's rest. Expect to pay around K25 for room and board. Get the key

from Ethel Kaniniba, Nita Taugopi or Delila Bogatu. For bookings write to Ethel Kaniniba, Dogura Post Office, Milne Bay Province.

There is no accommodation in Dogura, but it is worth a visit for the views from the plateau, and the cathedral is interesting. For good swimming and snorkelling ask people to show you the way to Gubanaona (a 45-minute walk). Mt Pasipasi, just behind the station, can be climbed (see the Other Suggested Walks section at the end of this chapter).

In Alotau, stay at the *KB Mission* guesthouse, a km or so towards Gurney from the centre of town, just off the main road. It's is a nice place on the bay and charges K25 or K40 with big meals. There's no phone but the Tourist Bureau (☎ 61 1503, PO Box 119, Alotau MBP) might be able to make a booking for you.

The *Government Hostel* has plain but decent accommodation and board for K45. Contact the Tourist Bureau to check they're not full of visiting members of the provincial parliament. To get there, walk up the steps in town to the hospital and keep walking uphill until you pass a big water tank on your left; the hostel is on the next street to the right. It's closer to town than the KB Mission, but the walk is very steep.

ACCESS
Air

Talair (☎ 61 1333 in Alotau) is the main carrier in this area, although there are also a few MAF flights. Talair flies between Gurney (Alotau) and Wedau on Monday, Wednesday, Friday and Saturday, charging K31. On Friday there are flights between Wedau and Port Moresby (K90), and on Wednesday and Saturday there are flights between Gurney and Lae, stopping at Wedau and a number of interesting places on the way. Wedau to Lae costs K156.

Both Talair and Air Niugini (☎ 61 1100 in Alotau) fly between Gurney and Port Moresby, and there's at least one flight every day, for K101.

Sea

Small boats coming from or going to Alotau usually call at Wedau at least twice a week. The trip takes some 12 hours and costs around K10. Bring your own food and water. It definitely is a very scenic trip but remember that most boats are small, some roll quite a bit, and others are likely to give off diesel fumes. Some boats don't carry life jackets and many won't have toilets. However, if you can put up with all these annoyances you'll be in for a good experience.

The best way to find out about who goes where is to go down to the wharf in Alotau and talk to people. Otherwise, tune in to Radio Milne Bay at 7 am or 7 pm and listen for shipping movements along the north-east coast.

Currently, no passenger boats operate between Port Moresby and Milne Bay Province, but there's a slight chance of arranging a ride on a cargo boat. See the Getting Around chapter for information.

STAGE 1: WEDAU TO LAVORA

Walking time: five hours, 20 km
Overnight: Lavora rest house

Leaving Wedau from the marketplace, the trail takes you first to the Wamira River, which is 25 metres wide and half a metre deep. Across the ford, the route follows the river down for a short distance, then swings sharply to the right and then heads at once towards Cape Girumia and the first houses of Wamira No 1.

Further on, the trail forks. Take the left fork and soon, after passing a cemetery and then a cross, you come to Mulawa Creek. Ford the creek near the mouth and follow the trail to Wamira No 2, a large village which straggles as far as the Uruam River.

Continue in front of the houses and leave the village from behind a group of houses roofed with galvanised iron. The route then carries on to nearby Wagamora Creek, best forded a little upstream, especially at high tide.

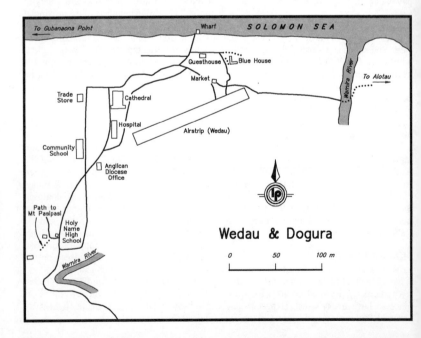

Crossing the Ali River, Western Province (YP)

Top: Village on a ridge top, Nomane, Simbu Province (YP)
Bottom: Mt Wilhelm, PNG's highest mountain, Simbu Province (YP)

Across the creek you're still in Wamira No 2 and (as is the case with most villages and hamlets you'll walk through from here) the route continues between the houses and the shoreline. Once past the last buildings, the trail turns inland and, past a large turn-off leading to the Pupuderi community school, heads towards the Uruam River, which is eight metres wide and half a metre deep. You can drink from the river.

A short distance further on you reach Bartle Bay. The route continues along the shore and passes many hamlets (Modawa, Iwagani, Ipugolo, Numaubu, Divari, Bodume, Gumadoudo, Babanai and Amedara) as it heads towards nearby Cape Girumia. This whole locality is usually referred to as Divari. You can drink from any of the streams along this section of the coast.

The trail can be a little difficult to follow between Babanai and Amedara, and a couple of times it ends at the foot of large rocks. When this happens look around the rocks

and you'll see the path continue on the other side.

While you will not see any more houses as you skirt around the base of Cape Girumia you won't be short of water, as you'll pass six lovely cascades. The fifth, called Vagawa, is the nicest; it falls into a large deep pool before reaching the sea. There are good views from the cape, as far as Cape Vogel to the west and East Cape to the east. To the north are the the d'Entrecasteaux Islands; from left to right these are Goodenough, Fergusson and Normanby.

Eventually, the route brings you to a large, dry creekbed filled with boulders. Follow it down some seven metres and then continue along the trail as it swings to the right and heads east again.

The rest house is now only a short distance away. The trail comes to the coast again and continues along a narrow pebble beach to the hamlet of Aihauwa. From here it carries on to nearby Irere and the rest house. Aihauwa

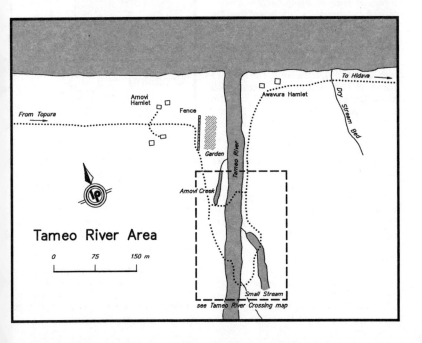

Tameo River Area

0   75   150 m

and Irere are two of several hamlets that make up Lavora No 1.

Irere is just a hamlet. You'll know you're there when you see a large, well-kept lawn surrounding a small church with two bright-yellow doors. The rest house is to the right of the church, beside the stream. It's a lovely bush-material house with two large rooms, an hearth and tap water outside. Just make yourself at home if no-one is around when you get here. A night's accommodation costs K5.

STAGE 2: LAVORA TO HIDAVA
Walking time: 5½ hours, 20 km
Overnight: village accommodation in Hidava

Lavora to Topura
Walking time: two hours
From the rest house, the trail continues along the beach for a while until, a short distance away, it swings a little inland and continues beneath the coconut palms. The route to Topura is fairly straightforward – a well-defined path running a little inland from the shore. Water from any of the streams along this section of the coast is drinkable.

After leaving the rest house and Irere the trail takes you to Tauoa, then to Wanaga; both hamlets of Lavora No 1. The next two places are Nade and Aigura, which are on Aigura Bay and are usually called Lavora No 2. As it continues from Aigura to Turi, the trail is edged with flowering hibiscus. From around Turi and lovely Parimeta Bay there are good views of the coast; Kea and Punipuni points and parts of East Cape can be seen to the east.

The next three hamlets you come to are Raratepana, Kiratepana and Varemutuna, just before you reach the small station of Topura. There is a store, a community school and an aid post in Topura.

Topura to Hidava
Walking time: 3½ hours
The trail continues right through the village, past a small trade store, then to the Topura hamlets of Riwabu, Moya and Amovi. At Amovi it swings inland then follows Amovi

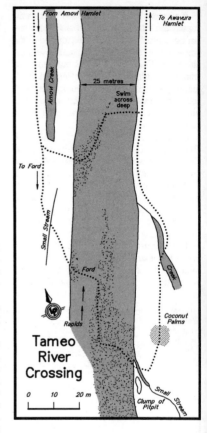

Creek until it reaches the large Tameo River. At one point you'll come to an intersection. The left-hand path leads to a bathing place where it's possible to swim across; continue straight ahead to the ford.

Although quite deep and wide near its mouth, the river is only half a metre or so deep and eight metres wide at the crossing. After fording, walk along the gravel bed as far as the rapids on your right. When you reach them, turn around and face the forest on the opposite bank. The trail here begins by the small stream which flows beside the clump of pitpit on your right.

If you can't find the trail, go back to the rapids and look for a group of coconut palms in the forest on the opposite bank. Once through the pitpit, the trail heads towards these palms, so if you can't find the trail, just make for these palms and you'll be on it. This small path, a little overgrown, then meets the main trail a little further down, on the other side of yet another small creek.

From that last creek the trail heads first towards Awavura, a hamlet at the mouth of the Tameo River, then towards nearby Gonopora. From here it continues to the Nevira Creek.

Although Nevira Creek is deep near its mouth, it is very easy to ford upstream. As the trail here might not be well defined, walk a little way upstream in the shallow water by the bank until you are opposite a large gravel bed. Ford across to the gravel bed and you'll see the path climb onto the bank. The water here is good to drink.

The trail then takes you back to the coast near the mouth of the Nevira Creek. If you can't locate it, just make for the shoreline and walk east for a short distance until you come to a dry creekbed. There, under the trees, you'll see the trail again. This place is called

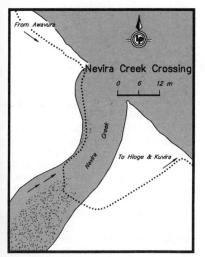

Hioge. Though there's not much here today this whole area used to be a large copra plantation.

The route then brings you to Kuvira Bay and the hamlet of Kuvira. There are only three or four houses here, all near a small stream. That stream, also called Kuvira, is basically the last drinking water before Wairanai Creek and Hidava. You will see many more streams, but most of them aren't suitable for drinking. To get fresh water, follow the path beside the copra drier, on the other side of the creek. Go upstream about 70 metres.

Further on, past Kuvira, the trail comes to a narrow ledge above the sea. It is usually bridged but the sea sometimes washes the logs away. If the bridge is out, the best way to get across is to scramble down the rock face and walk in the sea below. Right across the ledge, the path climbs a short crest known as Hiohioo by the local people. The water here is deep, and Hiohioo means 'the place where the octopus dwells'. From the top of the crest there are beautiful views of Kuvira Bay, one of the nicest spots along the coast.

The route then continues along the beach, first to the hamlet of Wairagaugau, then to Iomutuna, where you'll see a lonely house painted bright orange. From here it takes you towards Yagovani Point and the hamlet of Yagovani, then to Headugu. Between Yagovani Point and Headugu, the trail is again edged with lovely rows of flowering hibiscus.

At Headugu (two houses), the trail forks as it comes to the top of a small hill. The right fork goes to some gardens; take the left fork and immediately go down to another beach. From here, the trail continues to Ginahivuna, then Hogi Hogi Point and the hamlet of the same name, and finally small Wamawamana and the village of Hidava, which is by Wairanai Creek and is tonight's sleeping place.

Taupota No 2 is still two hours away. If you feel you can get there, carry on. If not, I recommend that you relax, take in the scenery and walk to nearby Omnawa Point which has good views of the coast back towards Kuvira Bay and Cape Girumia. People drink from and wash in Wairanai Creek; drinking water is collected upstream of the bathing area.

STAGE 3: HIDAVA TO TAUPOTA NO 2
Walking time: two hours, 8 km
Overnight: village accommodation

Get some water from Wairanai Creek before you leave the village. Most of the streams from now until Taupota No 1 are polluted by cattle, and good drinking water is scarce.

From Hidava the route continues past a small stream called Hawapa, then the hamlet of Bara, then the large, dry bed of Omnawa Creek and the point of the same name. There are good views back towards Kuvira Bay and Cape Girumia from the point.

Cross the creekbed, follow it up a few metres and you'll see the path continue on the left. A short distance away, in the kunai, the trail forks. The right fork goes to the hamlet of Omnawa, the left takes you towards Taupota. Continue on to Gerevaudi and the point of the same name, then walk along the beach to Awaula Point. There are more good views back towards Cape Girumia from here. Near the point is the hamlet of Awaula.

From now until you reach Taupota No 2 you'll also have good views towards Punipuni Point.

The route continues, mostly along the beach, past the hamlets of Tetebadona, Takakam, Arewabu and Taihuhuna, to the small station of Didiwaga. This part of the coastline, from Tetebadona, including Didiwaga and stretching as far as the mouth of Pori Creek, is usually referred to as Taupota No 1.

There is a school and a health centre at Didiwaga. It's only a short distance to Pori Creek and Taupota No 2, where the trail branches off for Alotau, so you could, if people invite you, spend the night here. A trail links Didiwaga with Alotau, but it's much more strenuous than the one described here. If people mention it to you, insist that you prefer to follow the Pori and Haumo Creek route.

The trail continues in front of the health centre and the church, then goes back down to the beach. The next hamlet you come to is Nuakata, the next bay Ginaihuna. Although there are four streams flowing into the bay, drink only from the last one. It's called Guga and is past the hamlets of Gehigehi and Igohi.

The next place, by Pori Creek and opposite the first hamlets of Taupota No 2, is Mudawa. You've now reached the turn-off to Alotau and have completed the third stage of the walk. There are lots of houses across the creek at Taupota No 2 and you could either sleep there or spend the night here at Mudawa. Ask around for a guide to Alotau. There are a couple of stores in Taupota No 2.

STAGE 4: TAUPOTA NO 2 TO ALOTAU
Walking time: 4½ hours, 15 km
Overnight: various options in Alotau

As some sections of the trail to Alotau are not well defined you will need a guide. The route to Alotau follows Pori Creek up to the top of the range and then Haumo Creek down to the lowlands and Milne Bay. It takes 2½ hours to reach the top of the range from Taupota No 2 and a further two hours to get down to Alotau.

After following and crossing Pori Creek 13 times, the trail brings you to the base of the mountains. From here it climbs along a steady, often steep, grade for 1¾ hours along the western wall of the valley to the top of the range.

A little above the last crossing of Pori Creek, disregard a small footpath on the left which goes back down to the stream. Further up, at a first small clearing, disregard the small path which branches off to the right. The correct route is fairly well defined and should cause no uncertainties. A little further up you'll come to an obvious resting place with a large mango tree growing in the centre of it. On the right of the tree is another turn-off; disregard it, as it goes back down the mountain. From here on, drinking water is plentiful all the way to Alotau.

Still further up, the trail brings you to a couple of places with views down the valley and towards the d'Entrecasteaux Islands.

Just before you reach the end of the climb you cross Pori Creek one last time. It flows through a small chasm.

The top of the range, the watershed between Milne Bay and the north-east coast of the province, is just a narrow ridge.

There is a small lookout to the left of the trail shortly after you begin the descent to Alotau. There are views of Haumo Valley and the coast, but Alotau is hidden behind the hill on the left.

A steep descent from the lookout takes you to the head of Haumo Creek. The route now follows the stream down to the coast and Alotau, either beside the creek or in its bed. The descent is somewhat slippery, at times steep and difficult. Bc very careful, especially when rock-scrambling.

On reaching the lowlands the trail continues along the gravel flats, through pitpit and secondary growth, until it eventually comes to a permanent house on the left-hand side of the creek. Here you'll see a small path branching off.

Follow the path past the house until it meets a larger vehicle track. Turn right and walk to the intersection ahead.

Turn left at the intersection and continue to nearby Gilmour Place, a street lined with government houses. At the next intersection turn left into Cameron St. It eventually meets the Alotau-Gurney road, where you turn left again to go into town.

OTHER SUGGESTED WALKS
Rabaraba to Wedau
It takes two days to walk from Rabaraba to Wedau. Talair flies from Gurney (Alotau) to Rabaraba most days for K44. For more details consult the Orangerie (8877) and Baniara (8878) sheets of the 1:100,000 topographic map series, or the Tufi (SC 55-8) and Samarai (SC 56-9) sheets of the 1:250,000 series.

Taupota No 2 to Alotau via East Cape
From Taupota No 2 it takes about three days to walk via East Cape to a village just east of Ahioma, where you can find vehicles running to Alotau. There is, I was told, a rest house at Garuahi, roughly two hours away from Taupota No 2. Consult the Hehego sheet (9077) of the 1:100,000 topographic map series, or the Samarai sheet (SC 56-9) of the 1:250,000 series.

Mt Pasipasi
The big challenge in Wedau and Dogura is to climb Mt Pasipasi, a 600-metre peak to the south-west of the Holy Name high school in Dogura. Five to six hours are needed to make a trip to the summit and back.

Take lots of water (a few litres) and be prepared to leave well before dawn in order to reach the summit before it gets too hot. There are fine views from the top: the d'Entrecasteaux Islands can all be seen, along with Cape Vogel to the west and East Cape to the east.

Menyamya to Kerema

Dramatically set in rugged ranges and lofty peaks, this beautiful walk takes the visitor through the very heart of Anga country. Providing a practical route to the south coast, it links Menyamya, a large government station in Morobe, with Kerema, a small coastal town in Gulf Province. It also offers a fascinating insight into the cultures of the Menya and Kamea people. Traditional round huts still dot the landscape, many people still wear tribal dress, and life goes on much the way it has always done.

HISTORY

Though Charles Higginson, a resident magistrate in Gulf Division, visited some Kukukuku villages at the head of the Lohiki River in 1907, the first Europeans to see much of these people in their own country were three Australian gold prospectors – Matt Crowe, Frank and Jim Pryke. In 1909 they went prospecting in the upper waters of the Tauri and Lakekamu rivers and were twice attacked by Kukukuku warriors.

In the following year Crowe returned with Hubert Murray, then lieutenant-governor of Papua, to establish a government station at Nepa, near the headwaters of the Lakekamu River. Some years later, this country was patrolled by Jack Hides, one of Murray's most famous 'outside men'.

In the meantime, in the Mandated Territory of New Guinea, a small patrol post had been established at Otibanda on the western side of the Watut River near Wau. In spite of this, it was not until 1933 that the exploration and 'pacification' of Kukukuku country in New Guinea really began.

JK McCarthy lead the first government patrol into the heart of the unexplored country to the west of the Watut. After leaving from Otibanda he explored the headwaters of the Langimar River, then the country at the confluence of the Yakwi and Tauri rivers where, during an earlier reconnaissance flight, he had located a flat expanse of grassland suitable for the construction of an airstrip. On that spot, at a place the local people called Menyamya, he established the first government patrol post in the forbidding Kukukuku country.

Four months or so after his first trip, McCarthy led another patrol to Menyamya to prepare a landing ground for Tommy O'Dea, who flew in a month later to the great wonderment of the local population. There was some more exploration of the area and McCarthy managed a trip along the Tauri River into Papua. To McCarthy's great disappointment, the government ordered that the newly established station was to be abandoned, following a report by government prospectors. New Guinea was run on a pittance and the government decided that there would be no expenditure on new posts or exploration unless dividends followed in the shape of gold.

It was not until 1950 that Lloyd Hurrell reopened the patrol post at Menyamya. The presence of his wife, Margaret, and their children had a startling effect on the local population who realised, perhaps for the first time, that the strangers were human.

The 1950s saw a great period of exploration throughout the region. Ian Sinclair, Ken Chester, Lance Vizard, Ian Downs, Ray Bamford and Lloyd Hurrell are among the celebrated names of that period. Hurrell patrolled around Menyamya, Bamford made several forays into Menyamya from his small patrol post at Bulolo, Downs made a trip in 1946 to the upper Banir River, and in 1951 Chester and Vizard spent 49 days exploring the country between Kerema and Menyamya.

In April I951 Sinclair left his patrol post at Mumeng, walked to the lower Watut River, travelled to the headwaters of the Banir, and ultimately reached Menyamya via the Tauri Valley. From Menyamya he returned to Mumeng through the Upper Watut area.

From July to September of the same year he made a more important, 70-day patrol to explore new regions of Kukukuku country. He walked to the headwaters of the Waffa River then, after visiting the area around Wonenara, reached the headwaters of the Vailala River and discovered the Marawaka Valley. From there he continued on to Menyamya, which he and his thin, hungry and footsore party reached 42 days after leaving Mumeng. The rest of the patrol consisted of getting back to Lae via the Tauri, Banir, Watut and Markham valleys.

Today, Menyamya is the largest and most important government station in Anga country.

PEOPLE & CULTURE

The origin of the word Kukukuku is uncertain. Some people think it means 'cassowary', others claim it derives from *kuku*, a Motu word meaning tobacco. What's certain, however, is that the Anga people today regard Kukukuku as a derogatory term – don't use it!

Traditional houses are still common in the area. There are two types: the house for sleeping, a round hut built on stilts and topped with a conical thatched roof – usually made of kunai but sometimes bunches of wild bamboo leaves; and a rectangular house which is built on the ground and is where meals are normally cooked. House compounds are often surrounded by clumps of bamboo and small gardens where sugar cane, corn, greens, sweet potatoes and other produce is grown.

The Menya and Kamea people once preserved the bodies of their dead by smoking. The corpse was smoked until it was hard and completely dehydrated and then placed in a sitting position on a burial platform, usually a small stand built on piles and topped with a roof to protect the corpse against the weather. Some were placed on protected limestone ledges overlooking their ancestral lands, again in a sitting position. Arrows were used to hold the bodies in an upright position.

Smoked bodies can still be found, usually concealed in inaccessible rock faces or on high mountain peaks. Although there are some in the country between Hawabango and Kaintiba, the best-preserved and most accessible are in Aseki, only a short distance from the station.

Anga warriors always carried a deadly stone club hidden in their waistband and covered by their cloak. Short but powerful bows and arrows, still used today for hunting, completed their weaponry.

Although the Kamea, Lohiki and Vori dress slightly differently from the Angan groups to the north, traditional dress throughout Anga country is fairly uniform. For men, it consists of many layers of beaten fibre skirts – square among the Kamea, Lohiki and Vori, triangular among the other groups – and sometimes, slung across their waists, a pair of cassowary thigh bones. The buttocks are covered with a strip of beaten bark which hangs down from a waistband. Around the waist and slung across the chest, bandoleer fashion, they wear bundles of finely plaited yellow bands made from tree orchids. Long, tapered lengths of cassowary bone, pitpit, or the leg-bone of an eagle are worn through the nose. Shell headbands are common and some men wear earrings made from the wing-bone of a fruit bat. Necklaces of dog's teeth, beads, kina or cowrie shells or fragments of bailer shells are also common.

Traditionally, men's hair was close-cropped except for a small top-knot from

Young girl wearing a *malo*

which the long bark cloak *(malo)* was suspended. Still worn today, the malo provides shade and protection against the sun, bitter winds and rains of the mountains. At night it is used as a blanket.

Women's traditional dress is generally less flamboyant, consisting of fibre skirts made from beaten strips of bark, a malo, and bead or shell necklaces. Some women from the Kamea area can still be seen with large ear ornaments made of several twisted loops of vine.

Although Western clothing is now usual, traditional dress is still worn in some areas, notably in villages around Menyamya, Marawaka and Wonenara. It's also common in the south-western part of Anga country but the people here (the Kamea, Lohiki and Vori) tend not to adorn themselves as much.

All Anga men and women smoke coarse tobacco in long bamboo pipes and chew wild betel nut *(kaipipi)*.

The staple food is sweet potato. Other important food items include: taro kongkong, cooking bananas, pumpkins, various greens, sugar cane and marita. Most food is still steamed in sections of bamboo (which explains the bamboo clumps found near settlements) or cooked in the hot ashes of a fire. However, cooking pots are becoming more common. Large-scale cooking, such as for a feast, is usually done in a mumu.

Note that the Kamea people are sometimes called the Kapau or Hamtai and that the Kapau people living near Wau are usually referred to as the Watut. The Kamea's neighbours are the Lohiki, the Vori and the Ankave to the west, the Opao, Kerema and Toaripi to the south, and the Yagwoia, Menya and Agaataha to the north. The Menya's neighbours are the Kamea to the south, the Agaataha to the east, the Kawatsa to the north and the Yagwoia to the west and the north. These are the names of the neighbouring language groups.

INFORMATION
Features

The entire length of the walk, except for the coastal strip behind the township of Kerema,

is through Kukukuku country – known today as Anga.

Several large, truly impressive valleys of kunai set amidst broken and rugged ranges characterise the country around Menyamya. It's the heart of Menya country and is largely dominated by the deep and dramatic Tauri Valley. The Menya people, one of some 12 different but closely related cultural groups that make up the greater Angan culture, still live in hamlets strategically perched on narrow, very steep spurs towering high above the flat expanses of below.

From the village of Koeyamaga, the trail takes you into Kamea country. The Kamea people inhabit the region that extends from the Tauri-Vailala Divide, as far east as the township of Wau and the upper Lakekamu River, and south to within a few km of the coast of the Gulf of Papua. The Kamea are an Angan group but they differ from the Menya in various ways, including language and traditional dress.

South of Koeyamaga, the great expanses of kunai give way to a timbered landscape. While primary forest still covers most of the ranges, secondary growth dominates along the trail and near settlements.

A fine panorama of the Tauri Valley can be enjoyed from Kanabea, the mighty Owen Stanley Ranges can be clearly seen to the east from several points between Hawakapia and Merapo, and views of the coast can be obtained from Mbauyia as well as from Didimaua, near Kerema.

As you reach the lowlands, the walk takes you through the customary lands of the coastal Kerema people. Unfortunately, little of their traditional way of life will be seen, as the trail takes the walker from the small station of Murua directly to the township of Kerema. However, those who choose to catch a motorised dugout down the Murua River to the coast will have the opportunity to see Kerema people at work in their gardens.

Standard

Despite its considerable length, most of this walk is fairly easy. For most of the way the trail basically follows a motorcycle track on which patrol officers in the '70s travelled between Menyamya and Mbauyia. There is no strenuous walking involved between these two points, the gradient is generally mild, the trail always follows the contours and water is plentiful.

A vehicle road now links Kaintiba, Kanabea and Paina, a small village half a day's walk south of Kanabea. Since it leads nowhere but from Kaintiba to Paina, you're unlikely to see much traffic – maybe one vehicle. The rest of the track is narrower, at times a little overgrown, but always clearly marked and easy to follow.

Between Mbauyia and Didimaua the trail follows a narrow, and strenuous path over very difficult terrain and, because of the lower elevation, it's very hot and humid and there are annoying bush flies. It's the most demanding section of the walk, and it requires a fair degree of fitness. However, it's possible to bypass it by flying out from Kamina, a small Catholic mission, half a day's walk due east of Ivandu. Flying out from Kamina would shorten the trip by two days.

From Didimaua, follow another vehicle track down to Murua station. Although vehicles go as far as the village of Aspopo, it's much better to continue on foot all the way to Murua itself. From there, Kerema can be reached by road or by motorised canoe down the Murua River.

Although the trail can be done either way, it's preferable to walk it from Menyamya to the coast. Not only is it much easier to walk from Mbauyia to the lowlands, it's also much easier to find a guide there than in Didimaua.

Days Required

The suggested itinerary requires eight days to walk but it can be shortened to six if you catch a flight out from Kamina rather than walking the last two stages to Kerema. Walking times listed are minimum walking times – unless you're very fit or carrying a light pack, you are unlikely to go much faster.

Season

The rainy season stretches from early November to the end of March. Kanabea tends to be wetter than other places along the trail. June, July and August are the best months, although May and September can also be reasonable.

Daytime temperatures in the mountains are quite pleasant but at night, especially around Menyamya, it can get very cold. In the lowlands and near the coast at Kerema daytime temperatures usually hover around 28 to 30°C.

Useful Organisations

There are telephones in Kerema and at the district office in Menyamya. You'll also find two-way radios, which can be used in case of emergency, at Hawabango, Kanabea, Kotidanga, Ivandu and Kamina. There are health centres in Menyamya, Hawabango, and Murua, small aid posts in Koeyamaga, Wemauwa, Manimago, Meware, Ivandu and Mbauyia, and good hospitals in Kanabea and Kerema.

The Menyamya PNGBC agency should have been upgraded to a sub-branch by now; if so you can change traveller's cheques. there. Check first at a PNGBC branch (preferably the Port Moresby head office) for up-to-date information. There is a PNGBC branch in Kerema.

Guides & Carriers

No guides are needed between Menyamya and Mbauyia, or between Didimaua and Murua. However, one is essential from Mbauyia to Didimaua – without a guide you haven't got the slightest hope of finding the trail. Expect to pay K5 per day for a guide/carrier, a little less for a guide only.

Elsewhere along the trail a carrier, if needed, should not be hard to find. Just ask around. Expect to pay about K0.50 an hour. In Menyamya, the people at the district office and at the Anga Development Authority (responsible for the guesthouse), can probably help you find a reliable carrier out of the station.

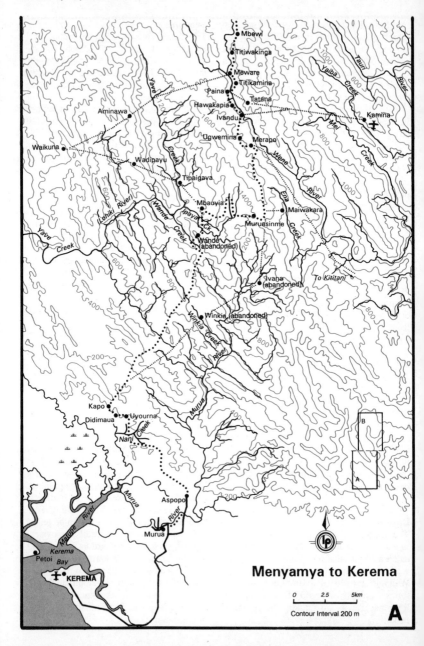

Mbewi
Titiwakinga
Meware
Titikamina
Paina
Tatana
Hawakapia
Ivandu
Ugwemina
Merapo
Kamina
Aminawa
Waikuna
Wadipayu
Tipaigava
Mbauyia
Maiwakara
Ipaya Ck
Muruasinme
Wande (abandoned)
Ivana (abandoned)
To Kititani
Winkia (abandoned)
Yaiba Creek
Tauri River
Mei Creek
Wene River
Eaa Creek
Yave Creek
Lohiki River
Wende Creek
Winkia Creek
Murue River
Kapo
Didimaua
Uyourna
Nani Creek
Aspopo
Murua
Maupe River
Murua River
Kerema Bay
Petoi
KEREMA

Menyamya to Kerema

0   2.5   5km

Contour Interval 200 m

A

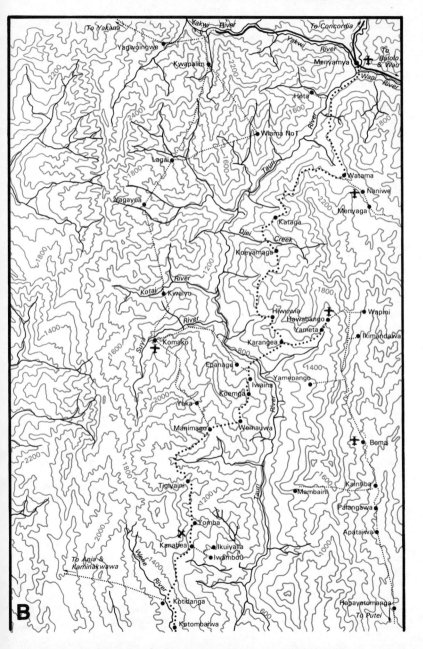

Equipment

Runners or very light boots are ideal footwear. Sunscreen and a wide-brimmed hat are advisable. A tent may be carried so as not to put pressure on village accommodation. Bring some sort of rain gear and a sleeping bag.

Food can be bought in villages along the trail but should not be depended on. Carry some of your own, especially for breakfast and lunch. There are reliable but poorly stocked trade stores in Menyamya, Hawabango, Kanabea, Kamina and Kerema. The small trade stores in Murua and along the road between Meware and Wemauwa are expensive and very unreliable.

Maps

The Kerema (8082), Armit (8083) and Aseki (8183) sheets of the 1:100,000 topographic map series cover the area described in the walk. The same area is also covered by the Wau sheet (SB 55-14) of the 1:250,000 series. There are problems with these maps. Many place names are misspelled and the position of many villages is no longer correct (villages tend relocate). Unless you want to find out more about the area, the map in this chapter should be sufficient.

Warning

Before taking a PMV between Lae and Bulolo, ask about the current situation, as there were many hold-ups on the road in 1992. Lae itself is extremely dangerous after dark and care is required during the day. See Lonely Planet's *Papua New Guinea – a travel survival kit* for more information.

PLACES TO STAY

In Menyamya, stay at the *Menyamya Guesthouse*. There are hot showers and a kitchen. A bed costs K15 and meals are available. The keys are kept at the Anga Development Authority office (☎ 44 0211). It's best to let them know when you're coming. If you arrive at the station at night and haven't made a booking, see the OIC (officer in charge), who lives next door to the guesthouse.

In Kerema, the *Elavo Inn* (☎ 68 1041, PO Box 25) might still have accommodation. Don't expect too much. The *Catholic Lodge*, situated within the Catholic mission compound near the market, offers bed & breakfast for about K25. Dinner is an extra K6. They have eight decent rooms, showers, cooking facilities and good views of Kerema Bay.

ACCESS

On Monday and Friday there are Talair flights between Kerema and Lae (K94 from Kerema), via Kamina (K32), Kanabea (K35), Kaintiba (K39), and Menyamya (K52, K60 from Lae). MAF and other outfits (such as Kiunga Aviation (☎ 42 6488) in Lae) service small strips in the area. Few of these flights are regular passenger runs but you can often arrange to go along on someone else's charter.

Talair flies between Kerema and Port Moresby daily except Sunday (K113). On Monday, Wednesday, Friday and Saturday, the outward flight from Moresby calls at small coastal towns including Malalaua (K96 from Moresby).

From Bulolo, PMVs for Menyamya leave from the road junction near the market. The 124-km, 5½-hour trip from Bulolo to Menyamya costs about K10. Bulolo is about 3½ hours from Lae and a PMV costs K4. It's a 30-km, 1½-hour, K6 trip from Aseki to Menyamya. From Bulolo to Aseki it's K10. The road actually bypasses Aseki, so if you're going there make sure the driver knows so he can take you into the village.

There are two ways of getting from Murua to Kerema. The most interesting is to catch a motorised canoe down the Murua River. They cost about K2 and though irregular are fairly common. The second is to catch a PMV for about K2. There usually is a first trip at around 6.30 am and another late in the afternoon.

It is fairly easy to catch a PMV from Kerema to Malalaua (K3), then a motorised canoe from Malalaua to Navara (Iokea) (K12) and last, a PMV from Navara to Port Moresby (K12). The trip through the swamps to Navara is very interesting. Expect two days of travelling.

STAGE 1: MENYAMYA TO KOEYAMAGA

Walking time: 5½ hours, 16 km
Overnight: village accommodation

The track to Koeyamaga begins at the Tauri River bridge. It follows the main road out then, from the top of the hill, continues straight ahead along a vehicle track to the Wapi River and the village of Watama. Do not follow the main road as it swings to the left towards Wau and Bulolo.

A short descent from the top of the hill immediately brings you to the Wapi River. A little to the left of the track, under the trees, is a suspended wire bridge. Across it, still

along a vehicle track, a steady but gentle uphill grade takes you up to Watama in about two hours.

From here, a clearly marked trail continues past the hamlets of Hakeyake and Hawignei to the villages of Kataga and Koeyamaga. A little off the trail, the first above it and the second below, Hakeyake and Hawignei are respectively 50 and 90 minutes' walk from Watama. Shortly after Hawignei, the trail goes around the side of a long slope leading down towards the Tauri River on the right. From here, as you climb gently towards a crest, there are magnificent

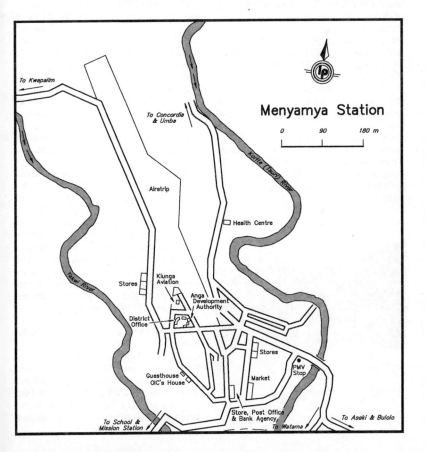

Menyamya Station

views of the Tauri Valley. Kataga is on the other side of the crest, and is an hour's walk from Hawignei.

On reaching the Kataga village square, disregard the track on the left which goes to the village proper. Continue along a fairly level grade, mainly through secondary growth, until you are opposite a group of houses on your right, built around the very top of a hill. From here you can see the Tauri Valley on the right and, across the small Djei Valley, some of the house of Koeyamaga.

Continue down to Djei Creek. In the near distance, on the left and a little above the track, you can see the galvanised-iron roofs of Koeyamaga's church and the aid post. These buildings constitute the centre of the village, as most of the population is widely scattered in the area. It takes three-quarters of an hour to walk from Kataga to Koeyamaga.

If you have a tent, the best place to pitch it is near the aid post and the church. Ask permission first. If you don't have a tent you'll have to find a family to sleep with.

Part of the border between the Menya and Kamea territories runs along Djei Creek. From now on, to within a few km of the coast, the people speak Kamea, a language a little softer than the harsh Angan languages to the north.

STAGE 2: KOEYAMAGA TO HAWABANGO

Walking time: 4½ hours, 17 km
Overnight: Hawabango Catholic mission
After about half an hour's climb out of the Djei Valley the trail levels off. From here, it follows a ridge-line down and falls gently towards Hiwuwia and a nearby stream. On your right as you approach the village you'll get a glimpse of the Komako airstrip. Situated in the Suya Valley, Komako is a small station on the other side of the Tauri River. It takes three hours to walk from Koeyamaga to Hiwuwia.

From Hiwuwia it's a 45-minute walk up and over the top of a small ridge and down to the village of Karangea, on the Kaintiba-Kanabea road. On reaching the road, go right to the Tauri River and Kanabea or turn left to Hawabango, a small Catholic mission station 45 minutes further on.

It is recommended that walkers spend the night in Hawabango. Father Flynn says he can provide a place for several travellers to sleep at the mission as long as they are not too fussy. Meals cannot be guaranteed but there is a place to cook. Make a donation.

STAGE 3: HAWABANGO TO WEMAUWA

Walking time: 5½ hours, 29 km
Overnight: village accommodation
First, walk back to Karangea. From here, a gentle downhill walk of 1½ hours brings you to the Tauri River bridge. Iwaina is now an hour's walk away. From Iwaina, Koemga is half an hour or so away along a gentle uphill grade. A mainly level walk of 1¾ hours takes you from Koemga to Wemauwa, the proposed overnight site, where there is a community school and an aid post.

STAGE 4: WEMAUWA TO KOTIDANGA

Walking time: five hours, 29 km
Overnight: village accommodation
It takes 1½ hours, along a mainly level stretch of road, to walk from Wemauwa to the large village of Manimago, then another 55 minutes to get to Tigiyaini. From here it's uphill to the top of the next ridge then downhill to Yomba, 20 minutes away.

Continuing downhill, first past the small village of Ipayu then the hamlet of Hatave, you come to Kanabea, a Catholic mission 1¼ hours' walk from Yomba. Contrary to what you might hear, there is no accommodation for walkers at Kanabea.

Kotidanga is now an hour's walk away. From Kanabea, past the hamlet of Kihamdia, the road climbs gently to the top of a small ridge. Along here, in addition to magnificent views down the Tauri Valley, you can see the Owen Stanley Ranges in the distance. From the top of the ridge, the road drops down to the small government station of Kotidanga.

There is no official rest house at the station. Contact the OIC (officer in charge) who will help you find a place to pitch your tent or a place to stay.

STAGE 5: KOTIDANGA TO IVANDU

Walking time: 4¼ hours, 25 km

Overnight: mission house

This section of the walk basically follows the Wene River – which rises in the country north-west of Kotidanga – down to Ivandu.

From Kotidanga the road continues past the hamlet of Aimagata and down to Kotombaiwa, a small village half an hour away. From here the road continues past the hamlets of Mbewi and Titiwakinga to Meware, a larger village with a community school. This section of the road is essentially level. It takes 20 minutes to reach Mbewi from Kotombaiwa, a further 30 minutes to reach Titiwakinga and from there another 25 minutes to reach Meware.

From Meware it's 20 minutes to the village of Titikamina and another 25 minutes to Paina. About 10 minutes before Paina is the nine-metre-wide Wene River. It's usually easy to ford, but if the river is in flood there is a bridge a little below Titikamina. Don't drink from the river.

If you're heading for Kamina, you could turn-off here. From the east side of the ford a small track continues along the left-hand side of the river towards Kamina. It first goes to Wambiyu, a nearby village, then to the hamlets of Tatana and Hindowe before eventually reaching Kamina. It takes between five and six hours to reach Kamina from the Wene River. A better marked trail leads to Kamina from Ivandu, a little further on.

Walkers heading for Ivandu and Kerema cross the river and follow the road, which becomes a large track. Follow it through Paina, then past the hamlet of Weuya to the large and pleasant village of Hawakapia. This section of the walk from the Wene River is mostly uphill and takes an hour.

From Hawakapia, past the hamlet of Yeka, it's an easy 50-minute walk to the small mission outpost of Ivandu. Here, the Kamina Catholic Brothers maintain a furnished house, available to visitors passing through. It costs about K4 per night per person and the keys are with the catechist in charge of the station. The Brothers are kind enough to lend their house, so make sure you keep it clean and tidy.

A good trail links Ivandu with Kamina, a small Catholic mission station roughly five hours' walk to the east. Flying out from Kamina shortens the walk by two days and avoids the most difficult section of it. Take a guide from Ivandu to Kamina. (See the Standard section in this chapter.)

STAGE 6: IVANDU TO MBAUYIA

Walking time: five hours

Overnight: mission house

On leaving Ivandu, there are good views of the Owen Stanley Ranges to the east. The mainly level trail continues past the hamlet of Ugwemina and reaches Merapo roughly 1½ hours later. From Merapo you can still see the Owen Stanleys in the east and to the north-east is a fine panorama of rugged ranges in the general direction of Wau.

From Merapo – built a little above the trail along a spur-line – a gentle downhill grade takes you first to the base of a large rock face, then to a stream (unsuitable for drinking) on the valley floor. This is followed by an equally gentle climb out of the valley. Shortly after reaching the highest point along that part of the trail, a large track branches off to the left. Don't take it; it leads to the village of Maiwakara.

From here the trail continues straight

ahead, gently down, until a second junction is reached. Take the right-hand track which leads to Muruasinme and Mbauyia; the track straight ahead takes you to Didimau by way of the abandoned village of Ivana. From the junction there are extensive views down the Murua Valley and at nearby Muruasinme, 100 metres or so away, you can see the coast near Ihu, a small government station roughly 50 km west of Kerema along the coast.

Mbauyia, the proposed overnight stop is 1½ hours away.

As you continue along the right-hand slope of a deep gully, the trail falls steadily towards the shallow, five-metre-wide Ipaya Creek. This is followed by a short climb, then the trail starts to go down again. From here, as the trail drops steadily but comfortably to Mbauyia, smaller paths leading to gardens and houses must be disregarded.

As in Ivandu, the Catholic Brothers of Kamina maintain a furnished house in Mbauyia which is available to visitors passing through. It costs about K4 a night and the keys are with the catechist in charge of the station. Make yourself at home, have a rest and enjoy the view to the coast. To the north-west, the village of Wauwekauke stands out in the foreground; much farther off and higher up is Tipaigava.

STAGE 7: MBAUYIA TO DIDIMAUA
Walking time: 8-9 hours

Overnight: village accommodation

It takes at least eight hours of sustained effort, through rugged country and a difficult trail, to reach Didimaua. There is possibly a rough campsite at old Wande and another one by Wande Creek where you last cross it to climb out of the valley. If you have neither a tent nor a large piece of plastic, then you have no choice but to walk the whole distance in one day. Both an experienced guide and an early start (at the crack of dawn) are imperative.

From Mbauyia the trail falls gently through gardens and houses at first, then drops steadily down, for 20 minutes or so, towards Ipaya Creek, which is crossed by a log bridge. This is followed by an equally steep 1½-hour climb, past several more houses and gardens, out of the Ipaya Valley to the very top of the next ridge. You immediately plunge steeply down to Ikuna Creek where, after a 30-minute climb out of a deep gully, you continue on down to the small Wande Creek. It's a gruelling descent and takes about 1¾ hours. On the way down, a little above Wande Creek, you go through the site of the abandoned village of Wande – easily recognisable by the extensive secondary growth and the areas of kunai.

At the valley floor the trail follows the creek for about 45 minutes, crossing it numerous times before starting one more ascent which, after 35 minutes or so, finally takes you out of the valley. From this point on, the going is much easier and the trail, which follows mainly along ridge-lines, now falls steadily down towards Didimaua. There are only two short climbs out of creekbeds along this section which, after 2½ hours of comfortable walking, sees you out of the forest onto a large track – the extension of the Kerema-Aspopo road.

As you now continue along that track, it takes 20 minutes along a gentle uphill grade to reach the hamlet of Kapo. From here it's downhill and only 15 minutes to Didimaua. Views of the coast can be enjoyed from here. There is no rest house in Didimaua so you'll have to find a family to stay with if you don't have a tent.

STAGE 8: DIDIMAUA TO MURUA
Walking time: 3¼ hours

Overnight: options in Kerema

From Didimaua, continue along the road, which runs gently downhill, for 15 minutes to Uyourna. From this hamlet the road falls gently at first, then more steeply, to Nani Creek where it levels off and continues to the village of Aspopo. Nani Creek, along with a few more streams in the immediate vicinity, is basically the last water until Murua. It takes roughly 2½ hours to walk from Uyourna to Aspopo.

Although PMVs do come to Aspopo it's preferable to continue on foot all the way to Murua. This very last section of the walk is

Top: Fording Arababou Creek, Southern Highlands Province (YP)
Bottom: Suspended vine bridge, Aku River, Southern Highlands Province (YP)

Log bridge over the Kitu River, Central Province (YP)

mainly level and takes no more than an hour to cover. Continue along the road past a turn-off on the right, then cross Murua River Bridge and, a short distance away, another smaller bridge. Shortly after the second bridge, look for a clearly marked track on the right which shortens the walk by 35 minutes. Via this alternative route, Murua is just 10 minutes away. If you can't find the short cut, keep following the road until you come to a T-junction and take the right turn to Murua.

OTHER SUGGESTED WALKS
Menyamya to Marawaka
Although the shorter route between Menyamya and Marawaka takes two days via the Lutheran mission Concordia and the village of Umba, a more interesting itinerary is to walk to villages west of Menyamya, then follow the Yiake River up to Male and Yamuru and climb over the top of a large mountain and then down to Marawaka. It's a fairly difficult, but very rewarding trip. Expect five or six days of walking. This route takes you through the villages of Yagwoingwe, Yakana, Andakombe, Gwalyu, Male, Yamuru and Wauko.

More information is available on the 1:100,000 topographic map series. The Armit sheet (8083) covers the area described by the walk, but Marawaka station itself appears on the Okapa (8084) sheet. Menyamya to Marawaka via Umba is covered by two sheets: Armit (8083) and Aseki (8183). These two routes are also covered by the Wau sheet (SB 55-14) of the 1:250,000 map series.

Ononge to Tapini

This beautiful walk through the heart of Goilala country links the Catholic mission station of Ononge with the large government centre of Tapini, which nestles on a short plateau abutting the deep, grassy Aiwara River valley.

Situated in the Owen Stanley Ranges north of Port Moresby, this area of Central Province is both carved and dominated by large, steep, awe-inspiring valleys. It introduces you to the beauty of the high country and its flora, and to the Fuyuge and Tauade people who live here.

HISTORY

The origin of the word Goilala is uncertain. Some people say that the name was borrowed from that of a small village near Kerau in the Aiwara Valley. It describes a large, upland administrative district in Central Province extending from Ononge in the south to Guari in the north.

The area is inhabited by numerous tribes (including the Ononge, Kambisi, Woitape, Kosipe, Kerau and Kunimaipa) which are collectively, although somewhat incorrectly, known as the Goilala. The numerous dialects spoken by these people can be grouped under three different languages: Fuyuge, Tauade and Kunimaipa.

Some people blame these short, muscular tribesmen for much of the criminal activity around Port Moresby, and this notoriety is not new. They were always greatly feared by their neighbours for their cunning, ferocity in war and contempt for human life. They were said to be obsessed with power, and to be very violent and aggressive. They fiercely resisted the Australian incursion into their territory, and it was not until the mid '40s that they finally succumbed to the colonial government. Even then, Goilala carriers on government patrols were always left well alone by other people.

At the turn of the century, following the establishment of mission stations along the coast and in the hinterland, the French missionaries of the Congregation of the Sacred Heart began exploration of the rugged Papuan mountains. Kubuna and Obaoba missions stations were established in 1899 in the Kuni district, followed by Malafu in 1905 and Ononge in 1913.

The Catholic Fathers played an important part in the development of the area. They gave the whole district an excellent network of well-graded trails, and it is they who lead the European push into this part of the country. Names like Boismenu, Dupuy, Dupeyrat, Fastré and Maye are famous, but dozens of lesser-known people, many still active, also contributed much.

The are still many mission stations throughout the Goilala area, including Kamulai, Kerau, Tapini, Fane, Kosipe, Yongai, Ononge and Fatima (near Woitape) and other, smaller stations.

PEOPLE & CULTURE

Two cultural groups, the Fuyuge and the Tauade, inhabit the country bisected by the trail. The Fuyuge live south of Kosipe, in the Auga, Dilava, Yaloge, Udabe, Savol and Sirima valleys; the Tauade live in the area north of there, reaching as far as Tapini and including the Ivani and Aiwara valleys.

The Fuyuge's neighbours are the Tauade to the north, the Kuni to the west, and the Koiari and Gabadi to the south. To the east of their territory lies an uninhabited area that extends from the top of the Otava Range down to the lowlands in Oro Province.

In addition to the Fuyuge to the south, the Tauade's immediate neighbours are the Kuni to the south-west, the Mekeo to the west, the Kunimaipa to the north, and the Guhu-Samane to the east.

Traditional dress has long been discarded, and all the Goilala now wear Western clothes. Traditional houses, however, are very common, and people still build large 'dancing villages'. These villages take many months to build and are easily recognisable by the tall, bare trees that are erected next to most houses. Feasts in these villages last months, and people travel great distances to attend them. They are occasions for celebration, making friends, allies or trading partners, and for discussing bride prices and marriages. For the hosts, however, they often cause a severe famine.

Gardening is an important activity, and kaukau is the staple food. Other important food items include: taro kongkong, cooking bananas, pumpkins, sugar cane, various types of greens, and the nuts of the karuka, either wild or cultivated.

The Fuyuge and Tauade languages are non-Austronesian or Papuan, and are unrelated to the coastal languages. Hiri Motu and pidgin are the lingua franca of the area, although English is understood by a few of the younger people and is spoken around the stations.

Banana tree

INFORMATION
Features

The Owen Stanley Ranges are the easternmost part of the central cordillera that runs roughly through the middle of the country along its entire length. To the east of the area bisected by the trail lies Mt Albert Edward, which at 3990 metres is PNG's sixth-highest mountain.

Tapini is 930 metres above sea level, Ononge 1789 and Woitape 1600.

Large, south-draining rivers dominate this part of the central range. These fast-flowing rivers have carved very deep, steep-sided valleys which are often covered with dense grassy vegetation. The Udabe, Savol, Ivani, Lova, Aiwara, Auga, Loloipa, Tapala, Jawataiza and the Kunimaipa are some of the most important rivers. The first two flow into the Vanapa, the next five into the Angabanga (St Joseph), the Tapala flows into the Biaru, and the last two into the Lakekamu.

The large Kosipe swamp extends south of Kosipe. The area around the base of Mt Albert Edward is surrounded by an extensive, grassy basin.

The vegetation along this walk varies considerably. Though most of the ranges are heavily timbered, secondary growth dominates along the trail. Grasslands are an important feature of the area, and lovely groves of karuka, the dark green pandanus nut palm, can be seen at higher elevations along the track and near villages.

Standard

The tracks in this area, made under the supervision of the Catholic missions, seldom exceed 5% in gradient and closely follow the contours. They are wide, well defined, and at one time took mule-trains.

This 116-km walk is easy. Except for the climbs out of the Ivani and Aiwara valleys there is little steep walking. Two routes between Ononge and Woitape are described here. The first and nicest takes you first across the Udabe and continues to Woitape via the village of Uruna; the second, easier route follows the vehicle track that links Ononge with Woitape.

Days Required

The suggested itinerary requires four days to walk, but it could be walked in three long ones if time is short. Alternatively, you could begin the walk in Woitape and walk three days to Tapini. There is also a nice two-day circuit between Ononge and Woitape.

This walk could be included in an 11 or 12-day walk from Tapini down to Port Moresby via Yongai and the Kokoda Trail. For more information see the Other Suggested Walks sections in this chapter and in the Kokoda Trail chapter.

Season

The rainy season stretches from mid-December to early May, and the average annual rainfall is about 2400 mm in Ononge, a little less in Tapini. In February you might encounter the *fidi* – two weeks of constant, non-stop rain. June, July and August are the best months, although September and October can also be quite nice.

Daytime temperatures often climb in to the high 20°Cs, but nights can be chilly, particularly around Ononge, Woitape and Kosipe. Both daytime and night-time temperatures get higher as you approach Tapini.

Useful Organisations

There are two-way radios, which can be used in case of emergency, in Ononge, Fatima, Woitape and Kosipe (but only if someone is living at the mission at the time of your visit), and there are two-way radios and telephones in Tapini. Ononge, Woitape and Tapini have health centres, and there are small aid posts in Kosipe, Tanipai, Minaru and Koluava.

Guides & Carriers

No guides are needed for this walk. The Goilala people are not always willing to act as carriers, and recruiting one can be a little more difficult here than in other parts of the country.

The mission people in Ononge and the government people in Woitape and Tapini should be able to help you find carriers.

Equipment

Runners or very light boots are ideal footwear. Sunscreen and a wide brimmed hat are advisable. Bring some sort of rain gear and a sleeping bag. A camping stove will come in handy in Ononge and Fatima. These two mission stations provide accommodation but have neither hearths nor stove to cook on. A kerosene (paraffin) stove might be available for hire in Ononge. Bring your own pots and utensils.

Food can be bought in villages along the walk, but should not be depended on. Carry some of your own, especially for breakfast and lunch. A mission-owned trade store in Ononge offers a fairly good selection of food items, and there are reliable but more basic stores in Fatima, Woitape and Tapini.

Maps

The Wasa (8380) and Albert Edward (8381) sheets of the 1:100,000 topographic map series cover the area described by the walk. Tapini itself appears on the Yule (8281) sheet of the same series. The same area is also covered by the Buna (SC 55-3) and Yule (SC 55-2) sheets of the 1:250,000 map series.

PLACES TO STAY

There is a wide range of accommodation in Port Moresby, one of the cheapest places being the *Salvation Army* (☎ 21 7683, PO Box 245, Port Moresby). The two-bed rooms cost K25 per person sharing, K40 for a couple or K30 if you want the room to yourself.

In Woitape, the *Fatima Mission* has in the past accommodated travellers for about K5 a night but the Father is due to be replaced and his successor might not continue the guesthouse. Dove Travel (☎ 25 9800, PO Box 6478, Boroko) or TransNiugini Airways (☎ 25 4791, PO Box 3779, Boroko), both in Port Moresby, might have information on this.

The Ononge Catholic mission in Woitape can provide accommodation for up to nine people for about K5 a night. There is running water, electricity between 6 and 9 pm, and beds with mattresses but no blankets. There is no stove or hearth to cook on but there might be a kerosene (paraffin) stove for hire. Bring your own pots and utensils, and your own sleeping bag.

The *Owen Stanley Lodge* (☎ 25 7999) in Woitape is a small place charging K110/180 a single/double, including meals, snacks, guides for walks, fishing, etc.

In Tapini there is no accommodation at the high school, the Catholic mission or the health centre. Ask around and you might find be able to stay with someone. You should make some small contribution to the household , such as K10 a night.

The small *Tapini Hotel* (☎ 29 9237, PO Box 19, Tapini) is near the airstrip and charges K115 per person, including meals.

ACCESS

There are airstrips in Ononge, Woitape and Tapini. The strip at Kosipe is now closed. TransNiugini Airways (☎ 25 2211 in Port Moresby) flies from Port Moresby to Woitape (K45), Tapini (K65) and many other strips in the area daily except Sunday.

The road linking Tapini to the coast is one of the most breathtaking in the country and is truly spectacular. PMVs leave early from Gordons Market in Port Moresby, but not every day. The five-hour trip to the station costs about K10.

STAGE 1: ONONGE TO WOITAPE VIA URUNA

Walking time: 5¼ hours, 27 km
Overnight: Fatima Catholic mission
From the mission, begin along the road that leads to Woitape. The trail to Uruna and Woitape begins roughly 10 minutes later, on the right, just a few metres past the smaller road that goes up to the community school. It first skirts around the hill on which the school is built, then carries on down the slope towards the Udabe River. A little further down, past a switchback, the trail forks; take the left fork. From here, just follow the trail, which is at times a little overgrown, as it falls steadily down to the river and the steel bridge spanning it. It takes 1¼ hours to reach the bridge from the community school.

Once across the bridge you immediately come to an intersection; the right-hand route leads to Kambisi and the left to Uruna, still 1¾ hours' away. Going left, you walk up the other side of the valley to a point where the overgrown trail becomes impassable. Here, you must continue along the smaller path on the left which is a diversion from the main trail and a short cut. It follows the spur-lines to the next village, and was made by local people who found the mission track too long and winding.

Further on, just before the final climb to Safala, is another small path on the left which quickly takes you back to the main trail. If you can't find this small path, continue to the village and ask someone to steer you in the right direction. Once back on the main trail, Uruna mission, a small Catholic sub-station, is roughly 45 minutes away. From near the church at Uruna you can see the whole upper Udabe Valley, including the mission station at Fatima and the government station at Woitape.

Only fifteen minutes past the Uruna mission sub-station, the village of Uruna proper is reached. From here it's a steady downhill grade as the trail falls gently towards Eru Creek, an hour's walk away, recognisable by its covered bridge. From the creek, it's another hour until the Udabe is crossed again. Close to the crossing, you pass Asuna on the left, built on a small hill. Just past the village, immediately across the river, you get back onto the road linking Ononge and Woitape. From the intersection nearby Fatima can be seen across the road and, as you continue up the valley, it's a 20-minute walk to Woitape.

Alternative Stage 1: Ononge to Woitape via Miku

Walking time: 5½ hours, 30 km
Overnight: Fatima Catholic mission
This route is much easier than the preceding one, as it follows the vehicle road to Woitape. After passing the Ononge school compound on a small hill on the right, a half-hour walk brings you to Yuwenis. At this hamlet, a smaller road branches off to the left; it leads

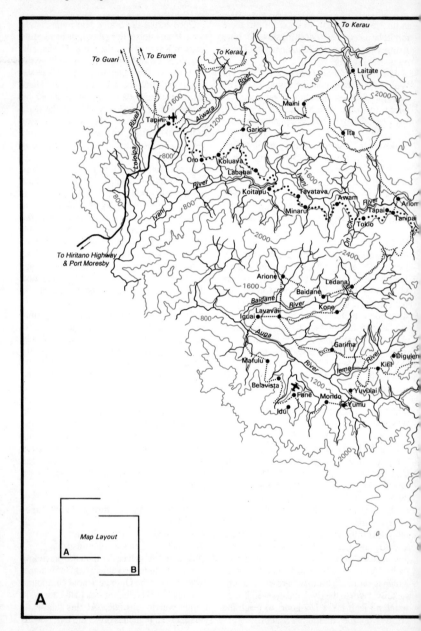

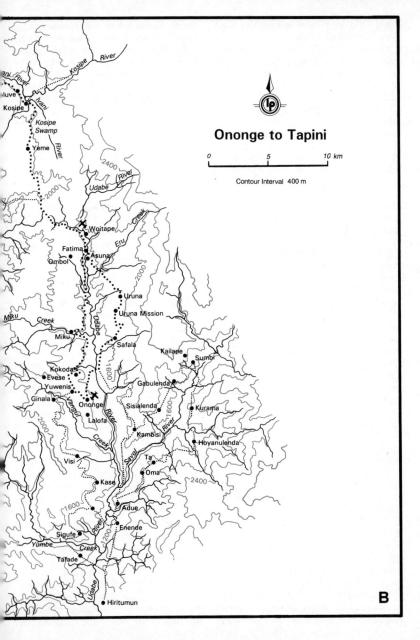

Ononge to Tapini

0   5   10 km

Contour Interval 400 m

B

down the valley to the villages of Visi, Kase, Horo, Sigufe and Tafade.

Continue for half an hour along the mainly level Woitape road to the village of Kokoda (not to be confused with the famous Kokoda in Oro Province). From here, it's a mild but steady two-hour downhill walk to Miku Creek and Miku village. After a mild climb followed by an equally gentle descent, the road levels off as it runs along the Udabe River and draws nearer to Fatima. A couple of streams are passed and further on, to the left-hand side of the road and nearly opposite the Udabe River bridge and the track leading to Uruna, Fatima comes into sight. From Miku to Fatima is a 2½-hour walk. The government station at Woitape is another 20 minutes further up the valley.

STAGE 2: WOITAPE TO TANIPAI
Walking time: 6¼ hours, 36 km
Overnight: Catholic mission's guestroom
Fatima is 20 minutes' walk from the government station at Woitape. From the top end of the airstrip in Woitape take the road on the left and follow it out of the valley towards the summit of the range. The steady, but gentle, climb takes about 1¾ hours. You'll find water at the beginning and end of the climb. At one point along the road there are good views of the upper Udabe Valley, including Woitape and Uruna. Roughly three-quarters of the way up you pass the first turn-off to Fane, another mission station two days' walk to the west. The start of this trail can be hard to find, as it's often hidden by dense grassy vegetation.

At the top of the ridge the road goes through a gap before opening onto the Kosipe Swamp, which it borders for the 45-minute walk to Yeme.

From Yeme, the mission station at Kosipe is 1½ hours' walk away, at the far end of the swamp. The track crosses several small streams and runs parallel to the Ivani River over precipitous mountainsides, for nearly two days, right up to the hamlet of Oro.

In Kosipe, the landing strip is now disused and the mission station is not permanently occupied. Past the school, the road swings

sharply to the left to climb another ridge. Koluve, the next hamlet, is on top of the ridge and is 25 minutes away. Just before reaching Koluve, there are good views of the swamp and of the Ivani and Kosipe rivers.

From here, it's a gentle downhill walk of about 1½ hours to Tanipai. Roughly 20 minutes before Tanipai a second turn-off to Fane is passed on the left, just before a bend. A little further on, and on the same side of the track, you come to the wide but short path that takes you to Tanipai's village square.

Visitors are usually given a small room at the rear of the church. Facilities are basic but private. There are two beds with mattresses, a table and a chair, and water is nearby. You will probably be offered a place to cook in one of the teachers' houses. There are no set charges but a donation is expected. If there's a Father in Kosipe give it to him; if not, give it to Father Duffey in Tapini. You need not give any money to the school teachers.

STAGE 3: TANIPAI TO KOLUAVA
Walking time: 6½ hours, 36 km
Overnight: village accommodation
Immediately on leaving Tanipai, in the direction of Tapai and Tapini, you pass a turn-off on the right to Ariome, Laitate and Maini, villages situated across the Ivani River. Past that intersection, the track continues along a gentle uphill grade and, within 15 minutes, comes to the village of Tapai. From here it continues (still overlooking the Ivani River) past some lovely groves of karuka, for another 25 minutes to Tokio.

From Tokio the track falls gently down to On Creek, then immediately goes up again, along an equally mild grade, to the top of the next spur and the villages of Awam, Kapaleve and Wasilip. Awam is on the left-hand side of the track, Kapaleve is opposite but a little lower down, and Wasilip is a stone's throw away, on the same side as Kapaleve.

An hour further on, you reach Minaru, on a small hill on the left-hand side of the track. From here the path continues along a mainly level grade for another 1½ hours to Koitapu. Just before the village there are dramatic views of the Ivani River as it rages into its junction with the Aiwara River.

Koluava is another 2½ hours' walk away. Past Koitapu, the track immediately descends to the Ivani, crossing it on a log bridge. The climb up the other side of the valley is equally gentle and involves several switchbacks until the hamlet of Lababai is reached. From here, to avoid the nearly vertical walls of the valley, the track continues to climb a little then levels off as it comes to a large, deep ravine. You skirt the ravine to reach the small village of Koluava, on the opposite side and high in the valley, overlooking the Ivani River.

On the right-hand side of the track, just before the school, you'll pass the turn-off to the villages of Garipa, Maini and Laitate.

STAGE 4: KOLUAVA TO TAPINI
Walking time: 2½ hours, 14 km
Overnight: options in Tapini
Just after you leave Koluava, you'll have a breathtaking view of the precipitous country surrounding the junction of the Ivani and Aiwara rivers. From here Oro is reached within half an hour along a gentle downhill grade. A few minutes past this hamlet, there are views of Tapini, situated on a short plateau on the other side of the Aiwara River and still two hours away.

The descent towards the river and the climb up the other side involve a series of switchbacks which considerably lengthen the walk. You could instead take the short cuts the local people have made through the grassy vegetation. The bridge is reached after roughly an hour's walk, and the climb up to Tapini takes about the same amount of time.

The only formal accommodation in Tapini is the expensive *Tapini Hotel* – see the Places to Stay section.

OTHER SUGGESTED WALKS
Woitape to Yongai
There is a large track (built by the Catholic Fathers) linking Woitape and Yongai. It goes via Murray Pass, then the villages of Yoribei, Belavista and Singgo. Murray Pass can be

reached on the first day after a six-hour hike, and Yongai on the second day after seven hours. You will need a guide.

The Father's track is seldom used today and your guide will decide whether you should follow it, or the shorter but more difficult trail that also connects these two areas. There is accommodation at the mission station in Yongai, but it's best to let them know you're coming. Like the other stations in the area, it can be contacted in the mornings and afternoons through the missions' two-way radios.

From Yongai you can walk to Kokoda in Oro Province in two or three days (see the Other Suggested Walks section of the Kokoda Trail chapter). Maps for this walk are the Wasa sheet (8380) of the 1:100,000 topographic map series or the Buna sheet (SC 55-3) of the 1:250,000 map series.

Mt Albert Edward
At 3990 metres Mt Albert Edward is PNG's sixth highest mountain. It can be reached from Woitape in a four-day return trip. Both guides and cold-weather gear are necessary. If you stay at the Owen Stanley Lodge in Woitape they will arrange guides free of charge. Bring your own tent and give the lodge two-weeks' notice. Trips can be arranged via either Murray Pass, Kosipe, or the Neon Basin, the last being probably the most interesting route.

Maps for this walk are the same as for the Ononge to Tapini walk.

Woitape to Fane
The turn-off to Fane is roughly an hour's walk north-west of Woitape, off the main track (see Stage 2 of the Woitape to Tapini walk). The trip, via the villages of Kiril, Yuvulai and Mondo, takes two days. The maps for this walk are the Wasa sheet (8380) of the 1:100,000 topographic map series or the Buna sheet (SC 55-3) of the 1:250,000 map series.

Accommodation is available at the mission station at Fane. There is running water, electricity between 6 and 9 pm, and beds with mattresses. Bedding is not supplied and neither is cooking gear. It is possible, if your party doesn't exceed two or three people, to have meals at the mission. There are no set charges but a donation is expected. It is best to let the Father-in-charge know you are coming. Like the other stations in the area it can be contacted in the mornings and afternoons through the missions' two-way radios. There is an airstrip at Fane.

Tanipai to Fane

The second turn-off to Fane is roughly 20 minutes' walk south-east of Tanipai, off the main track (see Stage 2 of the Woitape to Tapini walk). Fane is reached in two days via the villages of Ledana, Lavavai, Mafulu and Belavista, the first night being spent at Lavavai. The maps for this walk are the same as for the Ononge to Tapini walk.

The Black Cat Track

The Black Cat Track is the route along which hundreds of prospectors travelled from the coast to the goldfields of the Bulolo Valley after the discovery of gold at Koranga Creek in 1922. Today a popular, if arduous, walking trail, the Black Cat Track still links the township of Wau in the Bulolo Valley with Salamaua, a coastal village 35 km south of Lae near the mouth of the Francisco River.

HISTORY

The legendary prospector William 'Sharkeye' Park is credited with the discovery of gold at Koranga Creek, near Wau, in 1922. News of his strike triggered a gold rush that brought, in the 1920s and '30s, hundreds of gold diggers into the Bulolo Valley. Although there were other tracks into the goldfields, most diggers arrived at the newly established port of Salamaua and struggled, sometimes for eight days or more, up the steep ranges along the Black Cat Track to Wau, a mere 50 km inland as the crow flies.

Although Koranga Creek and many other small tributaries of the Bulolo River also bore gold, it's on upper Edie Creek and the Bulolo River that the richest claims were worked. Edie Creek, which rises at 2135 metres and falls into a gully to reach the Bulolo River near Wau, was said to bear gold of a distinctively light colour.

Although quick fortunes were made, it was soon realised that heavy equipment and large investments would be needed. There was no road linking the Bulolo Valley with the coast and the trail from Salamaua up to the goldfields was totally unsuitable for transporting heavy equipment, so the New Guinea Gold Company took the brave step of flying in the equipment.

Salamaua's airstrip at Laugui was only capable of taking small aircraft, so a new airstrip was made in Lae (then only a small mission station). From here, the triple-engined Junkers operated by Guinea Airways flew back and forth to Wau with countless heavy dredge parts that were to be reassembled and put to work at various sites along the Bulolo River. At one time, more air freight was lifted in PNG than in the rest of the world put together!

The goldfields continued to be productive until after the war when the yields fell, gold was pegged at an artificially low price (US$35 an ounce) and the costs of production increased. One by one, the eight huge dredges that operated along the Bulolo River were shut down, the last in 1965. Nevertheless, many individuals still work the fields.

In early '43, the Japanese, reeling from defeats at Milne Bay and on the Kokoda Trail and their naval power devastated in the Battle of the Coral Sea, decided to make one more attempt to take Port Moresby. This time they attacked towards Wau, marching up over the mountains from Salamaua. Australian troops in Wau were quickly reinforced by air from Port Moresby and the Japanese advance was repelled. Salamaua was recaptured later that year.

Lae, Wau, Bulolo and Salamaua were all destroyed during the war and Salamaua was never rebuilt. Today, with its airstrip out of service, it is just a very pretty village.

PEOPLE & CULTURE

Three cultural groups inhabit the country bisected by the trail. The Biangai live in the Bulolo Valley a little upstream from Wau, the Iwal (sometimes called the Kaiwa) occupy an area demarcated by the Kuper and Pioneer ranges, the Buyawem River and a point only a few km inland from the coast, and the Kela live along the coast from Kela Point in the north to Bnoto Point in the south.

To the north of the Iwal live the Yamap. Though the trail doesn't go into Yamap country, this people's lands and gardens can be seen to the north as you walk from the village of Kamoiyatum down towards the Francisco River.

As there has been a long history of European

contact throughout the region, little is left of the original cultures. Traditional clothing has long been discarded and rectangular houses with a two-slope thatched roof are now the preferred style of housing. Along the coast, galvanised iron is commonly used in the construction of houses.

Kaukau is the staple food of the Biangai; taro, kaukau and banana form a significant part of the Iwal diet. Some sago palms and breadfruit trees grow in the Francisco Valley and fish are an important item on the Kela menu. Coconut palms are commonplace in Mubo and along the Francisco River up to the Salamaua Peninsula.

Pidgin is the main lingua franca of the region and is understood by most people.

INFORMATION
Features
Running north-south and towering behind the townships of Wau and Bulolo, the Kuper Range is an imposing barrier between the Bulolo Valley and the Huon Gulf.

From its upper reaches rise some large rivers – notably the Bitoi, Buisavel, Buyawem and Francisco – which, as they follow their easterly courses to the sea, flow through dramatic steep-sided valleys covered with thick vegetation. In the shallow soils of the precipitous slopes, the towering, dark silhouettes of klinkii and hoop pines stand out; otherwise the forests are of mixed broad-leaved trees.

The trail reaches the lowlands by way of the Francisco River, leisurely flowing along a wide, flat valley. Tall, thick clumps of yellow bamboo are very common along this part of the walk.

The last section of the walk, from the mouth of the Francisco River to the nearby village of Salamaua, follows a sandy beach at the foot of the mountains. The walk ends at Salamaua, the name given to both a large village and a peninsula that juts into the Huon Gulf.

Standard
The Black Cat Track between Buidanima and Wapali is fairly hard. There are several

steep scrambles in and out of gullies, and progress along this section is generally slow and often hampered by loose ground, boulders and, on occasions, colonies of salat.

The remainder of the trail is generally easy to walk but caution must be exercised during the numerous crossings of the Bitoi River between Wapali and Mubo. The Francisco River is easily forded at its mouth at low tide; at high tide you may need someone to take you across in an outrigger. Water is plentiful throughout the walk.

Although this walk can be done in either direction, it's strongly recommended that you walk from the mountains down to the coast.

Days Required
The suggested itinerary requires three days to complete the walk, using private transport to the start of the trail near Wau. Alternatively, it can be done as an easy four-day walk.

Season
The rainy season stretches from the end of November to early May. While the average annual rainfall in Wau is in the order of 1600 mm, it is between 2500 and 3000 mm for most areas along the trail, and more as you near the coast. June, July and August are the best months, although May and September can also be quite nice.

The daytime temperatures in Wau often climb in the high 20°Cs, but nights can be quite cold. Temperatures rise steadily as you lose elevation and on the coast near Salamaua they usually hover around 28 to 30°C.

Useful Organisations
There are telephones and a good hospital in Wau, and there might still be a two-way radio in Salamaua. There are lots of trade stores in Wau and Salamaua, but none along the trail.

Guides & Carriers
Guides are not needed between Wau and Bitoi or between Mubo and Salamaua. However, a guide is necessary from Bitoi to

Mubo – without one you haven't got much hope of finding the trail. Between Wapali and Mubo, a guide will ensure safer crossings of the Bitoi River.

Hire a guide either at Black Cat or Bitoi, and make sure he understands you want him to go as far as Mubo, and that you want him to carry on right away and spend the night at Aulak. Say: *Mi laik baim wanpela man bilong soim rot long mi i go inap long Mubo. Mi laik go nau tasol bilong wanem mi laik slip long ples Aulak.* A carrier is a *wanpela kagoboi.*

Expect to pay about K5 per day for a guide who also carries, a little less for a guide who doesn't.

The director of the Wau Ecology Institute can probably help guests find a reliable carrier out of Wau to Bitoi, but it's unlikely that someone from Wau will know the route between Bitoi and Mubo well. Elsewhere along the trail, a carrier, if needed, should not be hard to find. Just ask around. Expect to pay at least K0.50 per hour.

Equipment
Light boots are ideal footwear, and sunscreen and a wide-brimmed hat, mainly for the section from Mubo to Salamaua, are advisable. Since the roof of the shelter at Aulak may not be in good repair, a tarp or a large sheet of plastic should be brought along. Bring some sort of rain gear and a sleeping bag.

Food (kaukau, taros, bananas, etc) should be available in villages along the trail, but should not be depended on. People in Mubo and along the Buirali and Francisco rivers will sell you green coconuts to drink, if someone capable of climbing a tree is available. Bring some small change.

Maps
The map provided in this chapter should be sufficient. For more information, the best maps are the Wau (8283) and Nasau (8383) sheets of the 1:100,000 topographic maps series. The same area is also covered by the Wau (SB 55-14) and Salamaua (SB 55-15) sheets of the 1:250,000 series.

Warning
Lae, which most bushwalkers will visit before and after this walk, is extremely dangerous after dark, and care is required during the day. See Lonely Planet's *Papua New Guinea – a travel survival kit* for more information. Wau and the immediate area have suffered a lot of rascal activity lately. The situation seems to have improved, but be careful. Before taking a PMV between Lae and Wau ask about the current situation, as there was a rash of hold-ups in 1992.

PLACES TO STAY
The *Wau Ecology Institute* (WEI) (☎ 44 6218, fax 44 6381, PO Box 77) is one of the better places in PNG for budget travellers. It's a couple of km out of Wau on the Mt Kaindi road, so get a ride or ask your PMV to take you to the 'ecology' – you'll have a steep walk if you don't.

There are many four-bunk rooms, where you'll pay K15 a night including breakfast, but they are sometimes booked out by groups so it pays to ring before coming. There's also a new accommodation centre where beds in three-bed rooms cost K20. You can use cooking facilities or buy meals; lunch is K5 and dinner K10.

In Salamaua, the *Salamaua Haus Kibung* (☎ 42 3782 for information) was a good place to stay but has been taken over by the provincial government and is falling into disrepair. The rates are supposed to be K20 per person but there are problems with water and food so they are charging only K10.

It's best to take your own food, but there is a local market near the school open from 7 to 8 am on Wednesdays and Saturdays where you can get fresh fruit and fish, and several small trade stores.

ACCESS
Wau is accessible by air and by road. PMVs leave from Eriku in Lae, usually early in the day, and the four-hour trip to Wau costs K5.

A Talair (☎ 42 2630 in Lae) flight from Lae to Wau costs K52. Talair also have a flight from Port Moresby, daily except

Sunday, to Wau which costs K95 (the same as the Port Moresby to Lae fare).

The Black Cat Track starts 14 km from the Wau Ecology Institute (WEI). Although PMVs do not go as far as the very start of the trail, the road leading to it is suitable for motor vehicles and private transport can be arranged. PMVs, if available, are unlikely to drop you any closer than the No 6 Escape Rd junction, half a km or so past the Bulolo River bridge. From there it's 5½ km, mostly along a steady uphill grade, to the start of the trail. Transport can be arranged through the WEI; talk to the director and expect to pay about K5 for the service.

From Salamaua there are irregular boats running to Lae, usually in the morning, for about K5. The trip takes about four hours.

STAGE 1: WAU TO AULAK CREEK SHELTER

Walking time: five hours
Overnight: bush shelter

From the WEI, drive to the start of the Biaru road, on the far side of the airstrip. There's a memorial at the junction. Continue along Biaru Rd for about a km to the No 6 Escape Rd junction, the first road junction on your left as you leave town. Follow the No 6 Escape Rd for about four km until, shortly after the Bulolo River bridge, you come to another major junction.

Go right at this junction and follow the forestry station road for about half a km until you reach a grass-covered track branching off to the left. Take this track and continue on for about five km, past a small junction on the left, until the track forks. This is the start of the Black Cat Track.

Take the right fork and walk along the track for about 45 minutes as it climbs steadily but comfortably, first in the sun then under forest cover, to the top of the range. Here there's a large resting place.

From here, the track continues for a short distance along a crest before it begins to

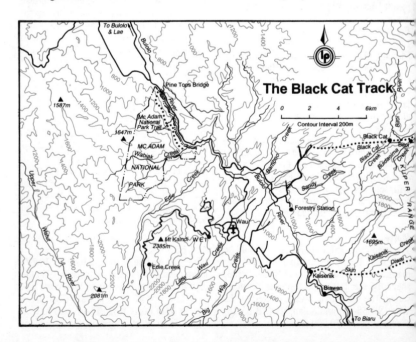

The Black Cat Track

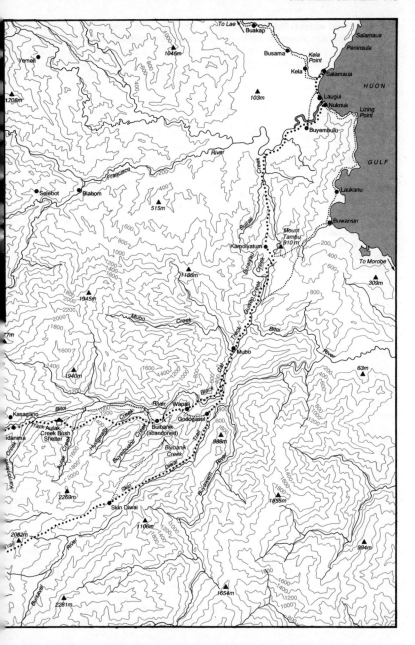

descend gently towards Black Cat. Soon after you begin to go down, the track you've been following ends, and you must continue along the smaller trail that clearly branches off on the left. Further down, a little past the grassy areas (from where views of the Black Cat Valley can be obtained) you reach Black Cat, nowadays also known as Niu Kem (New Camp). The walk from the top of the range down to Black Cat takes half an hour.

The main village is to the right of the trail, which continues straight ahead, passing a few houses, then down the right arm of a fork to the Black Cat Creek. You can drink from the creek but only upstream from where the trail meets it; downstream it is polluted by nearby small stream.

The trail continues down Black Cat Creek, crossing it 11 times, then reaches the Bitoi River which it follows to Bitoi, a small, rather dull place by the river and 15 minutes' walk from Black Cat.

At Bitoi find yourself a guide if you haven't yet got one, then carry on, past some gardens and several small groups of houses, until the trail drops into the shallow, eight-metre-wide Bitoi River. From here you can continue beside the river or in the riverbed.

The river is crossed 13 times, then you begin to climb steadily and steeply up a small ridge, at the top of which the hamlet of Buidanima comes into sight. It takes 1¼ hours to walk from Bitoi to Buidanima.

After Buidanima the trail passes through gardens then forest, then drops to the shallow, four-metre-wide Kamonlewe Creek, which it follows down until it meets the Bitoi River. This is followed by a short scramble out of the gully, from where the often narrow and difficult trail, continues along the contours, over several small streams, until it reaches an area of kunai overlooking the Bitoi and Aulak valleys.

Somewhere around here, either at the top of the kunai clearing or a short distance away under the forest cover, you should find at least one small bush shelter. These are built and maintained by the people of Bitoi who regularly come here to hunt and tend to their small plantations of betel nut. Your guide

will show you where to find water. It takes 2¼ hours to walk from Buidanima to the Aulak Creek shelter, the overnight stop.

STAGE 2: AULAK CREEK SHELTER TO MUBO

Walking time: 6¼ hours
Overnight: village accommodation
A trail beginning near the Aulak Creek shelter follows the Bitoi River down to its confluence with the Buyeibuanir Creek, then follows the creek up to its junction with the Black Cat Track. This route might be shorter but it is much more difficult. It follows the riverbed and in many places there is deep water, and lots of scrambling over slippery rocks and ledges is involved. Don't let your guide take you that way.

From the Aulak Creek shelter to Wapali, there is a sequence of spurs alternating with small and shallow streams. From the shelter, the trail descends for 20 minutes then fords Aulak Creek. After a steep climb it negotiates a series of mild ups and downs before it drops into a second creek, the Hudgwalbi, reached 1½ hours later.

It follows the Hudgwalbi down to its junction with the tiny Buyengo stream. The trail then swings sharply to the right, climbs steeply out of the ravine and follows the contours before it eventually opens onto a small kunai clearing. From here you can see the steep-sided Buyeibuanir Valley, your first view of the ocean and, straight ahead on the next spur, the old village site of Buibanik.

From the clearing, Buyeibuanir Creek is reached after an hour's walk. After fording this third stream, the narrow and difficult trail climbs steeply to the top of the next spur and reaches, after 20 minutes, the old village site of Buibanik, recognisable by its one house and the dense secondary growth.

A descent, mild at first then steeper, takes you down to a fourth stream, the Buibanik. Then there's an easy 40-minute climb, over several streams and past a trail junction leading to the Skin Diwai Trail, to the top of the next spur. From here there are beautiful views. To the west a fine panorama opens onto the dramatic Bitoi Valley; to the east the

Top Left: Necklace made from boar's tusks and cassowary bones (RE)
Top Right: Woman returning from market (JB)
Bottom: Lake Kutubu from Wasemi village, Southern Highlands Province (YP)

Top Left: Typical *haus pekpek* (toilet) (JB)
Top Right: Mendi man, Southern Highlands Province (YP)
Bottom: The Sui Valley from Wailep, Enga Province (YP)

Buisavel Valley stretches out amidst a wild tangle of mountains; straight ahead you can see the dark blue ocean.

Following this spur-line down, you reach Wapali in about 10 minutes. The bell in the church here is made from a WW II shell. From the village square you can see the neighbouring village of Godogasul, on another ridge to the east,

The remaining part of this stage, the walk up to Mubo, looks quite different. Leaving from the lower part of Wapali, the trail descends gently to the small Puipui Creek and, after following the creek for a short distance, drops sharply down to the Bitoi River, reached 20 minutes later.

From here the path essentially follows the Bitoi until it reaches Mubo village roughly two hours later. The route is easy but you have to cross the river seven times. A bridge of sorts might help at the first crossing but all the others are fords, the first four through a very strong, swift current. Past the so-called Mubo Gorge, the river is wider and much quieter.

Mubo, the proposed overnight stop, is situated at the confluence of the Bitoi River and Mubo Creek.

STAGE 3: MUBO TO SALAMAUA
Walking time: 5½ hours
Overnight: Salamaua Haus Kibung

Mubo to Kamoiyatum
Walking time: 2¼ hours
The trail begins at the Mubo school compound and leaves the village from the bottom right corner of the soccer pitch; from here, it continues to follow the river down.

Further on a little, after crossing a small stream, the path seems to end at a small promontory; look around it and you'll find a narrow walkway that will help you get across to the other side. Further still, past some old gardens where you'll need to take care not to trip on fallen trees hidden in the grass, the trail takes you back to the riverbank.

A second stream is crossed and, still a little further, where the Bitoi River make a 90° curve, you can see, on the left, the mouth of Guisep Creek (see the map of Guisep Creek

& Bitoi River Junction). The walk from Mubo to here takes half an hour.

The trail travels up the gravel bed of this small and shallow creek to its headwaters. There are, however, several short cuts through the forest which bypass long or obstructed bends.

Numerous merging streams are passed, that are larger at first then smaller. Eventually, you walk past two small waterfalls trickling down the right-hand wall of a small gorge. A little further on, roughly an hour's walk up from the mouth of the creek, the trail comes to a point where two streams merge

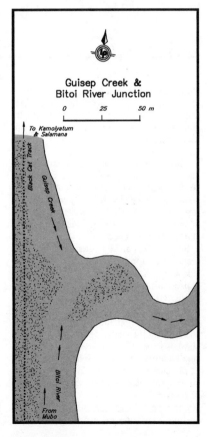

Guisep Creek & Bitoi River Junction

0   25   50 m

To Kamoiyatum & Salamana

Black Cat Track

Guisep Creek

Bitoi River

From Mubo

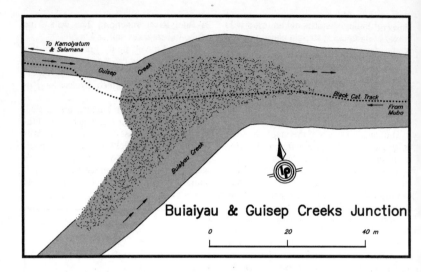

Buiaiyau & Guisep Creeks Junction

together, forming the letter 'Y'. The Buiaiyau, the larger of the two, is on the left; straight ahead, partly hidden and much smaller, is the Guisep, which you must keep following up. (See the map of the Buiaiyau & Guisep Creeks Junction).

This junction is not very obvious but if you pay attention to the signs mentioned before, particularly the small gorge, you should not have any difficulty in finding it. If you miss it you'll find yourself at the foot of a waterfall further up Buiaiyau Creek, about 20 minutes later.

Roughly half an hour after that junction, a second junction is reached. The right-hand side is the Kalangat and on the left is the Guisep, which you must keep following up. Hardly 40 metres up from that second junction, just before a large clump of bamboo and a bend in the stream, the trail leaves the creek and climbs up a small ridge on the right. The climb is steep at first, then easier. You pass a small intersection on the right-hand side and 15 minutes later reach the village of Kamoiyatum, also called Niu Kem (New Camp) or Kamoiyatum No 2.

Growing here are, among others things, coconut and betel nut palms, banana and breadfruit trees and a type of shrub whose fruits resemble those of a lychee. If you break open this fruit you'll find seeds which, when mixed with water, produce a red dye that is commonly used for body adornment.

The coast can be seen from Kamoiyatum but Salamaua is concealed behind a hill. To the north, along a trail that links Bulolo to the coast, is Yamap country.

Kamoiyatum to Salamaua

Walking time: 3¼ hours

After leaving Kamoiyatum, the trail climbs a little, and behind you are views of the Guisep Valley. The trail continues along the side of Mt Tambu, the site of a fierce WW II battle, and comes to a small stream. Fill your water bottle here, as there is no more drinking water until you reach the Francisco River, 1½ hours away.

Growing beside this stream are two sago palms and, about 15 metres away and by another stream, there are coconut palms. It is interesting to compare these two species of palm trees which, to many people, look nearly alike.

Continuing by some gardens, new and old, the trail eventually begins a steady descent down a spur-line to the lowlands. Lovely views of the coast, the Francisco Valley and Yamap country to the north-west can be enjoyed during the descent.

You'll see more sago and coconut palms, as well as breadfruit trees, when you come to a small, grassy plot, just before you reach the Buirali Creek. The creek is polluted by villages and cattle, so don't drink from it. Follow the creek down for 40 minutes until you come to the Francisco River.

The Francisco River is called Buyut by the Iwal people and Areng Wili by the Kela. On the right-hand side, at the confluence of the Buirali Creek and the Francisco River, the trail continues through a small clearing surrounded by clumps of bamboo. From here the route follows the river down for about 1½ hours, to the coastal village of Nuknuk.

Soon after the confluence you can see the Salamaua Peninsula on the left. Further on, as you walk past a large, sandy flat that stretches out to the foot of the mountains, you pass a small trail on the right which leads to Buyembulu. Further on again, close to the coast, mountains obstruct the way as they plunge directly into the river. At low tide, you can wade past and continue to Nuknuk village, but at high tide you have to follow the trail as it climbs up the side of the hill, then follows along the contours until the first houses are reached.

Nuknuk is on a beach between Lizing Point and the Francisco River; Salamaua is

on the opposite side of the river. At low tide you can easily wade across. If the water is high, you'll have to pay someone to take you across in an outrigger canoe. Expect to pay between K0.50 and K1 for the service. Once on the other side it's a 15-minute walk along the beach, through the village of Laugui, to a narrow isthmus and Salamaua.

OTHER SUGGESTED WALKS
Skin Diwai Trail

Also called the Buisavel Track, the Skin Diwai Trail, like the Black Cat Track, links Wau with Salamaua. Beginning about eight km up the valley from Wau at the Biangai village of Kaisenik, it passes over the Kuper Range, through the hamlet of Skin Diwai then the village of Godogasul, before it meets with the Black Cat Track near the village of Mubo.

Like the Black Cat, it takes three days to walk and offers good views at the beginning and end, with a rather dull and monotonous middle section. Although a little longer than the Black Cat Track, the Skin Diwai Trail is much easier to walk as it follows the surveyed route of a proposed road to the coast, and does not require much physical fitness. However, a guide is necessary for the first half of the walk to Godogasul. One can be recruited in Kaisenik. Hire him right through to Godogasul, as there might not be anyone in Skin Diwai. Take a tent fly, a tarp or a large piece of plastic as you might have to camp at Skin Diwai. Water is plentiful throughout the walk.

The first stage of the walk is a climb over the Kuper Range, reaching Skin Diwai from Kaisenik. From Kaisenik the trail climbs comfortably, for the first hour over dry kunai ridges then through cool mountain forest, to the summit of the range (1900 metres). This takes about 3½ hours. From the summit, the trail drops steadily for three hours, still through forest and over many streams, to Skin Diwai (1550 metres), the site of a small cattle project and half a dozen or so houses.

The second stage of the walk takes you to Godogasul then Mubo. Along the way you'll see precipitous mountainsides as the trail continues high above and along the deep valley of the Buisavel River until it reaches, roughly six hours later, the village of Godogasul (700 metres). There are dramatic views of the Buisavel and Bitoi valleys from the village. Mubo and Wapali can also be seen; Mubo down the Bitoi Valley, a little beyond the so-called Mubo Gorge, and Wapali high on a ridge to the north-west.

From Godogasul the trail drops steeply down to the Bitoi River and, after 35 minutes, meets with the Black Cat Track, coming from Wau by way of Bitoi and Wapali. From here the route is the same as for the Black Cat Track, with an overnight stop at Mubo and another day's walk to Salamaua.

The maps listed in the Black Cat Track section can also be used for the Skin Diwai Trail.

Salamaua to Lae

It is possible to walk along the beach between Salamaua and Lae, taking two days to cover the 45 km or so. Time your walk so that you arrive in Lae well before dark, when things become very dangerous, and ask about the current situation before you set out.

Two major rivers must be crossed, the Buang and the Markham. You can wade across the first but you must definitely get a boat across the second; agree on a price first (about K1).

Closer to Lae, the Labu Lakes, fringed with mangroves, are fairly interesting. Of greater interest are the leatherback turtles which come ashore from the end of November until early February along the beaches around Maus Buang and Labu Tali to dig deep nests and lay eggs.

A small, bush-material rest house may have now been built in Maus Buang, otherwise you can find accommodation at the school. Expect to pay around K10. This includes a contribution to the turtle guide and a donation to the conservation fund set up by lecturers from Lae Unitech. Maus Buang is five hours' walk from Lae.

Maps for this walk are the Nadzab (8284), Wau (8283) and Nasau (8383) sheets of the 1:100,000 topographic map series, or the Salamaua (SB 55-15) and Markham (SB 55-10) sheets of 1:250,000 map series.

McAdam National Park

Set back from the Wau-Bulolo road and fronting the Bulolo River gorge, McAdam National Park was established in 1962 to preserve the region's last virgin stands of hoop and klinkii pine. As well as these giant trees, the area is rich in cedar, silkwood, New Guinea oak, New Guinea beech and a wide range of smaller plants such as bamboo, ferns, various types of vines, and many varieties of orchids. More than 200 species of birds have been recorded in the park.

The disturbances in the Wau area have meant that this walk is sometimes unsafe. The WEI should have current information. The WEI can usually drive visitors to McAdam and back for K5. If you drive yourself to the start of the trail, don't leave your vehicle unattended by the side of the road. Find someone living nearby to leave it with, and pay them a kina or two when you get back.

A wide, well-defined road crosses the park. Marked by a sign on the side of the Wau-Bulolo road, it begins some 250 metres north of the Pine Tops bridge, the second and last bridge over the Bulolo River when

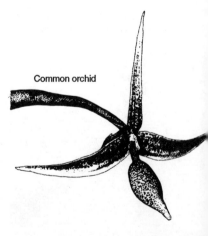

Common orchid

driving from Wau towards Lae. From the trail it climbs steadily at first then follows along the contours, past some gardens and through secondary forest, until it reaches a first stream. From here, the walk is much more interesting, with giant pines and more luxuriant vegetation.

The trail then runs above the Bulolo River, overlooking it for some distance, before it finally ends shortly after it begins to follow Wabiak Creek, a tributary of the Bulolo River. From here you have to head back to the start of the trail. Allow a little over four hours for the walk.

For further information on the park write to: the Ranger, National Park, PO Box 127, Bulolo, Morobe Province. The Wau (8283) sheet of the 1:100,000 topographic map series is the best for the park and the surrounding area.

The Sarawaget Massif

Dominated by Mt Bangeta and Mt Sarawaget, respectively PNG's third and fourth-highest mountains, the Sarawaget Massif is situated at the eastern end of the Sarawaget Range north of Lae.

Moderately easy to climb, the massif offers the walker a reasonable challenge and a good opportunity to discover both PNG's mountain-climbing conditions (although no technical climbing is required) and the high country's unique vegetation and fauna.

In addition to visiting the massif, this walk crosses the whole width of the Sarawaget Range, from Samanzing, a village inland from Lae, to Tipsit, a small community near Kabwum on the northern side of the range.

HISTORY

Traditional trade routes, running north-south across the range, have existed for a very long time. One such route crossed via the Kwama and Melambi rivers, with Sio pots from the north coast traded south and stone axe-heads traded north from the Wain country near Boana, north-west of Lae.

The Germans, during the years of their administration, made several exploratory trips into the Sarawaget Range from the north coast. Early European ascents of the massif include climbs of Mt Sarawaget by Keysser in 1913 and by Lane-Poole in 1925.

PEOPLE & CULTURE

Two cultural groups inhabit the area bisected by the trail. The Mosem people occupy the country around Samanzing, extending as far east as Zezagi; the Komba live in the foothills around Iloko and Tipsit, and north to within a few km of the coast near Sio.

Gardening is an important activity. Kaukau and taro are the staple foods, but cabbages, European potatoes, pumpkins and a wide variety of greens are also grown. Coffee is an important cash crop, and oranges abound in many of the villages.

Wallabies are common on the upland grasslands, and the people from the highest villages in the valleys commonly hunt on the slopes and summit plateau. Various communities lay special claim to the mountain, including the Zitali in Melambi Valley, the Iloko in Kwama Valley, the Honziuknan in Timbe Valley and the Ksituen in Tuembi Valley. Traditional clothing is not worn anymore, and many houses are built from non-traditional materials.

INFORMATION
Features

Towering behind the city of Lae, between the Markham Valley to the south and the Vitiaz Strait to the north, the Sarawaget Range originates near the headwaters of the Leron River near Wantoat in Morobe Province and extends for approximately 70 km east towards the Cromwell Mountains and the Huon Peninsula.

The Sarawaget Massif is mainly limestone and stands at the eastern end of the range. Dominated by Mt Bangeta and Mt Sarawaget, which at 4212 and 4020 metres are PNG's third and fourth-highest mountains, this large massif takes the form of a great, grassy plateau dotted with numerous tarns and sink holes.

Several large rivers rise high on the massif. They include the south-draining Melambi, Tuembi and Sanem rivers (all tributaries of the Busu), the east-draining Mana River (a tributary of the Mongi) and the north-draining Timbe and Kwama rivers. Kwama, a large river which flows into the sea near Wasu, has its source in Lake Guam, the lowest point on the massif plateau (about 3500 metres).

Standard

This walk can be described as moderately easy. No technical climbing is required, and anyone with a reasonable degree of fitness should be able to make it to the summit. The trail is well marked and easy to follow from the massif plateau down to Iloko, but some sections up from Zitali are more difficult to follow. The grade is steady and the route gains some 2300 metres up to the massif, losing them on the descent to Iloko.

However, the altitude and the climate must be respected, and proper preparation is essential to avoid serious trouble.

A party of at least two is recommended for the ascent of Mt Bangeta or Mt Sarawaget. Neither mountain should be underestimated. The weather at the top is very cold and highly changeable, and the summit can easily become fogbound. Snow can occur, although it is usually restricted to above 4000 metres.

Exposure can be a problem, whether it is from the intense sunlight or the cold. A combination of wind, wet clothing, fatigue and hunger, even if the air temperature is well above freezing, can lead to hypothermia. (See the Health section in the Facts for the Bushwalker chapter.) Likewise, you can burn deceptively quickly. There is less atmospheric protection at higher altitudes and the fact you're not hot doesn't mean you're not cooking.

As well as the weather, beware of altitude sickness, which is potentially extremely dangerous. Most climbers will suffer some degree of altitude sickness, and it is essential that you are familiar with the symptoms so you can assess the degree to which you are affected. See the Health section in the Facts for the Bushwalker chapter.

Days Required

The suggested itinerary takes four days. The route described here takes you over the top of the massif, but does not climb Mt Sarawaget or Mt Bangeta. These two mountains lie a little to the east of the proposed route. The first can be reached within 1½ hours from the trail, the second is four or five hours away and is reached by following the southern rim of the plateau. A more interesting trip would be to spend an extra day or two camping on the grasslands. This would allow you ample time to ascend either mountain, and wander around and explore the area.

This walk can be done either way, but it is recommended that you walk from south to north as guides are often reluctant to go any farther than the summit plateau and you may have to complete the second half of the walk without them. Unlike the trail up from Samanzing to the massif, the route down to Iloko is well defined and can be followed on your own.

Season

It can be very cold up on the massif. There is little natural shelter on the plateau, and strong cold winds are often blowing. Frosts occur above 2700 metres, and there are occasional snowfalls above 4000 metres. Rain is frequent, and mist can reduce visibility to nil. Daytime temperatures can be quite warm in Samanzing and Tipsit, but drop as you climb. The wet season is from November to March, and the rain can be heavy and abundant. Clear weather is likeliest in June, July and August, but May and September can also be quite nice.

While rain still occurs in the dry season, it is more frequent in the wet and tends to come earlier in the day. Temperatures during the rainy season, however, are not as low and the atmosphere is usually relatively haze-free. The dry season's haze means that views to the coast are less likely.

You're advised to make a very early start if you plan to climb one of the mountains. As on most high mountains in PNG, the sky around Mt Bangeta and Mt Sarawaget is usually clear in the early morning, with fog lying low in the valleys. By around eight or nine, the rising temperatures cause the fog to lift and large cloud formations gather at higher altitudes, enveloping the peaks. Later in the day, generally between 11 am and mid-afternoon, intermittent mist and showers may occur, often persisting until about sunset. The evening usually sees the cloud masses descend again to the valleys, and by midnight the skies are clear.

Useful Organisations

There are health centres and two-way radios in Samanzing and Kabwum. There are small trade stores in Samanzing, Iloko, Tipsit and Kabwum.

Guides & Carriers

A guide is not needed from Samanzing to Zitali, but one is necessary from Zitali up to the summit plateau. Both guides and carriers should be recruited in Zitali, as the Samanzing people don't have ownership rights to the mountain. They can be a little hard to recruit though, and are often reluctant to go any farther that the plateau itself. However, the route from the plateau down to Iloko is quite clear and it is not too difficult to follow it on your own, though it is still best to have a guide.

Since most visitors are not acclimatised to the altitude, carriers are strongly recommended. Expect to pay about K7 a day, and be prepared to spend a day negotiating their hiring.

Equipment

A comfortable, light pair of boots is recommended for this walk. You'll also need a warm sleeping bag (rated below 0°C) and cold-weather gear, including long trousers, a hat, a pair of gloves and a warm jacket. Rain gear is also essential, and a pair of nylon over-trousers is recommended for extra comfort in wet weather.

A compass and a copy of the Kabwum (8385) sheet of the 1:100,000 topographic map series are strongly recommended, and a camping stove as well as a large piece of plastic for waterproofing bush shelters along the trail are advisable. Sunglasses will come in handy. You should take a water bottle and some warm clothing for your guide or carrier. There are no bush shelters on the plateau itself and you will need a tent if you plan to camp on the grasslands or climb Mt Bangeta or Mt Sarawaget.

Local fruits and vegetables are usually available in Samanzing, Zitali, Iloko and Tipsit, but don't depend on them. Carry most of your food and bring extra rations in case the weather turns bad. Lightweight dried food is best. It can get very cold at the top, and you can easily be fogbound. It is vital that you have sufficient food and warm clothing and that you assess the weather and your physical state realistically.

Maps

The Kabwum (8385) sheet of the 1:100,000 topographic map series is the best map. The Huon (SB 55-11) sheet of the 1:250,000 series also covers the area described by the walk.

Warning

Lae, which most bushwalkers will visit before and after this walk, is extremely dangerous after dark, and care is required during the day. See Lonely Planet's *Papua New Guinea – a travel survival kit* for more information.

PLACES TO STAY

There is a wide range of accommodation in Lae. The YMCA's big *Haus Buabling* (☎ 42 4412, fax 42 2654, PO Box 1055) on Cassowary St is secure, clean enough and near the city centre. At K12 for a small single room, including breakfast and a good dinner, it's a bargain.

A few km from town (you'll need to take a PMV) the *Lutheran Guesthouse* (☎ 42 2556, PO Box 80) is at Ampo on Busu Rd, opposite the Balob Teachers' College. It's also very good, and it's a peaceful place. Bed and breakfast costs K25, with three good meals it's K33. The rooms are shared.

ACCESS

Samanzing is accessible by a short flight from Nadzab (Lae). MAF (☎ 42 1555 in Lae) flies on Tuesday and Thursday for K32, and Kiunga Aviation (☎ 42 6488) also has flights, mainly charter.

From the end of the walk at Tipsit, take a PMV down to Kabwum for K1. From there you can get a flight back to Lae or take another PMV to Wasu on the coast (about K5). Lutheran Shipping (☎ 42 2066, fax 42 5806) has passenger vessels which call in at Wasu on the run between Lae and Wewak, via Madang. Madang-bound boats currently depart from Wasu on Wednesday; Lae-

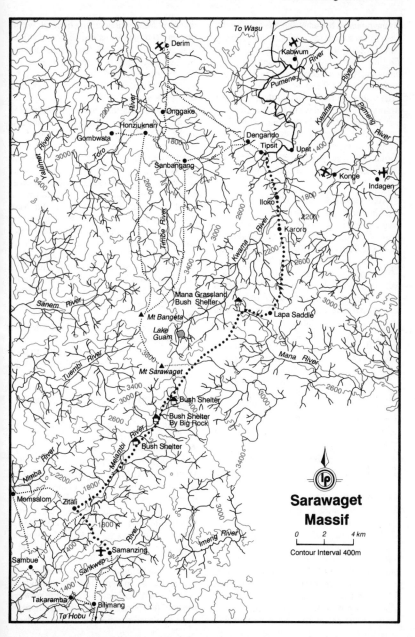

Sarawaget Massif

0   2   4 km

Contour Interval 400m

bound boats on Monday, but this can change. Deck/tourist class fares are K14.50/22 to Lae and K12/18 to Madang. There are also slightly cheaper passenger-carrying cargo boats, but their schedules are less reliable.

Talair (☎ 42 2630 in Lae) is the main carrier serving Kabwum and there are daily flights (except Sunday) to Lae for K45.

You can also walk to Samanzing from Lae. The trail starts at the end of the road at Hobu and requires eight steady, non-stop hours to cover. See the Other Suggested Walks section at the end of this chapter.

STAGE 1: SAMANZING TO ZITALI

Walking time: three hours

Overnight: village accommodation

From Samanzing (1737 metres) take the main track out of the village and follow it for a short distance until it forks. The right fork goes to the community school, take the left fork to Zitali. The wide and well-marked path, takes you over a ridge before it begins an easy descent down to the Melambi River and the bridge spanning it. As you go down, Zitali can be seen on the other side of the valley. Halfway down to the river the path takes you through a small hamlet and then continues more steeply down to the river.

On the opposite bank of the Melambi there are two different routes up to Zitali. One begins some 30 metres or so downstream from the bridge and goes steeply up to the main village; the other starts some 20 metres upstream and, after beginning as a climb, takes you more gently up to the village soccer pitch.

STAGE 2: ZITALI TO BUSH SHELTER

Walking time: nine hours

Overnight: bush shelter

The trail leaves Zitali (1700 metres) from the soccer pitch and continues along the contours, high on the left-hand side of the Melambi River until, after reaching a prominent flat area, it descends to the river and follows it for 100 metres or so to a small tributary. From here, after following the tributary for roughly the same distance, it

crosses it and continues close to the river for another 30 minutes to a bridge.

Across the river the trail immediately climbs a steep spur between the river and a parallel tributary. The going is hard at first but after 1½ hours it levels off a little and the walking is easier.

At the end of that section, before you descend to another small stream (a tributary of the Melambi), you go past a couple of bush shelters. These may or may not be in a good state of repair. If they still stand and you've had it, you can call it a day here. However, it is recommended that you continue for another hour to a cosier shelter.

As you come to the first shelters the trail forks; take the left fork and descend for 15 minutes until you reach another small creek. As you continue on from the creek, the path takes you back down to the river and, within 20 minutes, recrosses it. On the opposite side, and just after a steep but short climb over a bluff, one more creek is reached. This creek, also a tributary of the Melambi, descends from the V-cleft (called the *ai bilong maunten*) which penetrates to the summit plateau just east of Mt Sarawaget.

There, beside the stream and in the shelter of a large rock, you'll find the other bush-material hut.

STAGE 3: BUSH SHELTER TO MANA GRASSLAND

Walking time: 9½ hours

Overnight: bush shelter

From the shelter follow the stream up, criss-crossing it and avoiding narrow places by going up the valley sides until, roughly 1½ hours later, the path swings to the right and goes up a steep, narrow gully. From here, as it continues to climb, the path takes you through thick moss forest and, a couple of hours later, reaches yet another small shelter at the base of a large tree.

From this last shelter the path continues to go up through moss forest until it returns to the stream. From here it climbs steeply out to the right of the cleft to reach the plateau rim at 3700 metres within 2½ hours. This is a good point from which to begin a climb up either Mt Sarawaget or Mt Bangeta. The first lies just to the west of here and is reached within 1½ hours; the second is four or five hours away and is reached by following the southern rim of the plateau. On the summit grassland, follow the path in a north-easterly direction for 1¼ hours until you are just west of a small hill. As you cross it, check out the nice views over the high uplands at the head of the Mongi River. A well-marked track takes you down into a small clearing with tarns. From here it continues more steeply through forest to reach an open grassland at the head of the Mana River 2¼ hours later.

Somewhere nearby is the bush shelter where it is recommended you spend the night.

STAGE 4: MANA GRASSLAND TO TIPSIT

Walking time: seven hours
Overnight: village accommodation in Iloko
Having reached the Mana River and followed it down for some 20 minutes to a narrow ravine, the path climbs out to the left and continues up into moss forest. Forty-five minutes later, after having sidled to the left of a big hill, it brings you to a bush saddle high above the Kwama Valley at 3100 metres. Known as Lapa, the saddle offers views of the Kwama Valley and Iloko. This natural feature – and resting place – can be seen from Iloko. From here the route continues on a beautiful track with easy grades as it descends for 3¾ hours to the hamlet of Karoro (2000 metres). Iloko, a large and

friendly village with a trade store, and Tipsit, the final destination, are now respectively one and two hours' walk away, across the Kwama River.

OTHER SUGGESTED WALKS
Hobu to Samanzing

Hobu is the closest of the four roadheads to Lae, and is served by irregular PMVs. Eight hours of steady non-stop walking are required to walk this route, which passes through the hamlet of Tusilu and the villages of Kalau and Bilimang. At the last village the track divides; the path to the west runs to Takaramba and Sambue, and the north path continues to Samanzing and Zitali.

Maps for this walk are the Malahang (8384) and Kabwum (8385) sheets of the 1:100,000 topographic map series, or the Huon (SB 55-11) sheet of the 1:250,000 map series. Hobu does not appear on these maps; its position, however, is basically the same as that of the village marked as Kwapsanek.

Other Routes to Mt Bangeta

There are several other tracks leading up to Mt Bangeta but they are more difficult and guides and carriers may not be as easy to recruit. Two of them leave from around Derim on the northern side of the range and follow the Timbe River up; one from the village of Honziuknan, the other from nearby Sanbangang. A third track leaves from Ksituen, a village in the upper Tuembi Valley, and follows the Tuembi River up the mountain.

Mt Wilhelm

Mt Wilhelm is PNG's highest mountain. Rising to 4509 metres, the peak is the most northern summit of an extensive massif that stands astride the Bismarck Range and the Sepik-Wahgi Divide. Situated north-west of Kegsugl in the Simbu Province, it's also PNG's most accessible high mountain. Its great height, relative ease of access and the grandeur of the area make it a must for any visitor to PNG.

The ascent offers the walker a fair challenge and an excellent introduction to the Simbu people and the Highlands in general. The drive up the dramatic Simbu Gorge is spectacular, and the magnificent views from the summit are unforgettable.

HISTORY

The first European ascent of Mt Wilhelm was made in August 1938 by LG Vial, a government officer, and two Papua New Guineans whose names have been forgotten. The mountain received its European name in 1888 when Hugo Zöller, a German newspaper correspondent, and three other Europeans made the first ascent of the Finisterre Range south-east of Madang. From the top of the mountains the party saw the Bismarck Range and Zöller named its four highest peaks after the German chancellor and his children: Ottoberg, Herbertberg, Mariaberg and Wilhelmberg.

Mt Wilhelm is now a National Park. No hunting is allowed, no plants can be picked and no trees can be felled.

PEOPLE & CULTURE

The name Simbu refers to all the tribal groups who live in Simbu Province. It derives from the word *simbu*, which means 'very pleased'. The story goes that when the first Europeans walked through their valleys in the '30s, the locals were very pleased at the gifts they were being given and responded by saying *simbu, simbu*! Not knowing what that meant, the strangers named the area Simbu, which was temporarily corrupted to Chimbu, and finally changed back to Simbu.

The Kuman language is spoken throughout the Simbu Valley, around Kerowagi and in Kundiawa. Seven other languages are spoken in highland Simbu and there are several distinct dialects, especially south of the Highlands Highway.

INFORMATION
Features

The Wilhelm Massif is an enormous mass of rock culminating in several peaks rising well above 4300 metres. Its covers an area of more than 100 sq km and feeds the country's major river systems, the north-draining Ramu and Sepik, and the south-draining Purari.

The whole area underwent glaciation 15,000 years ago. Ice covered the massif, carved the valleys and formed the Pindaunde Lakes, headwaters of the valley of the same name. About 6½ km long, the Pindaunde Valley extends from Kegsugl to the base of an impressive cirque (semi-circular rock formation) that towers high above Lake Aunde, the upper of the two Pindaunde lakes. The valley is littered with morainic debris and colonies of prehistoric-looking tree ferns grow on its hummocky floor.

Lake Aunde discharges into Lake Piunde in a 90-metre cascade. Both lakes are flanked by Imbuka Ridge to the north and Bogunolto Ridge, Wilhelm's south ridge, to the west. Many large blocks of stone, left behind by the retreating ice, can be seen in and around Lake Piunde.

Standard

Considering the height of the mountain, this walk can be described as moderately easy. No technical climbing is required, and anyone with a reasonable degree of fitness should be able to make it to the summit.

However, the grade is a steady uphill and

the climb is very steep in places. The ascent is also made more difficult by the rarefied air, and most climbers will suffer some degree of altitude sickness. This is usually only annoying, but can be extremely dangerous.

Altitude sickness becomes noticeable at around 3000 metres, becomes more pronounced at 3700, and then requires adjustments at each further 500 metres of additional elevation. See the Health section of the Facts for the Bushwalker chapter.

A party of at least two is recommended for the ascent. Mt Wilhelm should not be underestimated. The weather at the top is very cold and highly changeable, and the summit can easily become fogbound. Snow can also be experienced, though it is usually restricted to above 4000 metres.

The route follows a road from the Kegsugl high school to the bridge over Komanemambuno Creek, then a well-marked trail to the Pindaunde Hut and Lake Aunde. A route marked with cairns and yellow, white, red, orange and blue markers painted on the larger stones leads from there to the summit. Water is plentiful from Kegsugl to the hut, but difficult to find between the second lake and the summit.

Days Required

Though the walk can be completed in two days, it is recommended that you take three or four. A two-day walk means that you get to the Pindaunde Hut the first day then reach the summit and walk back down to Kegsugl on the second day. This is both less interesting and less safe than taking an extra day or two.

A more sensible timetable is to reach the hut on the first day, climb the mountain on the next and walk back down to Kegsugl on the third day. It is even better to stay an extra day at the hut acclimatising to the altitude before you ascend the summit.

Season

It can be very cold up on the mountain. There is little natural shelter at the top and strong, cold winds are often blowing. Frosts occur above 2700 metres and there are occasional snowfalls above 4000 metres. Rain is frequent and mist can suddenly turn visibility to nil.

The dry season in the Highlands stretches from May to October, and the best months for a visit to Mt Wilhelm are definitely June, July, August and September. November to April are the wettest months. About 2600 mm of rain falls annually at the Pindaunde Hut.

While rain does fall in the dry season, it is more frequent in the wet and tends to come earlier in the day. However, temperatures are higher in the rainy season and the atmosphere is usually relatively haze-free, allowing views to the coast. These views are less likely in the hazy dry season.

As on most high mountains in PNG, the sky around Mt Wilhelm is usually clear in the early morning, with fog lying low in the valleys. By around eight or nine, the rising temperature causes the fog to lift, and large cloud formations gather at higher altitudes, enveloping the peaks. Later in the day, generally between 11 am and mid-afternoon, intermittent mist and showers may occur, often persisting until about sunset. The evening usually sees the cloud masses descend again to the valleys and by midnight the skies are clear.

It is advisable to begin the climb no later than 3 or 4 am (some guides like to leave as early as 1 am) to avoid the clouds which spoil the views and might make the descent difficult. The climb from the lakes to the summit takes four to six hours.

Useful Organisations

The traditional owner of the land charges walkers K4 a head to walk the trail.

Do not forget to contact the National Disaster, Surveillance & Emergency Service (☎ 27 6502; ☎ 27 6666 for emergencies) in Port Moresby to inform them of your plans and intended date of return. There is a health centre in Gembogl, some 10 km down the road from Kegsugl, and a hospital in Kundiawa. The trade stores near the high school at Kegsugl sell tinned meat and fish, noodles, biscuits, etc.

Treks up Mt Wilhelm can be arranged through various tour companies. These provide guides, carriers, food and equipment. Addresses and contact numbers of the major companies are given in the Useful Organisations section of the Facts for the Bushwalker chapter. For the latest information on National Parks you can write to the National Parks Service, PO Box 5749, Boroko.

Guides & Carriers

The path to both the Pindaunde Lakes and the summit is well marked and a guide is not strictly necessary, although climbing in the dark is much easier with a guide. Carriers, if needed, can be hired locally. The people at Kegsugl are keen to offer their services as guides and carriers. Guides and carriers are generally reliable and trustworthy, and both places to stay in Kegsugl can arrange them.

You can leave your gear at the hut while you ascend to the top, and carriers are not really needed beyond that point. You can arrange for a carrier to drop your gear at the hut and then return to take it back down to Kegsugl after you've climbed the summit.

A guide's fee to the summit is K12, and carriers ask K6 for taking your gear from Kegsugl to the hut. Expect to pay K18 if the guide you've hired to the top also carries your gear to the hut. Most guides now have warm clothes of their own but it is your responsibility to supply them with food and blankets and pay for their accommodation (K2 for guides) if they overnight with you at the hut.

Equipment

A comfortable, light pair of boots is recommended for this walk. You'll also need a warm sleeping bag (rated below 0°C) and cold-weather gear, including long trousers, a hat, a pair of gloves and a warm jacket. Rain gear is also essential, and a pair of nylon over-trousers is recommended for extra comfort in wet weather. Bring one or two changes of clothes.

A camping stove is required. Mt Wilhelm is a National Park and it is prohibited to

damage or cut trees. There is a kerosene (paraffin) stove at the hut but it doesn't work well and is sometimes locked away. In any case, you have no guarantee there will be kerosene.

A compass, sunglasses and sunscreen are recommended, and a good torch with a spare bulb and strong batteries are necessary, as you will be climbing in the dark. Candles are advisable, as the kerosene lamp at the hut is no more reliable than the stove. You might need to supply your guide or carrier with a water bottle and warm clothing and blankets. A tent is not necessary, although camping is possible (K4). Ice-climbing equipment is not required.

All food must be carried in, including food for your guide or carrier if they overnight with you at the lakes. Cooking and eating utensils are provided at the hut. You may be offered fresh carrots and strawberries along the first stretch of the walk from the high school to Komanemambuno Creek. Bring some small change.

Mt Wilhelm must not be underestimated. It can get very cold at the top, and snow is possible. You can easily be fogbound. It is vital that you have sufficient food and warm clothing and that you assess the weather and your physical state realistically.

Exposure can be a problem, whether it is from the intense sunlight or the cold. A combination of wind, wet clothing, fatigue and hunger, even if the air temperature is well above freezing, can lead to hypothermia.

Likewise, you can burn deceptively quickly. There is less atmospheric protection at higher altitudes and the fact you're not hot doesn't mean you're not cooking. (See the Health section of the Facts for the Bushwalker chapter.)

Maps

The best topographic map for this walk is the 1:100,000 Bundi (7986) sheet. The area is also covered by the Ramu (SB 55-5) sheet of the 1:250,000 map series.

PLACES TO STAY
Kundiawa

There are only two places to stay in Kundiawa and neither is cheap. The upmarket Simbu Lodge suffered the fate of many hotels in PNG and burned down, and the *Kundiawa Hotel* (☎ 75 1033, PO Box 12), now fills the top-of-the-market niche. Unfortunately, although its prices reflect this status, K56/78 for singles/doubles with attached bathrooms, its quality doesn't. Even so, as the only hotel in town it can be full.

The only other alternative is the *Simbu Women's Resource Centre*, where the people are friendly but the prices high – K35 per person in a seven-bed dorm! No meals are available but there are cooking facilities. Follow the road past the hotel and the government offices, and turn left onto a muddy track as you go down the hill. It's a pink building.

Kegsugl

Hermann, whose guesthouse near Kegsugl was a haven for backpackers, has gone back to Germany. Johnny Kail Dor, Hermann's brother-in-law, has taken over the guesthouse and charges about K10 a night. Good meals are available. There is also a good new guesthouse near the airstrip, run by Henry Agum. It's very clean and a bed costs K10 a night. There are cooking facilities. Both places can arrange guides and porters, and you can store unneeded gear while you climb the mountain.

There used to be a good guesthouse in Niglguma village, at the junction of two streams on the Kundiawa-Kegsugl road, past Gembogl, but it burned down. Let us know if it has been rebuilt.

ACCESS

Access to Mt Wilhelm is from Kegsugl, in Simbu Province near Kundiawa.

Kegsugl

Kegsugl, at the foot of the mountain, is about 57 km from Kundiawa along a road that has to be seen to be believed. Irregular but frequent PMVs make the two-to-three-hour trip anytime between 8 am and 3 or 4 pm, and the fare is K5. They leave Kundiawa from the Shell service station, on the highway near the police station.

The airstrip at Kegsugl, once the highest in PNG at 2469 metres, has been shut down. but check with TransNiugini Airways (☎ 25 2211 in Port Moresby), as they want to have the strip re-opened.

Just before Kegsugl a road leading to Bundi in Madang Province branches off to the right. This is a relatively easy way of getting between the Highlands and the north coast. See the Other Suggested Walks chapter for information on this route.

Kundiawa

Kundiawa is on the Highlands Highway and is accessible by road and air.

Kundiawa's airport is on a sloping ridge surrounded by mountains. Air Niugini (☎ 75 1273) has a weekly flight to/from Port Moresby (K113) and Talair has flights to/from Port Moresby (K113), Goroka (K34) and Madang (K68) about once a week. Simbu Aviation took over many of Talair's local routes, but they might not still be in business. TransNiugini Airways might fill the breach.

PMVs are fairly frequent on the Highlands Highway, and the fare between Kundiawa and either Goroka or Mt Hagen is K4; both are two hours away. From Goroka you can get PMVs down to Madang or Lae, and from Mt Hagen you can continue as far west as Tari, and perhaps on to Kopiago if the road is OK.

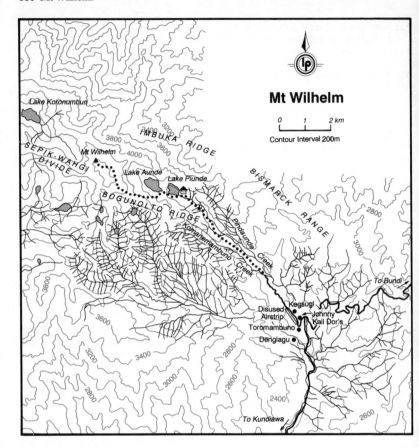

Because accommodation in Kundiawa is expensive and scarce, try to arrive as early as possible to ensure that you get to Kegsugl the same day. An early start is always preferable when travelling on the Highlands Highway, whether you're in a PMV or a private vehicle, as the danger of hold-ups increases dramatically after dark.

STAGE 1: KEGSUGL TO PINDAUNDE HUT

Walking time: 2¾ hours
Overnight: Pindaunde Hut
You first have to get the key to the hut at the lakes from the head ranger at the National Parks camp. From the high school, the road runs alongside the old airstrip, then past a trout hatchery and several houses, before it reaches the National Park camp 25 minutes later. This is a double-storey house with a galvanised-iron roof and woven pitpit walls. The office is open from 8 am to 4 pm. If the head ranger isn't here, he's probably on the trail or at the hut. People on the road from the high school to the camp might know his whereabouts.

Five minutes on from the camp you reach the end of the road and a last house. From

Top: Women with *bilums* (string bags), Southern Highlands Province (RE)
Bottom: Butterfly at Kundiawa, Mt Wilhelm, Simbu Province (RE)

Top: The Strickland Gorge as viewed from Kunanap, Sandaun Province (YP)
Bottom: Mendi House, Southern Highlands Province (YP)

here, after crossing the small Komane-mambuno Creek bridge (the last watering place until the Pindaunde Valley, still 1¼ hours' walk away), the route is a wide and well-defined track that takes you up to the Pindaunde Lakes and the hut in about 2¼ hours.

From the bridge the track begins to climb, through a delightful moss forest, a steep spur that runs between Komanemambuno and Pindaunde creeks. The route is easy and involves numerous switchbacks, some of which can be bypassed using narrow short cuts. On your way up you'll see two wooden benches, one about 35 minutes from the bridge, the second 20 minutes further on.

The track eventually leaves the forest and brings you to an open area from where Kegsugl and the Simbu Valley can be seen. A couple of minutes on from here, you pass a sign which tells you (in pidgin) that, 'It is forbidden to pick flowers or take anything from the park. Offenders are liable to go to court, or to pay a K10 fine'. A little further still, after seeing the first water since Komanemambuno Creek, the path comes to the lower reaches of the grassy Pindaunde Valley at 3210 metres.

This place is called Kombuglomambuno and it offers a magnificent view down the Simbu Valley, including Kegsugl and its airstrip. To the right of the strip you can see the road that links Kegsugl to Bundi and Brahmin in Madang Province. The hut is an hour's walk away and water is now plentiful.

As you continue through a landscape of tussocks and prehistoric-looking tree ferns, you soon reach the valley proper. The path is well defined but, because it becomes water-logged after rain, it divides a lot. All these different paths lead to the hut, just choose the driest.

Soon, Pindaunde Creek, a tributary of the Simbu River, comes into sight. The route continues on the left-hand side of the creek and brings you to a pretty waterfall called Nigledembuglokuglo, which is the first of two rock steps which have to be crossed before the hut is reached. The hut comes into view just after the second rock step is climbed.

Just before arriving at the hut you walk past the latrine on the right and the trail leading to the summit on the left. The hut is some 50 metres from Lake Piunde which, at 3475 metres, is the lower of the two Pindaunde Lakes. Roughly 400 metres to the east of the lake is the research station belonging to the Australian National University. Walkers can't use its facilities.

The hut is beautifully situated, with magnificent views over both the summit ridge and the 300-metre, near-vertical walls of the impressive cirque that towers behind Lake Aunde.

There are mattresses (plus lots of floor space) and cooking and eating utensils are provided. The kerosene stove and a lamp should not be depended on, as they might be locked away or there might be no kerosene. Nightly fees are K4 for walkers, K2 for guides (paid by the walker).

STAGE 2: PINDAUNDE HUT TO SUMMIT & RETURN

Walking time: four to six hours
Overnight: Pindaunde Hut
Take the path which you passed just before you reached the hut, and a couple of minutes later you cross Pindaunde Creek. From here the route continues through a grassy area before it enters a narrow, timbered strip along the left-hand shore of Lake Piunde. Coming out of this strip, it carries on towards the upper lake, Lake Aunde (3625 metres).

The path is now somewhat ill-defined. Basically, it follows along the left-hand side of a small stream until, at the foot of a rock face, it swings to the right, crosses the stream, and continues up and along the 90-metre cascade which separates the two lakes. It takes about 45 minutes to reach Lake Aunde from the hut.

Fill your water bottle at the top of the cascade. Although there may be water further up during the rainy season, there is usually none during the dry.

Past the cascade, the path swings sharply to the left and turns towards Wilhelm's south ridge (Bogunolto Ridge), north-west of the Pindaunde Valley. A little further on you come to a sign and, behind it, the small turn-off leading to nearby Lake Aunde.

The next section of the track climbs some 400 metres to the top of the ridge and is quite steep and unrelenting. It is marked by cairns and orange, white, blue, yellow and red markers painted on some of the larger stones.

Towards the end of this section you will see, on both sides of the path, the remains of an American WW II bomber. From here, if it is still dark, you can see the lights of the Ramu sugar refinery down in the Ramu Valley in Madang Province.

A little further on, at around 4000 metres and about 2½ hours after leaving the hut, the path climbs briefly onto Bogunolto Ridge. Early risers will see dawn breaking and a fine panorama of rugged mountain country. To the left you can see the Guraugulakugl Valley and its lake, which flows down towards the Denglagu Catholic mission near Kegsugl; to the right, the Pindaunde Lakes and the route travelled so far. On the left, a little to the east of south, is the tip of Mt Elimbari, near Chuave in Simbu Province.

From here the route turns off the ridge and continues at the foot of the large rock faces which tower high above the upper Pindaunde Valley. Despite the elevation, this relatively level section is easy to walk.

An hour later, as you continue to walk among towering rocky buttresses, the path swings sharply to the left and passes through a gap at 4400 metres. Here, cemented onto a large rock on the right, there is a plaque in memory of an Australian soldier who became lost and died on the mountain in 1971. The summit of Mt Wilhelm is now directly ahead, roughly 45 minutes away.

A little further on, the route brings you to a spot from where parts of the Wahgi Valley can be seen in the distance. Then it passes underneath two large outcrops at the head of a U-shaped valley and, after circling around the upper end of this valley, turns up and

heads more directly towards the summit of Mt Wilhelm, which can soon be seen. The summit is easily recognisable by the trigpoint marker.

A few minutes later, after a steep but easy scramble, the summit is finally reached. You're now at 4509 metres.

On a clear day the panorama is magnificent. Just to the west of north, you'll see Manam Island. Clockwise from Manam is Karkar Island and the Ramu Valley (northeast); the Bundi country, the airstrip at Moki and the Bundi road (north-east, near); the coast near Madang; the Finisterre and Sarawaget Ranges (east, distant); the coast near Lae; Mt Otto (south-east, near); the Kratke Range (south-east, distant); Mt Kerigomna, nearby across the Simbu Valley; Mt Kubor and the Kubor Range (southwest); Mt Giluwe (south-west, distant); Mt Hagen (west, distant); the Sepik-Wahgi Divide (just north of west); the upper Jimi Valley and Lake Koronumbun (north-west, near); and Mt Herbert (north, near).

Descent to the Hut

The descent back to the hut follows the same route and is a pleasant two or three hours of walking. You don't need to hurry: wander around, sit down and just take in the scenery. Though some walkers might want to immediately head back down to Kegsugl, I recommend that a second night be spent at the lakes.

Pindaunde Hut to Kegsugl

The descent back to Kegsugl takes about two hours. Again, walkers should feel free to dawdle around and explore the area.

PMVs from Kegsugl back to Kundiawa leave any time, morning or afternoon. If there are none waiting at the road-end when you get there, walk down to the market at nearby Denglagu, where you are more likely to find a PMV.

Nipa to Lake Kutubu

Renowned for its serenity and set in rugged limestone ranges dropping steeply down into its deep sheet of sapphire-blue water, Lake Kutubu is a magnificent and enchanting freshwater lake situated south-west of Mendi in the Southern Highlands.

The lake is accessible along an old trading route that still links Halhal, a small village north-west of Nipa, with Tage Point, the site of an excellent lodge built on a small promontory overlooking what is regarded as the most beautiful sheet of water in all of PNG.

In addition to offering a reasonable challenge and a superb introduction to the Southern Highlands, this walk provides the visitor with an excellent opportunity to view two well-made suspended cane bridges and to observe the fascinating culture of the Foi people of the Lake Kutubu-Mubi River area.

The big oil project near Lake Kutubu is changing the face of the Mendi area. Oil began flowing through the pipeline down to the Gulf of Papua in 1992, and the Chevron company is fulfilling its agreements with the local landowners, the Foi and Fasu people, which include building a road from Mendi to Pimaga and eventually on to Moro, the company headquarters near the north-west end of Lake Kutubu. Moro airstrip will be upgraded and given to the government, so more flights will go there in future.

HISTORY

In 1935 Jack Hides, accompanied by Jim O'Malley, led a seven-month patrol that went up the Fly, Strickland and Rentoul rivers, crossed the area of the Huli, Mendi and Kewa people, and returned to the coast via the Purari River.

The following year, both to trace Hides' trip and to plot the route of Ivan Champion's Bamu-Purari patrol, several reconnaissance flights were made over the area. During one of these flights Lake Kutubu, which Hides had missed on the ground, was first sighted by Europeans.

Later in the same year Champion and CJ Adamson, in the course of an eight-month patrol that took them up the Bamu River, across the Leonard Murray Mountains and the Wagi Valley and up to the country around Mt Giluwe, were the first Europeans to reach the lake.

Its large sheet of water proved suitable for flying boats and in June 1937, after an eight-week journey from Kikori, Claude Champion, Ivan's brother, and FWG Andersen, in the course of a patrol that took them through the Wagi Valley and the Tari Basin, established a police camp on the shore of the lake at Tugiri.

War forced the closure of the station in 1940, but it was re-established in 1949 at Tage Point. Flying boats served the patrol post and it was the base for much reconnaissance work, both by air and foot, throughout the Nembi Plateau, the Tari Basin and the country around Mendi and Erave.

It was from the Kutubu base that Syd Smith and Des Clancy located the airstrip sites at Mendi and Tari in 1950, and on 20 October of the same year the first plane landed at Mendi.

PEOPLE & CULTURE

Two cultural groups inhabit the area bisected by the trail. They are the Mendi and the Foi. The first occupy a territory that extends from Mendi and the base of Mt Giluwe as far west as the headwaters of the Nembi River and Mt Ambue, as far south as the Wagi River, and as far north as the border with Enga Province. The Mendi language is fragmented into several dialects, and around Nipa and the area traversed by the walk the people speak West Mendi.

Numbering about 5000, the Foi people live around Lake Kutubu and on the flood plain of the Mubi River. Roughly a fifth of their population live in some six villages on the lake, the rest in the country around Pimaga and Orokana.

The Legend of Lake Kutubu

In the beginning Lake Kutubu didn't exist, there were only mountains and forests. A group of women lived there who hunted, gathered fruits and nuts and led a peaceful life. However they had no water and were always thirsty.

One day, their dog Niyibe returned home with a wet nose. Sure he had found some water, the women tied a string to one of his legs and followed him to a small hole at the foot of a huge fig tree. Inside the hole there was water, but the women could not reach it.

They set to work with their stone axes and after several days of hard work cut the tree down. Water gushed wildly out of the hole and started to flood the whole valley, forming Lake Kutubu. The women fled up a mountain and made magic to stop the water rising further. The magic worked, but the women turned into palm trees, which can still be seen growing on the rocky slopes around the lake. ■

The two cultures are very different. The Mendi live in scattered farmhouses, low and well built to protect them against the bitter cold of the mountains. They put a great deal of emphasis on pig husbandry and wear beautifully made wigs adorned with bird feathers. Though the wigs are now worn only on special occasions, many people, particularly men, still wear traditional dress, which consists of an apron hanging from a wide bark belt and a large bunch of tanget leaves covering the buttocks. Armbands are also commonly worn.

The Mendi cultivate neat gardens and kaukau is their staple food, although a wide variety of European vegetables are now grown. Karuka is also a valuable food item and an important source of protein. It is not uncommon for tribes to fight over ownership of the palms.

The Foi live in villages made up of a large longhouse (up to 50 metres in length) flanked on either side by numerous smaller family houses. These longhouses can only be entered by men, the women living in the adjacent family dwellings. The Foi do not really cultivate gardens, other than a few greens, vegetables and bananas. Their staple food is sago, a starchy extract washed from the pith of sago palms, which are plentiful around the lake and near Pimaga. They do raise pigs, but the animals are not overwhelmingly important. Crayfish abound in the Mubi River and Lake Kutubu, and sago grubs are also an important source of protein.

Several old trade routes linked the Lake Kutubu/Mubi River area with the Highlands. Stone axes, pigs, salt, tobacco and kina shells came from the north in exchange for tigasso oil, sago, feathers, black palm bows and cowrie and kina shells from the south.

Tigasso oil was, and still is, the most important trade item along these routes. It is widely used by Highlanders, particularly the Mendi, as body decoration. Mendi brides, for instance, coat themselves with soot and tigasso oil for their wedding.

It takes a long time to collect the oil. A deep hole is cut into the trunk of a large tree, then left to heal for several years until the owner decides it is time to collect the oil. The hole is again scraped and the oil flows in and collects at the bottom. After the oil is scooped out and filtered, it is put into short sections of bamboo or gourds. When enough oil has been collected, it is poured into long bamboo tubes then traded to the Highlands.

INFORMATION

Features

The country between Nipa and Lake Kutubu is mainly limestone and is dominated by the expansive Nembi Plateau and the deep valley of the south-draining Wagi River.

Lake Kutubu is 19 km long and up to 4½ km wide, and is 800 metres above sea level. Its depth varies, but is said to be more than a hundred metres deep in places. Hemmed-in by steep mountains, it lies south of the Central Range, north-east of both the Great Papuan Plateau and Mt Bosavi, a large volcanic cone clearly visible from Yalanda, a village three hours' walk north of Tage Point.

A large, poorly drained upland plain dominates the country around Pimaga, the site of an airstrip and the end-point of the walk. The plain extends along the course of the Mubi River to a little beyond the mission station of Orokana, east of Pimaga. Numerous colonies of *tigasso* trees and sago palms grown on the plain, the first providing a much-prized oil, the second the staple food of the local people,

The region traversed by the walk is densely timbered with lower montane vegetation. Black and sago palms and tigasso trees are plentiful around Lake Kutubu and Pimaga. Karuka are a common sight on the Nembi Plateau, and freshwater crayfish abound in the Mubi River and Lake Kutubu.

Standard

The trail between Halhal and Ungubi and between Yalanda and Pimaga is very easy to walk. Between Ungubi and Yalanda, however, it is hard and rather gruelling. Steep, unrelenting ascents alternate with equally difficult descents, and the path is narrow and often strewn with stones. Large blocks of sharp, slippery limestone make the descent down towards Sagip Creek particularly hazardous.

The route described follows a vehicle track from Halhal to Ungubi, from the Mubi River to Tage Point, and from Gesege to Pimaga. Between Ungubi and Yalanda, it follows a small path.

Days Required

In addition to the 1½-hour walk from Halhal to Ungubi, it takes three days to reach Tage Point from the Highlands Highway near Nipa. From Tage Point, after resting at the Lake Kutubu Lodge, a motorised dugout is taken to Gesege, a village at the eastern end of the lake. From there it's three hours' walk along a road to the airstrip and government station at Pimaga.

If time is short, and only if you're fairly fit, the section between Sagip and Tage Point can be walked in one long day instead of two. This walk, if time and fitness allow, can be used in conjunction with any of the other trails mentioned in the Other Suggested Walks section at the end of this chapter. You can, for instance, walk down to Lake Kutubu from Nipa, then walk back up to the Highlands via Benaria and Tari Gap, or Pimaga and Poroma.

Season

The rainy season around Nipa stretches from early November to late April. The weather is less predictable around Lake Kutubu, and rainy and sunny days can occur at any time of the year. The annual rainfall is about 3500 mm in Nipa, a lot more around Lake Kutubu.

Daytime temperatures around Nipa often climb into the high 20°Cs, but the nights can be fairly chilly. Both day and night temperatures get substantially higher as one descends to the lowlands and draws closer to Lake Kutubu (800 metres above sea level).

Guides & Carriers

A carrier, if needed, from the Highlands Highway to Ungubi, can be recruited at the small market at Halhal.

A guide is not necessary between Halhal and Ungubi and Gesege and Pimaga but is essential between Ungubi and Yalanda, and is recommended between Yalanda and Tage Point.

It costs K20 (K10 a day) for a guide/carrier from Ungubi to Yalanda, K5 from Yalanda to Tage Point; guides-only are not available. It is your responsibility to feed your guide, his to carry your gear. Insist if he's reluctant to do so and refuse to pay any additional fees. If the guide doesn't have friends or relatives in Yalanda you might have to pay for his accommodation there.

Pastor Tom in Ungubi will help you find a reliable person to accompany you to Yalanda. Establish both his wages and responsibilities in public before you set out, it's the best way to avoid misunderstandings.

Though someone will undoubtedly offer to guide you, many people are reluctant to travel to the lowlands, for fear of sorcery. This is not mere superstition, as a trip to the lowlands often means a bout of malaria for Highlands people.

The Yalanda people feel that they should get their share of the walker's kinas and do not take kindly to guides from Ungubi going further than their village. Two guides must therefore be recruited, the first from Ungubi to Yalanda, the second from Yalanda to Tage Point.

Yalanda guides are fairly easy to find, and are strongly recommended for the crossing of the Mubi River. The Mubi is a large river and fording it can be difficult, particularly if it is high. Your guide will not only ensure a safer crossing, but will also take your bag securely to the other side.

Carriers from Gesege to Pimaga charge K5.

Equipment

A light pair of walking boots, sunscreen and a hat are recommended for this walk. It is your responsibility to provide your guide/carrier with food. Bring lots – he can eat nearly twice as much as you. Neither dugouts nor water-sports equipment are available at the Lake Kutubu Lodge. It is OK to swim in a Western-style bathing costume at the lodge, but elsewhere you'll need to wear a laplap.

If you stay with Pastor Tom in Ungubi, he will provide your evening meal. There are small, poorly stocked and unreliable trade stores in Ungubi, Gesege, Hegeso and Barutage. The stores in Pimaga are more reliable, though still poorly stocked.

Lake Kutubu Lodge at Tage Point provides meals and has a small store selling some basic food. The nightly rate at the Pimaga Lodge includes all meals. Local food can normally be purchased in Ungubi and Yalanda but all other food must be carried in. There are usually small weekly markets in Pimaga and Inu, a small station 30 minutes south of Tage Point.

Useful Organisations

For information on Lake Kutubu Lodge and the Pimaga Guesthouse, contact the Foi Diagaso Oil Company (☎ 59 1328, fax 59 1305) in Mendi. This company belongs to the Foi people and handles their side of the Chevron development, as well as running the accommodation.

There are two-way radios at Lake Kutubu Lodge and Pimaga, and a two-way radio and a telephone can be found in Nipa. There are aid posts in Ungubi, Yalanda and Barutage (near Herebo), and health centres in Nipa, Pimaga and Inu.

There are excellent lodges at Tage Point and Pimaga, and a small rest house in Gesege (see Places to Stay). In Ungubi you can stay at Pastor Tom's place. There is a small rest house at Yalanda.

Maps

The best map for this walk is the Kutubu (7585) sheet of the 1:100,000 topographic map series. The Kutubu (SB 54-12) sheet of the 1:250,000 series also covers the area described by the walk.

Warning

The big Chevron oil project near Lake Kutubu has changed the character of this area somewhat, and local people are used to dealing with (or hearing exaggerated stories about people dealing with) oil workers with fat wallets and expense accounts. There have been frequent instances of travellers being asked by the bridge owners to pay a fee to cross the Wagi River bridge between Ungubi and Sagip. These have been as high as K20 per person. Similar fees may also be asked at the Aku River bridge. However, the latter is a full day's walk from Ungubi, so its owners don't usually bother to chase you that far down the track. People whose house you will be sleeping in at Sagip may also demand comparable payments.

The people are quite within their rights to request money from you; they've seen many tourists walk down this trail over the years and they feel that all foreigners are rich and can't comprehend that some may be poorer than others. Never refuse to pay; try instead to agree on a sum that is reasonable to the two parties.

You may end up not having to pay anything at all. However, if you feel you can't really take that risk, either fly in to Pimaga (or take a PMV on the soon-to-be-completed road from Mendi) and walk to the lake, or follow a different route down to the lowlands (see the Other Suggested Walks section at the end of this chapter).

PLACES TO STAY

Mendi

The *Pentecostal Guesthouse* (☎ 59 1174, PO Box 15) is in town, not far from the airport. There are only a few rooms and church workers have priority, so it's sometimes full. The rooms are small but clean enough and there are cooking facilities. It costs K8 for a bunk bed or K15 for a room to yourself (if available). If this is full, check out the *Training Centre* across the road, which is cheap but very run-down.

The *Educational Resource Centre* (☎ 59 1252) also has reasonable value rooms with meals and cooking facilities.

The *UCWF Guesthouse* (☎ 59 1062, PO Box 53) is a 20-minute walk from town and costs K10 in a shared room or K15 per person in a twin room with attached bathroom. There are no cooking facilities and meals are expensive. Walk out Old Hagen Rd past Mendi Motors, take the left fork after the bridge, pass the turn-off to the large Menduli Trade Store and it's further up the hill on your right, across from the hospital.

Muruk Lodge (☎ 59 1188, PO Box 108) is the revamped version of the old Mendi Hotel. It's comfortable and has a licensed restaurant. Singles/doubles are K75/95.

A few km out of town, on the Highlands Highway just beyond the turn-off into Mendi, *Kiburu Lodge* (☎ 59 1077, fax 59 1350, PO Box 50, Mendi) costs about the same (K75/85) but is much nicer. The 12 rooms are in quasi-traditional style and the lodge has pleasant grounds and views.

Ungubi

You can stay at Pastor Tom's place. He has a fairly large, spacious, Western-style house and his family is good company. Expect to pay about K8 for your accommodation and evening meal. Fix your own breakfast.

Lake Kutubu

The comfortable *Lake Kutubu Lodge*, on a ridge overlooking the lake, is attractively designed and constructed from bush materials. Prices have risen quite a lot lately, and might rise further – there are hopes of a tourist boom. Currently, for full board you pay K60 for the first night, then K55 for each additional night. There's also a backpackers' bunkhouse, where a bed costs K8 a night or K12 if you need sleeping gear (mattress, pillow, mosquito net). Meals are available and cost K8 for breakfast, K9 for lunch and K15 for dinner. To book, contact the Foi Diagaso Oil Company (☎ 59 1328, fax 59 1305) in Mendi. If you don't book there might not be anyone there when you arrive.

If you're cooking for yourself it's best to bring some food. However, you can often buy things from the lodge and Kutubu's perfect climate means there is never a shortage of fresh fruit and vegetables.

One of the reasons why the lodge was built was to control visitors. The local people are quite traditional, and segregation is maintained between the sexes – this segregation, among other things, was undermined by travelling couples staying in the villages. The lodge means that the people can now more easily accept visitors on their own terms, and maintain their privacy. If you do

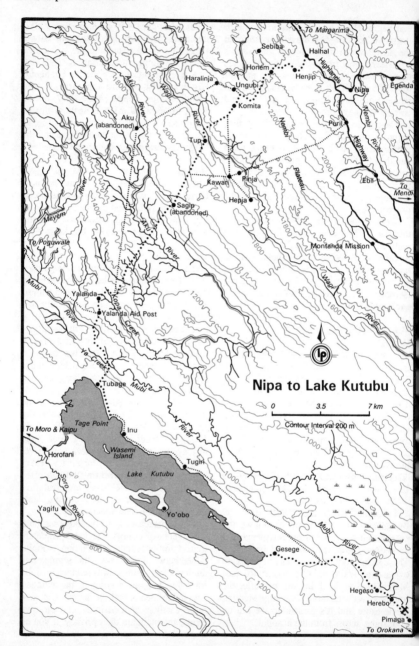

Nipa to Lake Kutubu

0   3.5   7 km

Contour Interval 200 m

visit Lake Kutubu, do not try to stay in the villages; that would defeat the purpose of the lodge.

The lodge has a motorised dugout and can arrange tours to various sights around the lake. You can travel down the Soro River, see some burial caves or visit Wasemi village which has a 50-metre-long longhouse and the best views over the lake. The cost of these trips is about K20, and picnics can be arranged. From March to October, a Raggiana bird of paradise can be seen displaying on a tree near by the lodge.

Gesege

There is a small *rest house* in Gesege, convenient for those who walk in from Pimaga and can't manage to get to the lodge the same day. Its all right, but neither bedding nor cooking utensils are provided. Expect to pay about K8.

Pimaga

At Pimaga you can stay at the *Pimaga Guesthouse*, also owned by the Foi people. The place is charming and set in superbly landscaped flower gardens along Sura Creek, a few minutes' walk from the station. A large sign just behind the first store shows you the way. Linen is provided and room and board is around K25 per night. It's a truly beautiful spot, perfect for just lazing around. Ask Kofe, the caretaker, about visiting nearby villages. There's also a cheaper and more basic *council guesthouse*.

ACCESS

The start of the trail at Halhal is about five km north-west of Nipa, and is accessible by PMV along the Highlands Highway. PMVs can be found near the PNGBC office in Mendi and the 1½-hour trip costs about K5. Nipa-bound PMVs don't normally go as far as Halhal, so find yourself a vehicle that goes through to Margarima and Tari. If you take a Nipa-only PMV, make sure that the driver knows that you want to be dropped at Halhal.

There is an airstrip at Pimaga. Southwest Airlines (☎ 59 1031) in Mendi has a regular passenger flight to Pimaga and MAF also

flies there. The 15-minute trip costs K30 and takes you over classic limestone pinnacle country. Southwest is a Talair agent, so you can book through Talair offices. Milne Bay Air (MBA) flies from Mendi to Moro, the Chevron headquarters are an hour's walk from the west end of the lake, for K52. From here to Tage Point (for Lake Kutubu Lodge) it's K25 by boat if you charter, or K5 if there's a boat going to the lodge.

There will probably be PMVs running between Pimaga and Mendi when the new road is completed.

Although a large track links Tage Point with Gesege it is fairly overgrown and not much used. It is much better to take a motorised dugout across the lake. The trip takes just over an hour but can cost up to K45 for the boat, whether you're by yourself or with four other people. If you arrange a boat at Lake Kutubu Lodge it will cost much less and you might be able to call in at two very interesting burial sites on the way. If you arrive from Pimaga and have let the lodge know you were coming, it will send someone to pick you up for about K5. Otherwise you will have to arrange a ride with people in Gesege. Several people have outboard motors and it should not be too hard to line something up, but the cost might be sky-high.

As you've now probably come to appreciate, the trip will cost you about the same whether you fly in or walk down. However, the walk is much more challenging and interesting, and is worth the trouble.

STAGE 1: HALHAL TO UNGUBI

Walking time: 1½ hours
Overnight: Pastor Tom's house
This first stage of the walk takes you along a vehicle track from Halhal to Ungubi. From the Highlands Highway, the route first takes you down to a small stream then goes up to Henjip, reached 15 minutes later. As with Honem, the next village on, Henjip is easily recognisable by a large, rectangular church, topped with sheets of galvanised iron, on the village square. From Henjip, the route continues up a gentle slope. There is some nice

scenery to the east – groves of casuarina and karuka, pitpit, fences, gardens and houses – and within 35 minutes you reach Honem.

From Honem the route continues up a gentle slope to a small marketplace. Take the turn-off on the right and after a little way you go down to Ungubi's community school and aid post, and Pastor Tom's place. You can stay here for about K8, including dinner. Situated 35 minutes from Honem, and topped with a galvanised-iron roof, Pastor Tom's house stands on the last level of the descent.

You must take a guide from here to Yalanda and Lake Kutubu. Let Pastor Tom know your plans and ask him if he can help you find a reliable person.

STAGE 2: UNGUBI TO SAGIP
Walking time: at least 5½ hours
Overnight: garden house
From Pastor Tom's place, turn right onto the road and continue gently up towards the village proper.

Two different routes lead from Ungubi to Yalanda. The first is a small path that branches off on the left a little before the village. This is the route described here, and

is probably the best. It leads first to the hamlet of Komita, then the Wagi River and, eventually, Yalanda. The second route begins in Ungubi village, heads first to Haralinja, then takes you through the abandoned village of Aku, and finally meets the other trail a little before Yalanda.

Depending on the state of the vine bridges spanning the Wagi River (which rot with time and become dangerous if they're not properly maintained) and the conditions of the unbridged Aku River (fairly large, rather swift and often in flood), your guide will choose the best route.

Thus, roughly 30 minutes after leaving Pastor Tom's place, you take the first turn-off on the left on the road to Ungubi. The path climbs gently up towards the hamlet of Komita, passing several houses, gardens and groves of karuka. Komita, 20 minutes' walk from the road, is on top of a ridge, at the edge of the forest. From Komita the route drops down to the Wagi River.

The descent lasts about 50 minutes. The grade, steep at first, eases a little halfway down and the trail goes through an area of poor drainage. Mild ups and downs follow.

On the left you soon pass a turn-off leading to Kawari and Pinja; just a little further, on the right, you'll find a watering place close to some colonies of karuka. The trail continues its descent after passing the watering place. It is often steep and stony, but always clearly marked.

The Wagi is a large, 20-metre-wide river spanned by a suspended vine bridge. As the river draws closer you can get some views, poor though, of the deep valley it flows through and some gardens on the right.

Just after crossing the Wagi, the trail goes over a small stream, through some old gardens and climbs for 30 minutes, quite steeply and unrelentingly, to the top of a first ridge. There's a 15-minute descent to Tup village, with its several houses and gardens, then there's a second climb.

In all, this scenario of laborious descents and climbs repeats seven times, and takes nearly 1¾ hours. Between the sixth and seventh ridge a path from Kawari merges in on the left; at the top of the seventh and last ridge you can at last see Lake Kutubu in the distance.

From the top of the seventh ridge an unrelenting descent follows that is very steep and hazardous through nasty blocks of sharp and slippery limestone. After 45 very trying minutes and past three small streams, the trail brings you to Sagip Creek, which is six metres wide, but easy to ford.

About 10 minutes on from the creek a house comes into sight. It is possible to stop here; however, it is recommended that you spend the night a little further on. A further 15 minutes through gardens in fallow will take you to Sagip, where you'll find a watering place and two more houses. From here you can see Yalanda on a ridge to the distant south-west and Yagifu, site of the oil project. Accommodation is in a bush-material house.

Alternative Place to Stay

An hour's walk on from Sagip there is a small bush shelter a little above the Aku River. This might no longer be standing, so consult your guide and the villagers.

STAGE 3: SAGIP TO YALANDA

Walking time: 3¾ hours
Overnight: village rest house

After an hour on a gentle downhill grade, past a couple of streams, you reach the Aku River, which is 20 metres wide and spanned by a suspended vine bridge. Kopa Creek is now an hour's walk away. Another five small streams have to be crossed before it comes into sight; the first after a short climb up from the river, the other four as the path continues along a series of mild ups and downs. From the last stream the trail follows spurs and ridge-lines gently down to Kopa Creek. Just before reaching the creek, the other route from Ungubi (by way of Haralinja and Aku) comes in on the right.

Follow the small, shallow creek past several houses and gardens for about 15 minutes. Then the path starts to climb steeply through old gardens. After a first ascent it goes down to a small stream then, up an equally steep grade, it climbs to the top of second ridge, reached an hour later. From here Yalanda is only a few minutes away, and is reached by walking along the top of the ridge.

If you found this last section of the walk extremely laborious, imagine the extraordinary work of the women who, besides regularly coming down to the creek to work in the taro gardens, often have to climb back up to the village carrying more than 20 kg of taro roots.

From Yalanda the whole country just traversed can be seen to the north-east and Mt Bosavi can be seen rising above the Great Papuan Plateau to the south-west.

There is a small rest house in the village. It's fairly basic but expect to pay around K10.

STAGE 4: YALANDA TO TAGE POINT

Walking time: 2¾ hours
Overnight: Lake Kutubu Lodge

On leaving Yalanda the trail descends along a ridge-line to the aid post, 20 minutes away. Mt Bosavi still stands out to the south-west, and Wasemi Island and Lake Kutubu can now be seen to the south. From the aid post, a gentle descent takes you down to the Mubi River in about 20 minutes. The large metre-deep river must be forded. It's easiest to cross level with an island which splits the river into two arms, 15 and 18 metres wide.

The next hour's walk, along a mainly level grade, brings you to the six-metre-wide, half-a-metre-deep Ya Creek. Across the ford, the trail goes up a little then descends to the village of Tubage, 25 minutes on.

Tubage is on the shore of Lake Kutubu, and is only 30 minutes from Tage Point and Lake Kutubu Lodge. Next to the water tank and the memorial, the route continues and now follows an old vehicle track. Further along is a small wooden bridge over a ditch; to its right a turn-off leads to Tage Point. Just before reaching the lodge the path forks: the right path leads directly to the lodge; the left takes you first to the helipad.

STAGE 5: GESEGE TO PIMAGA
Walking time: three hours, 18 km
Overnight: guesthouse

To spare yourself a long and difficult walk, cross the lake in a motorised dugout from Tage Point to the village of Gesege, from where it's a three-hour walk on a road to Pimaga, a small government station with an airstrip.

From Gesege the road goes up, gently but steadily, for half an hour to a first top. After a short descent, it goes up again to reach a second ridge. At the top, the abandoned and overgrown Tugiri-Inu-Tage track merges in on the left.

After a short descent, the road levels off as it continues towards Pimaga. Further on, past some paddocks, tigasso trees, and black and sago palms, Hegeso comes into sight. Situated by Fayaa Creek, a tributary of the Mubi River, this village is roughly three-fifths of the way to Pimaga.

Hegeso is a typical Foi village, with a longhouse nearly 45 metres long. On the road, across the bridge over the Fayaa, is a tank of drinking water. Ask first before you take some. A little further on, the road takes you past the Mubi River again, easily recognisable by the numerous dugouts tied

along the banks. After a short walk along the river, you come to Barutage, on the right-hand side of the road, and a little further on, on the left-hand side, is Herebo.

A large river is soon crossed, then the road continues on to a community school before it reaches the government station at Pimaga 10 minutes later. In the distance you'll see some large houses roofed with galvanised iron. These are at Orokana, a mission station 30 minutes' walk east of Pimaga.

There are plenty of small trade stores at Pimaga and there is accommodation at the *Pimaga Guesthouse* and the *council guesthouse*.

OTHER SUGGESTED WALKS
Poroma to Pimaga
Poroma is on the Highlands Highway, halfway between Mendi and Nipa. This walk follows an old trade route and takes three days. A kiaps' motorbike track once linked Poroma and Pimaga, and traces of this old road, made of tree trunks, still remain. Starting at Poroma, the track takes you first to the village of Toyawaro where you can see the Awale Falls, then to Kunduru, across the fast-flowing Wagi River, and finally to Orokana and Pimaga.

The first night is spent at Kunduru, the second probably by the Wagi. On the last day, after climbing out of the Wagi Valley, Orokana and Pimaga can be seen. A steep descent, past a large sago swamp, eventually brings you across the Mubi River onto a road at Orokana.

The going is hard and the mainly limestone terrain is fairly rugged. A guide is necessary. This walk, if you're keen, can be used in conjunction with the Nipa to Lake Kutubu walk. You could, for instance, hike down from Nipa to Lake Kutubu and, after a rest at the Lake Kutubu Lodge, walk back up to the Highlands by way of Pimaga and Poroma.

The Mendi (7685) sheet of the 1:100,000 topographic map series is the best map for this walk. The Kutubu (SB 54-12) sheet of the 1:250,000 series also covers the area described by the walk.

Note The new road linking Pimaga and Mendi might mean significant changes to the standard and routing of this walk. Ask around in Mendi or Pimaga for the latest information.

Tari to Lake Kutubu

This trail starts at Tigibi, a village near Ambua Lodge on Tari Gap, and takes you to Tage Point and Lake Kutubu by way of Benaria station, Homa, Poguwale, Yalanda and Tubage. It takes four days. The first stage is a five-hour walk along a cut, clay-surfaced track to Benaria. From Benaria it takes two fairly hard days, with an overnight stop at Homa, to reach Poguwale, a day's walk from Lake Kutubu. From Poguwale, the route follows the Mubi River down and the going is easier (see Stage 4 of the Nipa to Lake Kutubu walk).

The Kutubu (7585) and Doma (7586) sheets of the 1:100,000 topographic map series cover the area described by the walk. The same area is also covered by the Kutubu (SB 54-12) and Wabag (SB 54-8) sheets of the 1:250,000 map series.

Puril to Lake Kutubu

It's possible to walk from Puril, a village on the Highlands Highway a little before Nipa, to Lake Kutubu. Starting at what is known as the Ai Gris Market, this trail takes you first from Puril to the villages of Pinja and Kawari. From there, after meeting with the main trail coming down from Nipa to Lake Kutubu, it follows the route described in the Nipa to Lake Kutubu walk description. The maps needed for this walk are the same as for the Nipa to Lake Kutubu walk.

Koimal to Maramuni

This beautiful walk through montane forest and lovely upland scenery provides an excellent introduction to the people and culture of Enga Province.

Set in rugged ranges dominated by deep, steep-sided valleys, the route links Koimal, a large village north-west of Laiagam, with Ilia, a small community high on a ridge overlooking the dramatic Maramuni Valley. In addition to taking the walker over the Central Range, this hike offers the opportunity to cross several interesting bridges and wander through many well-kept hamlets and villages.

The name Maramuni refers to the large administrative district around the upper Maramuni River, and is the official name of the district's government station and airstrip. The local people call the airstrip and government station Pasalagus, and that usage is followed here. However, this name is not widely known outside the area.

HISTORY

The Maramuni Valley was first visited by Europeans in 1930, when members of the Akmana expedition, after travelling up the Karawari and Arapundia rivers from the north coast, reached the junction of the Tarua and Maramuni rivers, south-west of present-day Pasalagus. After building a palisaded base-camp, the four members of the party, Reg Beazley, EA Shepherd, HV Seale and Bill MacGregor, spent some time exploring the area and prospecting for gold in the Tarua and Maramuni rivers and many of their tributaries.

Lake Sirunki and the Lagaip Valley were first seen by Europeans in 1938, when assistant district officer James Taylor and patrol officer John Black walked from Mt Hagen to the Upper Sepik district of Telefomin. Their Hagen-Sepik patrol, from 9 March 1938 to 19 June 1939, was easily the largest, longest and best-equipped ever mounted in PNG.

PEOPLE & CULTURE

The Enga are the largest single cultural group in PNG. Their territory extends from the Hagen Range, Wapenamanda and Kompiam as far west as Kandep, Longap and Tumundan, south to the border of Southern Highlands Province, and north to the border of East Sepik Province. To the west of their territory, living in the vicinity of Porgera and Paiela, are the closely related Ipili.

The Enga live in scattered farmhouses, low and well built to protect them against the bitter cold of the mountains. They put a great deal of emphasis on pig husbandry, and are renowned for their elaborate wigs and vigorous dances. Most people now wear Western clothes but the traditional dress, which consists of an apron hanging from several loops of rope and a large bunch of tanget leaves covering the buttocks, is still worn by many men in more remote areas.

Neat gardens are cultivated, and kaukau is the staple food. Other important foods include European potatoes, cabbages, pumpkins, sugar cane, various types of greens, and the nuts of the karuka, either wild or cultivated.

Most people understand pidgin, although many of the women and older men speak

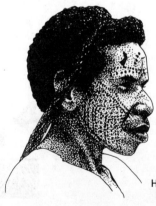

Highland woman

174

only their own language. English is understood by a few of the younger people and is spoken around the stations.

INFORMATION
Features

The Central Range, the backbone of PNG, is the broad cordillera that runs roughly through the middle of the country along its entire length. Ranging in width from approximately 50 km in eastern Papua to about 300 km in the provinces of Southern Highlands, Enga and Western Highlands, it is made up of a complex system of ranges, upland valleys and volcanoes.

Wide, deep rivers dominate the area around this walk, including the south-flowing Lagaip, a tributary of the Strickland and Fly, and the north-flowing Sui and Maramuni, both tributaries of the Yuat and Sepik. The valleys of the Lagaip and the Sui are broad, but the Maramuni flows through heavily timbered, precipitous mountainsides plunging dramatically down to the wide, fast-flowing river, which is laden with alluvial deposits. The area immediately north of the range is characterised by a wide upland valley dominated by the deep Sui River.

The vegetation throughout the walk is interesting, with secondary growth and numerous passion-fruit vines, delightful lower montane forest and some areas of grassland.

Standard

The trail follows the proposed route of a road. It follows a large track from Koimal to Otel Creek and then a small path to Pasalagus (Maramuni station) and Ilia. Although not difficult to walk, it requires a certain degree of fitness. The 800-metre climb to the top of Mt Poapia and the Central Range is fairly steady, and the section between Wailep and Pasalagus has a series of short ridges, which are often steep and tiring to climb under the hot sun.

Although this walk can be done either way, walking from Koimal to Pasalagus is easier, as there is less climbing. The only airstrip in the Maramuni district is at

Pasalagus so, having reached Ilia, you have to walk back to the station to catch a flight out. Alternatively, you could walk all the way back to Koimal or continue on down to the Sepik plains (see the Other Suggested Walks section at the end of this chapter).

Days Required

In addition to the 1¾ hours' walk from the Laiagam-Porgera Road to Lambusalam, it takes two days to get to Pasalagus. From there it takes two short days or one fairly long day to make a trip to Ilia and back.

Season

The rainy season stretches from mid-November to mid-April and the area averages around 3000 mm of rainfall a year. June, July and August are the best months, although May and September can also be quite nice.

Daytime temperatures often climb in to the high 20°Cs, but night-time temperatures can be very cold – particularly around Koimal and Lambusalam. Nights are much warmer in Wailep and Pasalagus, but can be fairly chilly in Ilia.

Useful Organisations

There is a two-way radio and a health centre in Pasalagus. Koimal, Wailep and Ilia have small aid posts.

Guides & Carriers

Apart from the short walk from the Laiagam-Porgera road to Lambusalam, you'll need guides, especially for the crossing of the Central Range from Lambusalam to Wailep.

Carriers can be recruited in Koimal (Paitingis), Kililam, Torenam, Lambusalam, Wailep, Pasalagus and Ilia. Expect to pay around K5 a day.

Equipment

Runners or very light boots are ideal footwear, and sunscreen and a hat are advisable. A tent provides an alternative to the limited village accommodation. Bring a water bottle, rain gear, a sleeping bag and a warm sweater.

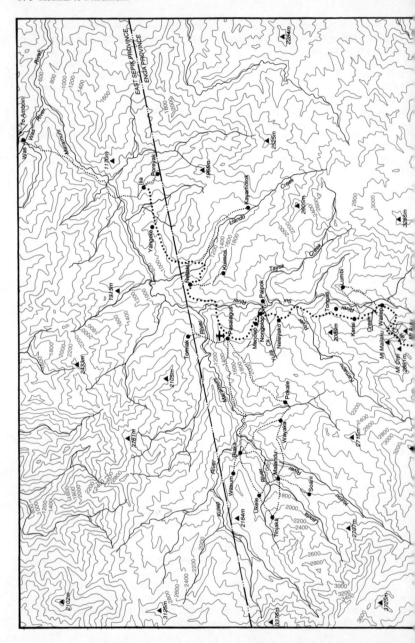

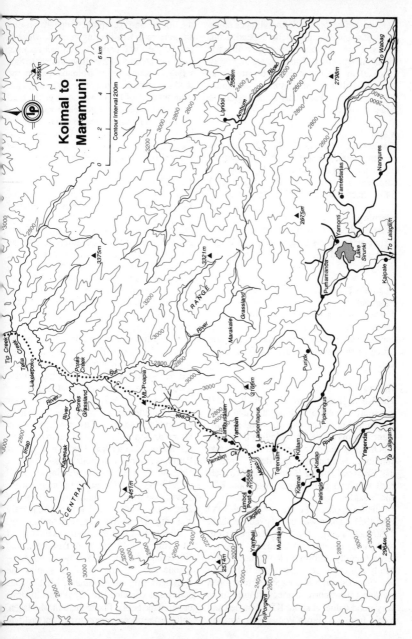

Koimal to
Maramuni

Contour Interval 200m

Food can be bought in the villages along the walk, but should not be depended on. Carry some of your own, especially for breakfast and lunch. There are small, poorly stocked and unreliable trade stores at Koimal, Kililam and Torenam. The more reliable stores at Pasalagus and Laiagam are better stocked.

Maps

The Porgera (7587) and Wabag (7687) sheets of the 1:100,000 topographic map series cover the area described by the walk. The same area is also covered by the Wabag (SB 54-8) sheet of the 1:250,000 map series.

Warning

Tribal fighting is quite common in Enga Province. Outsiders are not usually affected, but you should ask about the current situation.

PLACES TO STAY
Pasalagus

There is no rest house at Pasalagus so you have to stay with a family. Ask around, perhaps at the health centre, the government office or the school. Leave a gift of a few kina.

Wabag

The *Malya Hostel* (☎ 57 1108, PO Box 237) is a short way out of town on the road to Mt Hagen and is run by the provincial government. Rooms cost K50, including breakfast; lunch is K5 and dinner K8. It isn't in great condition. Not far from the Malya Hostel is the *Teachers' Transit Hostel*, which charges K20 a night; a good dinner costs about K10 and breakfast is K5.

The *Kaiap Orchid Lodge* (☎ 52 2087, PO Box 193) is some way out of Wabag. About 2700 metres above sea level, it is built from bush materials and is surrounded by gardens. It's a friendly, informal place, but unfortunately it was closed due to tribal fighting in late '92. Although it is expected to re-open we don't have current prices. It used to be very good value, at about K20 for a bed and meals from K8. From Wabag you can ring

the lodge and get picked up (if no-one answers go to Kol Trading in town, which is run by the same people). You can also get there by catching a PMV from Wabag to Sari village, a couple of km from town along the road to Laiagam. From there it's a tough but pleasant walk of 1½ to two hours on the road up to the mountain ridge. The road crosses the Lai River, passes gardens and houses and there are good views along the climb up to the ridge. Before you do this, check that the lodge is open and that the area is safe.

ACCESS

The walk begins at Paitingis, a hamlet of Koimal. Paitingis is 19½ km north-west of Laiagam, and is accessible by PMV along the road running between Laiagam and Porgera. Some PMVs run direct from Wabag but you usually have to change at Laiagam. Both the 1½-hour trip from Wabag to Laiagam and the half-hour trip from Laiagam to Koimal cost about K4. The 2½-hour trip from Mt Hagen to Wabag costs K5. PMVs also go through to Porgera and the two-hour trip costs K7.

A road links Lake Sirunki, 25 km north-west of Wabag, with Torenam, a village halfway between Koimal and Lambusalam. No PMVs travel on this road but private transport can sometimes be arranged. It's best to take a 4WD. Do not leave your vehicle unattended by the side of the road as it might be vandalised. Pay someone to look after it or, better still, get a friend to drop you off. Starting the walk at Torenam instead of Paitingis saves you an hour's walk.

There is an airstrip at Pasalagus. MAF (☎ 55 1506 in Mt Hagen) is the main carrier serving the strip and usually flies in from Mt Hagen on Tuesday and Friday, frequently stopping over at Wapenamanda on the way.

Flights cost K68 between Pasalagus and Mt Hagen, K47 between Pasalagus and Wapenamanda, and K38 between Wapenamanda and Mt Hagen. MAF knows the Pasalagus strip as Maramuni. MAF flights sometimes continue from Pasalagus to strips down in the Sepik. Phone them in Mt Hagen, or talk to the pilot in person, to find out the flight schedule. This route can be a real money saver.

Talair (☎ 52 1347 in Mt Hagen) flies to Wapenamanda from Mt Hagen on Tuesday and Thursday for K42.

STAGE 1: KOIMAL TO LAMBUSALAM
Walking time: 1¾ hours
Overnight: village accommodation
From Paitingis, a hamlet of Koimal, the walk begins with a gentle 15-minute descent to the Lagaip River, crossed on a large bridge designed to take vehicles when the road is completed. Across the river, 15 minutes walking on a gentle but steady uphill grade brings you to the village of Kililam, recognisable by its school, a large, white building.

Keep following the road up. After passing the school on the right, you come to a bush-material house and the road comes to a sudden end. Here, instead of continuing straight ahead, take the large, climbing trail on the left, opposite the house.

This trail is clearly marked and should pose no problems as long as you disregard any smaller paths branching off it. It leads to another road in about half an hour. You'll pass several houses on the right and, just before reaching the other road, there are beautiful views down the Lagaip Valley, including Paitingis at the foot of the quarry near the village of Kasap.

This second road links the village of Sirunki, a fair distance away on the right, with Torenam, five minutes away on the left. Turn left and, just before you reach the first houses of Torenam, take the road that branches off on the right.

This road quickly becomes a large track, which descends to the floor of the Moko Valley then gradually climbs out of it. The village of Yambim is now 40 minutes away and Lambusalam is some 10 minutes further on.

While descending to the valley floor, shortly after having taken the new road, you pass scattered houses belonging to the hamlet of Langentapus. The first creek crossed is the Komaip, the second the Moko.

Immediately after the bridge over the Moko you come to an intersection. The left-hand path leads to Lumbol Post; take the right-hand path. Yambim Creek is soon crossed and the path climbs a spur between Yambim Creek on the left and Moko Creek on the right.

The vegetation here is almost entirely pitpit. Further up, on a peak of the spur, sits the village of Yambim, from where there are good views down the Lagaip Valley. The Laiagam-Porgera Road is also visible, as are the few houses of Langentapus, on the other side of the Moko Valley.

Lambusalam, 10 minutes away on a second top, is a much larger village with about 20 houses, many of which are of traditional design. It is the last village before the crossing of the Central Range, and this is the proposed overnight stop.

STAGE 2: LAMBUSALAM TO WAILEP
Walking time: 6½ hours
Overnight: village accommodation
The route linking Lambusalam and Wailep goes through very diverse country. It first descends to the floor of the Moko Valley then climbs to the top of Mt Poapia, the highest point along the trail. From there you reach Wailep by way of the Sui Valley, passing the Marakale Grassland, the Pores Grassland, Mt Likelepoko, Mt Otel, and an impressive collection of limestone cliffs.

After climbing a little from Lambusalam, you begin to descend along the side of the valley. The trail follows the contours and overlooks the creek for some time before finally crossing it, an hour or so after leaving Lambusalam. From near the end of this section until the second bridge over the Sui River, you'll see passion-fruit flowers, with lovely pink petals and yellow stamens. Locals say that the liquid in the flowers' ovary is thirst-quenching.

A steady, slow 1½-hour climb up the other side of the valley brings you to the top of Mt Poapia. About three-quarters of the way up, you should fill your water bottle, as there is no water between here and the Sui River, still an hour's walk away. There are good views of the Lagaip Valley from just below the top of the range. The galvanised-iron roofs of Kasap are still visible, as is the route just travelled.

From Mt Poapia the route descends into the Sui Valley, then twice crosses the deep river which it will follow beyond Wailep to Pasalagus.

As you go down you'll see a large grassland on the right called Marakale, the headwaters of the Sui River. Further ahead, you can already see the much smaller Pores Grassland.

After 45 minutes the first bridge over the Sui River is crossed. The path goes up a little then falls to the small Pores Creek and the Pores Grassland. Mild ups and downs follow. Eventually, after travelling over numerous small streams and about an hour after the first crossing of the Sui, the route brings you back to the Sui and crosses it a second time.

From here, the path goes up again for 20 minutes to the top of the next ridge, Likelepoko. After a short level section, it falls to Telia Creek and continues to follow the Sui River down. Further on, Tip Creek then a much larger tributary, Otel Creek, are crossed. This is as far as the proposed road has been cut, and from here the route follows a small trail.

From Otel Creek, a steeper uphill grade through a beautiful forest brings you to Mt Otel. The walk from Likelepoko to Mt Otel takes about 55 minutes. From Mt Otel, the small Yak Stream is followed down. After passing a pretty cascade, the path swings to the left and climbs for 20 minutes to a resting place and lookout also called Yak. This overlooks an impressive collection of cliff-faces and both Wailep, still an hour's walk away, and the Sui Valley can be seen.

The route now drops down along a narrow and rather stony path over numerous small streams. Eventually, the trail brings you to Wailep's watering place and a creek that has been dammed for bathing. Wailep is now a few minutes away.

The village has many traditional bush-material houses and offers magnificent views. To the south rise the limestone cliffs of Mt Aulu on the left and Mt Mailaku on the right; to the north the lower Sui Valley stretches majestically.

STAGE 3: WAILEP TO PASALAGUS

Walking time: 4½ hours

Overnight: village accommodation

The trail to Pasalagus begins from a large grassy area at the lower part of Wailep village. Ten minutes later, having crossed a wooden bridge over a small gully, it brings you to a second grassy area. It passes a turn-off on the right leading to Lumbi, a village situated across the Sui Valley, and continues along the contours high above on the left-hand side of the Sui River.

Walk over the gullies of three small streams. After the last, the path goes up by a garden to reach a resting place at the foot of a tall hoop pine. This is about 45 minutes from Wailep. Most of the streams crossed in this section of the walk are polluted by people living upstream, so drink only from small rivulets.

From the hoop pine, Wailep and the large cliff-faces behind the village are clearly visible to the south. Straight ahead you can see the trail undulate along the contours then climb to the top of a ridge; this is the first of a series of ridges to be crossed before Pasalagus is reached.

The trail goes down and crosses a stream before levelling off. After a second stream and a second turn-off on the right to Lumbi, you cross a third stream then climb the first ridge. At the top, 20 minutes' walk from the hoop pine, is the hamlet of Kerai. As with all the other hamlets along this route, it is made up of scattered houses.

Beyond a turn-off which leads to a last house on the right, the trail begins to descend again. Three small streams are crossed, after which the route climbs a second ridge. At the top is a large, grassy clearing called Tongati, also the name of the hamlet a little lower down on the right. From here, 25 minutes' walk from Kerai, you get another spectacular view of Wailep and the whole lower Sui Valley. You can also see the hamlet of

Neleyako on top of the next ridge, 1½ hours' walk away.

The route descends, passing a turn-off to Tongati on the right and crossing numerous streams, to the Kamapu River. Fill your water bottle at any of these streams, as the next good drinking water is about two hours away, near Yulis Creek. The grade is steady, often steep. At one point there is a small lookout offering beautiful views down the Kamapu Valley. You can make out an extensive landslide that apparently killed many people in the '60s.

Soon after the lookout, the trail forks. Both routes lead to the river but it is better to take the left fork. Several houses are passed near the end of the descent, and the path soon brings you to a narrow log bridge that spans the river at its junction with the Sui. On the other side you first follow Onomal Creek, then climb to the top of the next ridge, the third. The ascent is tiring, but your discomfort will be offset by the beautiful views of the upper Sui Valley.

Near the top, soon after walking through another grassy area, you come to a turn-off. As at the next three junctions, you must keep to the right and stay on the main path. If you want to visit the nearby hamlet of Neleyako, turn left down the fourth turn-off.

From this ridge, 25 minutes of walking down a gentle downhill grade brings you to the hamlet of Nongolop, situated by the small Yulis Creek. Just before reaching it, you cross a small stream called Ansualem, the first source of drinking water since Tongati.

After Nongolop, the trail takes you across Yulis Creek and over several small tributaries as it gently rises for 15 minutes to the hamlet of Mendep. Mendep, on the fourth ridge, is recognisable by its tiny church topped with a galvanised-iron roof.

Pasalagus is an hour on from Mendep. At the end of a gentle downhill grade, and after having followed the contours for a while, the trail climbs to the fifth and last ridge. For the first time, the station can be seen. The narrow and stony path now falls a little and continues along the contours to the hamlet of Nengeyo.

From here, the route crosses several small streams, then forks twice; bear to the right at both forks. The path becomes much wider after the first junction, and Pasalagus is now only a very short distance away.

There is no rest house at the station, so accommodation must be found with a family. Ask around, perhaps at the health centre, the government office or the school.

STAGE 4: PASALAGUS TO ILIA
Walking time: 3¾ hours
Overnight: village accommodation

The trail to Ilia starts at the district office, at the bottom end of the airstrip, with a gentle 30-minute descent to the suspended wire bridge over the Sui River.

Passing two small streams (both unsuitable for drinking), the trail brings you to the village of Malikama. After reaching the grassy village square it continues behind a tanget hedge which is just to the left of the church, a rectangular house with a yellow door. A little further down, the path forks; take the left fork. As you continue down you'll soon pass a watering place on the right, and shortly after you'll come to the bridge over the Sui River.

Across the bridge, the route climbs the opposite side of the valley and heads for Neliaku, 50 minutes from the bridge. A gentle climb brings you to a small group of marita, a breadfruit tree and some wild bamboo. A little further up is a small stream bordered with a red-purple plant, often used to make a red dye. Finally, the route levels off and soon after reaches the hamlet of Neliaku, recognisable by the croton hedge and the many *yar* (casuarinas) that surround its few houses.

The continuation of the trail begins on the right, a few metres before the fence surrounding Neliaku, so if you've entered the hamlet you'll have to backtrack a little. This narrow and stony trail falls gently for 15 minutes to the 12-metre-wide Liando Creek, which is spanned by a log bridge. Across the creek, the trail climbs a gentle slope out of the valley.

Shortly after the bridge you'll come to an

intersection; the right-hand path leads to Kayamotok, a small village further up the valley; take the left to Ilia. About 50 minutes later, having passed a resting place and crossed many small creeks, you come to a second intersection. The left-hand path leads to the nearby hamlet of Yangere; take the right-hand path to Ilia, still 1¼ hours' walk away.

After walking past several small paths that obviously lead to nearby houses, you come to a third intersection – take the right-hand path. Shortly after this, Ilia comes into sight. Still following the contours, you continue over several small creeks and eventually come to a lovely cascade, where you can bathe and rest.

Having reached Ilia, you'll enjoy magnificent views over the whole Maramuni Valley from the village square.

The walk ends here, but if you aren't too tired it's worth walking down to the fast-flowing Maramuni River, where there is a superb 25-metre suspended cane bridge. Leave your gear with someone in the village. The descent takes 50 minutes, the climb back to Ilia about 1½ hours. This is also the way to Amboin and the Sepik plains, and across the river the trail continues to Was, an old abandoned village two day's walk away. Most walkers, however, will overnight in Ilia then retrace their steps to Pasalagus.

There's a community school in Ilia, which might be a good place to begin asking about accommodation.

OTHER SUGGESTED WALKS
Pasalagus (Maramuni) to Amboin

It takes five days to walk from Pasalagus to Imboin, where you might find someone to paddle you down the Arapundia and Karawari rivers (one or two days) to Amboin, site of a small government station, an airstrip, and the luxurious Karawari Lodge.

This walk is tough and should not be undertaken lightly. Good views are rare, the trail is difficult, and the place can get pretty hot. The only villages, Kupina, Namata and Imboin, are small and there's a chance that everyone will be away working sago and hunting.

Guides are essential. Many Penale people, who come from the Kupina and Namata areas, live in Pasalagus. Look for them at the station and try to recruit one to take you to at least as far as Kupina or, better still, to Namata. No-one lives in Was, and guides may be difficult to find in Ilia and Kupina.

From Ilia continue down to the Maramuni River, cross the bridge, and spend the first night at either Kopas (2½ hours from Ilia) or Tanol (four hours from Ilia). Both places have small bush shelters. The second day takes you to Was, an old village site by the river of the same name. Was is five hours from Tanol, 6½ hours from Kopas.

On the third day you cross a low divide between the Was and Arapundia rivers, and come to Kupina. From here, follow the Arapundia down to Imboin and the Karawari. The river needs to be forded seven times, first soon after leaving Kupina, then six more times between Namata and Imboin. Namata is a day's walk from Kupina, and Imboin is a day on from Namata.

At Imboin, try to hire someone to paddle you down the Arapundia and Karawari to Amboin. It's likely, however, that you'll have to travel in stages. Rates per paddler are about K3 between Imboin and Yamantim, K3 between Yamantim and Yimas, and K3 again between Yimas and Amboin. However, you might be asked for a lot more.

For those with the money, the *Karawari Lodge* (run by Trans Niugini Tours, (☎ 52 1438, PO Box 371, Mt Hagen) at Amboin is recommended. The cost is K141/182 a single/double, plus K12 for transfers from the airstrip. Meals are extra, K11 for breakfast, K13 for lunch and K27 for dinner.

Few motorised canoes travel from Amboin down the Karawari to the Sepik River, so you will probably have to fly out of the station. Because of the up-market Karawari Lodge, flights are fairly frequent. Talair flies to Tari (K88) on Monday, Wednesday and Friday, Tarangau Airlines (☎ 86 2203 in Wewak) flies to Wewak (K55) and Sandaun Air Services (SAS) (☎ 86 2793 in Wewak, (☎ 87 1268/79 in Vanimo) flies to Wewak and Vanimo (K160).

See Lonely Planet's *Papua New Guinea – a travel survival kit* for details of travel on the Sepik and its tributaries.

The Wabag (7687) and Yimas (7688) sheets of the 1:100,000 topographic map series cover the area described by the walk. The same area is also covered by the Wabag (SB 54-8) and Ambunti (SB 54-4) sheets of the 1:250,000 map series.

Other Suggested Walks

KEGSUGL TO BRAHMIN

This a relatively easy way of getting between the Highlands and the north coast. Following a 4WD track (the proposed route of a highway), this 96-km walk takes you from Kegsugl, north-east of Kundiawa in Simbu, to Brahmin, a mission station 21 km off the Ramu Highway in Madang.

The track is quite rough, but occasional vehicles do drive to Bundi and sometimes all the way to Brahmin. You may be lucky enough to get a lift. If so, expect to pay about K3 to Pandebai, K4 to Bundi and around K7 to Brahmin. There are PMVs running between Brahmin and Madang (K6), and between Kundiawa and the start of the track (K5). The turn-off for the Bundi road is a km or so before the high school at Kegsugl (see the map of the Mt Wilhelm walk).

Though the walk can be done either way, walking up means a long, hot climb – most people walk down. Make sure you take a hat and sunscreen, as there is no shade on the road.

Guides are not necessary.

Despite the hot sun, the walk is relatively easy and takes three days. Meals are available at Bundi, but otherwise you'll need to take your own food.

The first stretch is largely uphill and there are few villages. From the turn-off at Kegsugl the track climbs 10 km to Bundi Gap, known to the Simbu people as Mondia. From here it's another 10 km, gently downhill, to Pandebai, a village four hours' walk from the Kegsugl road.

Bundikara is seven km and 1¼ hours on from Pandebai. Here there's an attractive waterfall and you can apparently stay in the village. There are good views towards the Ramu Valley and the mountains near Madang.

A further 13 km and 3¾ hours takes you to Bundi, a large Catholic mission station and site of a group of lodges known as the *Mt Sinai Hotel*. These cost K10 per person

with breakfast or about K18 for full board. The meals are good.

Brahmin is still 35 km away. From Bundi the road descends, past the small village of Pupuneri, for 2½ hours to Ua, which is just after a large bridge over the river of the same name. From here it's 3½ hours, up and over a small range, to Brahmin.

Brahmin is 21 km from the Ramu Highway, the road linking Lae and Madang. A PMV from Brahmin to Madang costs K6 and takes about 1½ hours.

The Bundi (7986) sheet of the 1:100,000 topographic map series covers the area described by the walk. The same area is also covered by the Ramu (SB 55-5) sheet of the 1:250,000 map series.

LAKE KOPIAGO TO OKSAPMIN

This is a very difficult but particularly interesting walk. Starting at the end of the Highlands Highway at Lake Kopiago it takes you across the Strickland River's spectacular gorge to Oksapmin, a small government station in Sandaun Province.

In addition to being hard, this walk is potentially dangerous and should not be undertaken unless you're pretty fit. The river is crossed on a 65-metre-long suspended vine bridge and dense kunai grasslands cover the steep slopes of the gorge, a staggeringly rugged and awe-inspiring stretch of country. The trail is very steep and slippery, even in the dry season, which is definitely the best time to walk it. Guides are essential; expect to pay them around K5 a day.

The Highlands Highway beyond Tari is a rough 4WD track, and the 75-km, six-hour trip to Lake Kopiago costs about K10. Very few vehicles make the trip and rain often closes the road. The best way to find out about vehicles going to the lake from Tari is to call in at the PTB (Plans & Transport Branch) and have a chat with Jack, himself a Kopiago man. The PTB is next to the Tari's

Women Guesthouse, roughly opposite the MAF terminal.

You might decide to fly in. MAF is the main carrier serving the strip and a flight from Tari to Kopiago costs about K40. There are also flights between Oksapmin, Tari (K63) and Kopiago (K30). Talair flies from Oksapmin to Green River on the Upper Sepik for K73, to Telefomin for K33 and to Vanimo for K109. Oksapmin to Tari costs K60 with Talair.

In Lake Kopiago you can stay at the Hirane Apostolic Church *mission*, 2½ km from the government station, or at the *council guesthouse*, next to the police station. The mission costs K10 per night and is a lovely place by the lake, with bedding and cooking facilities. Swimming is possible. The council guesthouse costs K5, and also has bedding, showers and cooking facilities. Get the keys from the council clerk, who works in the green house on the right-hand side, below the district office.

The walk takes four or five days. The first day is a three or four-hour walk to Waip, a small village beyond Kaguane, where there's a rest house. Day two is a six or seven-hour walk through beautiful rainforest to Yokona, where there's a haus kiap (a small bush-material house used by visiting government officers).

The third stage is a very hard 10 to 12 hours to Gaua, or you can break the walk by camping at the Strickland River. It's a steep and dangerous three hours down the Strickland Gorge to the bridge. A fee (about K5) for using the vine bridge across the river will be requested by the Yokona people. There's a small cave near the bridge where you can sleep. From the bridge it's a steep, unshaded, uphill walk to Gaua that takes six to eight hours. There's a hut at Gaua. If you overnight at the river you can start early in the morning and avoid the worst of the heat. The last day's walk is a reasonably easy three hours to Oksapmin.

There's an Agricultural Centre at Oksapmin run by the Peace Corps and there are plans for a guesthouse: expect to pay around K5.

The Oksapmin (7387) sheet of the 1:100,000 topographic map series covers this walk. The same area is also covered by the Ok Tedi (SB 54-7) sheet of the 1:250,000 map series.

Note

The bridge over the Strickland River collapsed a while ago and rebuilding it seems to be taking a long time, so it might not be possible to follow the route outlined above. Ask around before you set out.

MANAM VOLCANO

The island of Manam, or Vulcan, is only 15 km off the coast from Bogia in Madang Province. It is 83 sq km in area and is an almost perfect cone, rising to 1829 metres. The soil is extremely fertile and supports a population of about 4000, but from time to time the volcano erupts and everyone has to be evacuated. Even when it's quiet, the volcano's tip glows and occasionally spurts orange trailers into the sky. There is a seismological observatory on the side of the cone.

The volcano can be climbed from the village of Warisi on the southern side of the island. The steep trail follows a gully until it reaches the tree line, from where it continues along scree slopes to the top. Above 1600 metres the scree gets more slippery and the gases become more noxious. There are good views on the way up but the summit is nearly always in the clouds, because of steam from the volcano. Bring lots of water as there is none at all along the climb, and allow four or five hours for a trip to the top and back.

There is a lovely bush-material guesthouse in Warisi. It belongs to the Kabung Youth Group (Warisi Village, Manam Island, PO Box 20, Bogia, Madang Province) and costs K10 per night. This includes a guide up the volcano and, if there are enough visitors, traditional dancing. Bring your own food, bedding and cooking utensils. The village is right by the sea and there is good snorkelling.

Access to the island is from Bogia, 193 km north-west of Madang. Note that there is now no formal accommodation at Bogia. A PMV from Madang to Bogia costs K6, and a boat from there to Manam costs about K3 to K5. Boats travel to Manam most days (not Sundays) from the wharf near the old Bogia Hotel, usually departing between one and 3 pm, and taking about two hours. Tell the captain you want to get off at Warisi village and which day you want to be picked up again. Boats normally leave Manam at around 8 am.

MT GILUWE

Situated south-west of Mt Hagen and rising to 4367 metres, Mt Giluwe is the second-highest mountain in PNG. Though trails to the summit leave from many villages around its base, you should climb from the DASF agricultural station, about 18 km south-west of Tambul in Western Highlands Province. The station is accessible by PMV along the Mt Hagen-Tambul-Mendi road, and the trip from Mt Hagen costs around K6. A few PMVs also run here from Mendi.

Two separate summits share the name of Mt Giluwe. The route up from the agricultural station leads to the lower of the two, the East Summit (4280 metres). Views from the top are quite good, and on a fine day you can see the Hagen Range, Mt Ialibu, the Kubor Range, the Sepik-Wahgi Divide, parts of the Kaugel Valley, and the Sugarloaf to the north.

A trip to the summit and back takes two days. An easy walk of 2¾ hours takes you from the road to the alpine grasslands at about 3500 metres; from here a further 2½ hours brings you to the summit plateau, an expansive area of grasslands dotted with numerous small tarns. From here it's a little over an hour to the East Summit.

A guide is necessary, and bring cold-weather gear, including a hat, a pair of gloves, a warm jacket and a good sleeping bag. There are bush-material shelters along the trail, but these may not be in good repair, and so some form of shelter should be carried just in case.

Read the warnings about altitude sickness and extreme climates in the Mt Wilhelm section, as they apply equally to Mt Giluwe.

Both the Mendi (7685) and Wapenamanda (7686) sheets of the 1:100,000 topographic map series cover Mt Giluwe.

POMIO TO ULAMONA

This beautiful walk crosses the island of New Britain from Pomio on the south side to Ulamona on the north side. The people are friendly, their culture interesting, and the trail passes the foot of Mt Ulawun, an impressive, sometimes active volcano. Pomio can be reached by boat from Rabaul or you can fly to Pamalmal, the nearest airstrip, then walk one day along the coast to Pomio.

The walk can be completed in four days. Day one takes you past Marmar, a large village half an hour's walk above Pomio, to the top of the range. The first night is spent in a small bush-material shelter. The second day's walk takes you to Pakia, a large village with many traditional houses. On day three you walk for six or seven hours to Muela, a beautiful village with magnificent views of both Mt Ulawun and the extinct Mt Bamusi, and the coast towards Open Bay. The last day brings you to Bago, a large village superbly located at the foot of the volcano. From Bago you can catch a PMV to Ulamona and the road leading west to Bialla and Kimbe.

The Ulawun (9187), Ludtke (9186) and Jacquinot (9286) sheets of the 1:100,000 topographic map series cover the area described by the walk. The same area is also covered by the Pomio (SB 56-6) and Talasea (SB 56-5) sheets of the 1:250,000 map series.

Glossary

This glossary is a list of pidgin (p) and basic bushwalking terms.

aumak (p) – a chain of tiny bamboo rods worn around the neck. (It is a form of traditional wealth.)

bagi (p) – elaborate shell jewellery that is ritually traded around the islands. (It is a sign of prestige and wealth.)
bihainim kil (p) – to follow a spur or ridge
bihainim wara (p) – to follow waterways (usually involves making many crossings)
billum (p) – coloured string bag
buai (p) – betel nut

cirque – a semicircular or crescent-shaped basin with steep sides and a gently sloping floor (formed by the erosive action of ice).
contour – the outline of a mass of land

doba (p) – traditional leaf money (made from a bundle of etched and dried banana leaves).

fidi (p) – a two-week period of solid rain

galip (p) – a type of nut
grassroot – slang term for the people. (A grassroot lives in a village or town on a low income.)

haus tambaran (p) – spirit house
haus kiap (p) – patrol officers' house

kaikai (p) – food
kaipipi (p) – wild betel nut
kanda (p) – lawyer vine
karuka (p) – fruit from one variety of pandanus palm
kaukau (p) – sweet potato; a root crop that forms a staple food in PNG.
kiap (p) – patrol officers
kina (p) – traditional shell money
kunai (p) – a type of grass

laplap (p) – a length of fabric worn around the body, similar to a sarong

malo (p) – a long bark cloak.
mami (p) – lesser yam.
marita (p) – fruit from one variety of pandanus palm
moraine – a mass of debris, carried by glaciers, that forms ridges and mounds when deposited
mumu (p) – an earth oven in which food is cooked

okari (p) – a type of nut

pitpit (p) – wild cane

tok ples (p) – a person's 'home' language

rascal (p) – usually young, unemployed men who have drifted to the city and then become involved in petty crime.

saksak (p) – sago
salat (p) – stinging nettles
sanguma (p) – sorcery
saitim kil (p) – to follow contour lines
scree (p) – an accumulation of weathered rock fragments at the foot of a cliff or sloping hillside
sing-sings (p) – traditional ceremonies and dances

tanim tok (p) – translator
tarn – a small mountain lake or pool
taro kongkong (p) – Singapore taro
taro tru (p) – taro
traverse – to move sideways or crossways across a hill or mountain

wantok (p) – system of clan responsibility

yam (p) – a tuber that is a staple food in PNG

Index

Keep in touch!

We love hearing from you and think you'd like to hear from us.

The Lonely Planet Newsletter covers the when, where, how and what of travel. (AND it's free!)

When...is the right time to see reindeer in Finland?
Where...can you hear the best palm-wine music in Ghana?
How...do you get from Asunción to Areguá by steam train?
What...should you leave behind to avoid hassles with customs in Iran?

To join our mailing list just contact us at any of our offices. (details below)

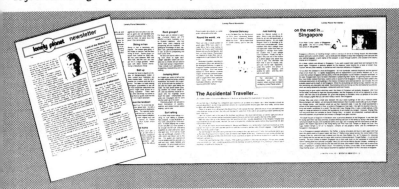

Every issue includes:

- *a letter from Lonely Planet founders Tony and Maureen Wheeler*
- *travel diary from a Lonely Planet author - find out what it's really like out on the road*
- *feature article on an important and topical travel issue*
- *a selection of recent letters from our readers*
- *the latest travel news from all over the world*
- *details on Lonely Planet's new and forthcoming releases*

Also available Lonely Planet T-shirts. 100% heavy weight cotton (S, M, L, XL)

LONELY PLANET PUBLICATIONS
Australia: PO Box 617, Hawthorn, 3122, Victoria (tel: 03-819 1877)
USA: Embarcadero West, 155 Filbert Street, Suite 251, Oakland, CA 94607 (tel: 510-893 8555)
UK: Devonshire House, 12 Barley Mow Passage, Chiswick, London W4 4PH (tel: 081-742 3161)

Guides to the Pacific

Australia – a travel survival kit
The complete low-down on Down Under – home of Ayers Rock, the Great Barrier Reef, extraordinary animals, cosmopolitan cities, rainforests, beaches ... and Lonely Planet!

Bushwalking in Australia
Two experienced and respected walkers give details of the best walks in every state, covering many different terrains and climates.

Islands of Australia's Great Barrier Reef – a travel survival kit
The Great Barrier Reef is one of the wonders of the world – and one of the great travel destinations! Whether you're looking for a tropical island resort or a secluded island hideaway, this guide has all the facts you'll need.

Sydney city guide
A wealth of information on Australia's most exciting city; all in a handy pocket-sized format.

Hawaii – a travel survival kit
Share in the delights of this island paradise – and avoid some of its high prices – with this practical guide. Covers all of Hawaii's well-known attractions, plus plenty of uncrowded sights and activities.

Melbourne city guide
From historic houses to fascinating churches and famous nudes to tapas bars, cafés and bistros – Melbourne is a dream for gourmands and a paradise for party goers.

New Zealand – a travel survival kit
This practical guide will help you discover the very best New Zealand has to offer – Maori dances and feasts; some of the most spectacular scenery in the world; and every outdoor activity imaginable.

Tramping in New Zealand
Call it tramping, hiking, walking, bushwalking, or trekking – travelling by foot is the best way to explore New Zealand's natural beauty. Detailed descriptions of 20 walks of varying length and difficulty.

Fiji – a travel survival kit
Whether you prefer to stay in camping grounds, international hotels, or something in-between, this comprehensive guide will help you to enjoy the beautiful Fijian archipelago.

New Caledonia – a travel survival kit
This guide shows how to discover all that he idyllic islands of New Caledonia have to offer – from French colonial culture to traditional Melanesian life.

Solomon Islands – a travel survival kit
The Solomon Islands are the best-kept secret of the Pacific. Discover remote tropical islands, jungle covered volcanoes and traditional Melanesian villages with this detailed guide.

Rarotonga & the Cook Islands – a travel survival kit
Rarotonga and the Cook Islands have history, beauty and magic to rival the better-known islands of Hawaii and Tahiti, but the world has virtually passed them by.

Micronesia – a travel survival kit
The glorious beaches, lagoons and reefs of these 2100 islands would dazzle even the most jaded traveller. This guide has all the details on island-hopping across the north Pacific.

Papua New Guinea – a travel survival kit
With its coastal cities, villages perched beside mighty rivers, palm-fringed beaches and rushing mountain streams, Papua New Guinea promises memorable travel.

Tahiti & French Polynesia – a travel survival kit
Tahiti's idyllic beauty has seduced sailors, artists and traveller for generations. The latest edition provides full details on the main island of Tahiti, the Tuamotos, Marquesas and other island groups. Invaluable information for independent travellers and package tourists alike.

Tonga – a travel survival kit
The only South Pacific country never to be colonised by Europeans, Tonga has also been ignored by tourists. The people of this far-flung island group offer some of the most sincere and unconditional hospitality in the world.

Samoa – a travel survival kit
Two remarkably different countries, Western Samoa and American Samoa offer some wonderful island escapes, and Polynesian culture at its best..

Also available:
Papua New Guinea phrasebook.

Lonely Planet Guidebooks

Lonely Planet guidebooks cover every accessible part of Asia as well as Australia, the Pacific, South America, Africa, the Middle East, Europe and parts of North America. There are five series: *travel survival kits*, covering a country for a range of budgets; *shoestring guides* with compact information for low-budget travel in a major region; *walking guides*; *city guides* and *phrasebooks*.

Australia & the Pacific
Australia
Bushwalking in Australia
Islands of Australia's Great Barrier Reef
Fiji
Melbourne city guide
Micronesia
New Caledonia
New Zealand
Tramping in New Zealand
Papua New Guinea
Bushwalking in Papua New Guinea
Papua New Guinea phrasebook
Rarotonga & the Cook Islands
Samoa
Solomon Islands
Sydney city guide
Tahiti & French Polynesia
Tonga
Vanuatu

South-East Asia
Bali & Lombok
Bangkok city guide
Myanmar (Burma)
Burmese phrasebook
Cambodia
Indonesia
Indonesia phrasebook
Malaysia, Singapore & Brunei
Philippines
Pilipino phrasebook
Singapore city guide
South-East Asia on a shoestring
Thailand
Thai phrasebook
Vietnam, Laos & Cambodia
Vietnamese phrasebook

North-East Asia
China
Mandarin Chinese phrasebook
Hong Kong, Macau & Canton
Japan
Japanese phrasebook
Korea
Korean phrasebook
Mongolia
North-East Asia on a shoestring
Seoul city guide
Taiwan
Tibet
Tibet phrasebook
Tokyo city guide

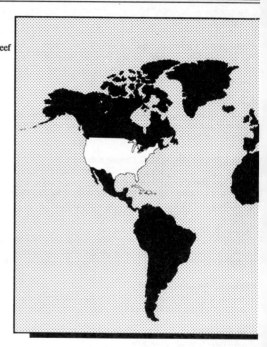

West Asia
Trekking in Turkey
Turkey
Turkish phrasebook
West Asia on a shoestring

Middle East
Arab Gulf States
Egypt & the Sudan
Egyptian Arabic phrasebook
Iran
Israel
Jordan & Syria
Yemen

Indian Ocean
Madagascar & Comoros
Maldives & Islands of the East Indian Ocean
Mauritius, Réunion & Seychelles

Mail Order

Lonely Planet guidebooks are distributed worldwide. They are also available by mail order from Lonely Planet, so if you have difficulty finding a title please write to us. US and Canadian residents should write to Embarcadero West, 155 Filbert St, Suite 251, Oakland CA 94607, USA ; European residents should write to Devonshire House, 12 Barley Mow Passage, Chiswick, London W4 4PH; and residents of other countries to PO Box 617, Hawthorn, Victoria 3122, Australia.

Indian Subcontinent
Bangladesh
India
Hindi/Urdu phrasebook
Trekking in the Indian Himalaya
Karakoram Highway
Kashmir, Ladakh & Zanskar
Nepal
Trekking in the Nepal Himalaya
Nepal phrasebook
Pakistan
Sri Lanka
Sri Lanka phrasebook

Africa
Africa on a shoestring
Central Africa
East Africa
Kenya
Swahili phrasebook
Morocco, Algeria & Tunisia
Moroccan Arabic phrasebook
South Africa, Lesotho & Swaziland
Zimbabwe, Botswana & Namibia
West Africa

Central America
Baja California
Central America on a shoestring
Costa Rica
La Ruta Maya
Mexico

North America
Alaska
Canada
Hawaii

South America
Argentina, Uruguay & Paraguay
Bolivia
Brazil
Brazilian phrasebook
Chile & Easter Island
Colombia
Ecuador & the Galápagos Islands
Latin American Spanish phrasebook
Peru
Quechua phrasebook
South America on a shoestring
Trekking in the Patagonian Andes

Europe
Dublin city guide
Eastern Europe on a shoestring
Eastern Europe phrasebook
Finland
Iceland, Greenland & the Faroe Islands
Mediterranean Europe on a shoestring
Mediterranean Europe phrasebook
Poland
Scandinavian & Baltic Europe on a shoestring
Scandinavian Europe phrasebook
Trekking in Spain
Trekking in Greece
USSR
Russian phrasebook
Western Europe on a shoestring
Western Europe phrasebook

The Lonely Planet Story

Lonely Planet published its first book in 1973 in response to the numerous 'How did you do it?' questions Maureen and Tony Wheeler were asked after driving, bussing, hitching, sailing and railing their way from England to Australia.

Written at a kitchen table and hand collated, trimmed and stapled, *Across Asia on the Cheap* became an instant local bestseller, inspiring thoughts of another book.

Eighteen months in South-East Asia resulted in their second guide, *South-East Asia on a shoestring*, which they put together in a backstreet Chinese hotel in Singapore in 1975. The 'yellow bible' as it quickly became known to backpackers around the world, soon became *the* guide to the region. It has sold well over half a million copies and is now in its 7th edition, still retaining its familiar yellow cover.

Today there are over 100 Lonely Planet titles – books that have that same adventurous approach to travel as those early guides; books that 'assume you know how to get your luggage off the carousel' as one reviewer put it.

Although Lonely Planet initially specialised in guides to Asia, they now cover most regions of the world, including the Pacific, South America, Africa, the Middle East and Europe. The list of *walking guides* and *phrasebooks* (for 'unusual' languages such as Quechua, Swahili, Nepalese and Egyptian Arabic) is also growing rapidly.

The emphasis continues to be on travel for independent travellers. Tony and Maureen still travel for several months of each year and play an active part in the writing, updating and quality control of Lonely Planet's guides.

They have been joined by over 50 authors, 48 staff – mainly editors, cartographers, & designers – at our office in Melbourne, Australia and another 10 at our US office in Oakland, California. In 1991 Lonely Planet opened a London office to handle sales for Britain, Europe and Africa. Travellers themselves also make a valuable contribution to the guides through the feedback we receive in thousands of letters each year.

The people at Lonely Planet strongly believe that travellers can make a positive contribution to the countries they visit, both through their appreciation of the countries' culture, wildlife and natural features, and through the money they spend. In addition, the company makes a direct contribution to the countries and regions it covers. Since 1986 a percentage of the income from each book has been donated to ventures such as famine relief in Africa; aid projects in India; agricultural projects in Central America; Greenpeace's efforts to halt French nuclear testing in the Pacific and Amnesty International. In 1992 $45,000 was donated to these causes.

Lonely Planet's basic travel philosophy is summed up in Tony Wheeler's comment, 'Don't worry about whether your trip will work out. Just go!'